SINGER/RANDOM HOUSE LITERATURE SERIES

SINGER / RANDOM HOUSE LITERATURE SERIES

APPROACHES TO LITERATURE
Volume One   Studies in the Short Story
Volume Two   Studies in Drama
Volume Three   Studies in Poetry
Volume Four   Studies in Nonfiction

PATTERNS OF LITERATURE
Volume One   The Short Story
Volume Two   The Novel and Nonfiction
Volume Three   Dramatic Literature
Volume Four   Narrative and Lyric Poetry

THE LITERATURE OF AMERICA
Volume One   Beginnings 1620-1865
Volume Two   Coming of Age 1865-1914
Volume Three   Modern Fiction
Volume Four   Modern Drama, Poetry, and Essays

THE LITERATURE OF ENGLAND
Volume One   Heroes and Pilgrims 449-1485
Volume Two   Poets and Critics 1485-1789
Volume Three   Visionaries and Realists 1789-1900
Volume Four   The Twentieth Century

THE LITERATURE OF AMERICA - VOLUME TWO

Coming of Age
1865-1914

SINGER / RANDOM HOUSE LITERATURE SERIES

THE LITERATURE OF AMERICA - VOLUME TWO

Coming of Age
1865-1914

Julian L. Maline, James Berkley, *General Editors*

Vernon Ruland
Marion T. Garretson
Chloe A. Morrison
Dictionary of Questions for Understanding Literature
by Vernon Ruland

Random House, Inc.
New York

SINGER / RANDOM HOUSE LITERATURE SERIES

Contributing Editors to the Series

George L. Ariffe
Dwight L. Burton
Lydia G. Goforth
John W. Ragle
Thomas J. Shanahan
William Shurr
John S. Simmons
Thomas J. Steele
David Stryker
Paul A. Thetreau
Jerry L. Walker

Contents

Unit Two - Growth of the Democratic Idea

Unit Three - The Triumph of Regionalism

Unit Four - The Naturalistic Vogue

Unit Five - The American Design

Introduction

"So, then, to every man his chance—to every man, regardless of his birth, his shining, golden opportunity—to every man the right to live, to work, to be himself, and to become whatever thing his manhood and his vision can combine to make him—this, seeker, is the promise of America."

Thomas Wolfe

In defining American literature the terms we must deal with—*American* and *literature*—are deceptive. Because they are familiar terms we are apt to believe they are also simple ones. Nothing could be further from the truth. Is "American literature" literature by Americans? about Americans? Should the works of Crèvecoeur, a European writing about America, be considered a part of American literature? Is Bradford's "Of Plimoth Plantation" as "literary" as Hawthorne's "Ethan Brand"? What are the distinctions? For our purposes it is enough to say that American literature is that written art which is the result of the experience of America by persons who have considered themselves Americans.

Literature, as a written art, has one fundamental requirement: the consciously creative process. This creative process is distinguished from the analytic process by being about and for things totally unlike those with which the latter is concerned. In the analytic process, one takes a thing apart to see of what it is made. In the creative process, one begins with the germ of an idea, and proceeds to clarify or crystallize it; first by excluding from the idea the inessential, meaningless, or misleading, then by exposing the residue (the aspect of the idea which the artist wants to express) to certain elements. These elements (for example, plot, character, action, dialogue) are the *achievements* of the idea *if the work is successful.* The poet achieves tone meter, balance, imagery through the working out of his theme. In the same way the dramatist achieves plot and tension, and the essayist achieves lucidity, logic, and coherence, if his idea or theme is successful. In other words, the writer does not begin with the parts to create a whole. He begins with an idea of the whole and creates its parts. And his creation is a result of his own imagination and his experience in the world of which he writes. American writers experience America in some phase, understand it in some way, and represent a facet of it by some means.

Whatever is *American* of this country's literary tradition must be obviously continuous and traceable. Each generation of American writers fed upon and was nourished by the preceding generation. We are wise, therefore, to begin with John Smith and Bradford in order to understand the literature that followed. The same things that disturbed Jonathan Edwards about human frailty as expressed in his "Resolutions" disturbed Hawthorne in *The Scarlet Letter*, just as the issues that concerned legislators Hamilton and Jefferson were the issues that preoccupied the poet Whitman. It is important to know how these American writers translated these various awarenesses into literature. What Irving, Poe, Hawthorne, and Melville had done to and for the literature of America before 1865 was not undone or discarded by the writers who followed — it was redirected, redefined, and reappraised. The ante-bellum anxieties about discipline and human weakness, illustrated in the works of Edward Taylor, Benjamin Franklin, and Ralph Waldo Emerson, could not exist on the frontier. There was a different code of values in the new territory of the West and this code provided material for the raw humor in much of the literature of the West.

The call for self-reliance that Emerson made in 1841, "Nothing is at last sacred but the integrity of your own mind . . . " became a curious kind of "integrity" and a stern, indeed, self-reliance in the hands of Bret Harte. The central character of "The Outcasts of Poker Flat," for example, attributes the circumstances that brought about his suicide to a streak of bad luck: "Luck is a mighty queer thing. All you know about it for sure is that it's bound to change. And it's finding out when it's going to change that makes you." Melville's and Hawthorne's brooding and philosophic melancholy became doubt and denial among some of the ante-bellum poets, such as Stephen Crane, and cosmic confidence in others such as Whitman and William Vaughn Moody. The romantic themes of Cooper and Irving, placed in New World settings with an Old World flavor became

another kind of romanticism—the naturalistic-realism
of the local color school. Unlike Irving, who borrowed
a literary style from the British neoclassicists, the local
colorists listened to and recorded the American language
with its cadences enriched by decades of European im-
migrations and uncultured native voices. They tried
to portray in depth the uniqueness of a particular region,
taking their cue from the European realists-naturalists
Zola, Balzac, and the British Trollope, to name a few.
These local colorists believed their realistic-natural-
ism was a revolt against the entrenched romanticism of
Melville and Hawthorne, Irving and Poe. Actually they
were simply re-defining the Romanticist Man, who himself had rebelled against the formalism of neoclassicism.
The pioneer industry and energy revealed in the writings
of Bradford, Winthrop, and John Smith became technologi-
cal competence which was reflected throughout the land
in railways, waterways, factories, and a rising leisure
class, the subject of much American literature. There was
a vast gulf existing between the rich and the poor and this
social unrest soon found a waiting ear for Marxist and other
social doctrines at the end of the 1890's. Man's freedom,
that had been so nobly taken for granted by Jefferson and
the American Constitution, that had formed the basis of
Emerson's and Thoreau's romantic rebellion, was now almost explained out of existence.

But something more was happening to Americans between 1865 and 1914. The seeds had been planted—Americans knew the answer to the question "Whence Came We?"
Now that the roots had spread their tendrils deep into the
soil, Americans asked "Whither Goest We?" An American
character was about to emerge.

Early idealism, energy, and concern for morality, religion,
and social justice had precipitated the War Between the
States. Subsequent developments of these early virtues—
notably the industrial expansion, which attracted large
numbers of immigrants—contributed much to molding the
character of this infant nation. Out of this mixture of Puritan
restraint and romantic exuberance, perhaps the outstanding

symbol of what American character had become was the simple, yet complex, figure of Abraham Lincoln. This manly, unrefined gentleman from Illinois seemed to epitomize the discoveries Americans were making about themselves. American writers were among the first to articulate these discoveries: Whitman discovered that beneath what seemed to be enduring hatreds was often great generosity and affection. As a result of the influx of immigrants, the local colorists discovered that the melting pot produced not cosmopolitanism, but different kinds of provincialism. Mark Twain, for all his championing of realism, surpassed himself only when writing nostalgically and romantically of his boyhood. Henry James, William Dean Howells, and Edith Wharton discovered that mechanical competence and financial prowess produced something less than a serene leisurely existence; Jack London discovered that the initial pioneer conquests of nature did not leave man fully in control of the forces of nature; Emily Dickinson, under an inveterate shyness, revealed a bitter, razor's edge perception akin to quick-silver.

Lincoln, Whitman, Twain, James, Wharton — they were all Americans reacting to their country and representing what they understood to be "truth." It is important for us, then, in order to understand the national characteristics of our literature, to know how American writers looked at America and what they saw.

Unit One

POETRY OF ASSURANCE
AND DOUBT

According to Emerson, "the experience of each new age requires a new confession, and the world seems always waiting for its poet." Perhaps of all the poets in American literature, Walt Whitman (1819-1892) most consciously strove to become the poet of his era. It was Whitman who said the driving purpose behind his poetry was "a feeling or ambition to articulate and faithfully express in literary or poetic form, and uncompromisingly, my own physical, moral, intellectual, and aesthetic Personality, in the midst of. . . . current America."

Whitman in his twenties had all the earmarks of the stereotyped Old World poet; as a society reporter for the Brooklyn *Eagle* he dressed meticulously—a frock-coat with a flower in the lapel, a high hat, and a cane. In his late thirties, however, he was wearing work-trousers and high boots, and calling himself "a rude child of the people," and "one of the roughs." His early imitative verse abruptly gave way to the new poetry of the first edition of *Leaves of Grass* (1855), with cadences and themes native to the everyday American man. Little in Whitman's earlier writing or in much of the world's literature seemed to anticipate it. It is interesting that Whitman himself attributes his inspiration chiefly to Emerson: "I was simmering, simmering, simmering; Emerson brought me to a boil." Perhaps Emerson found in Whitman the very bard of the people, the poet of nationalism and individualism that Emerson himself had always hoped to become. "I greet you at the beginning of a great career," he wrote to Whitman. "I am not blind to the worth of the wonderful gift of *Leaves of Grass*. I find it the most extraordinary piece of wit and wisdom that America has yet contributed, and I am very happy in reading it, as great power makes us happy. . . ."

Whitman epitomized a major aspect of the American character of the latter nineteenth century—optimism. He could sing with vibrant hope:

Come, I will make the continent indissoluble;
I will make the most splendid race the sun ever shone upon;
I will make divine magnetic lands,
        With the love of comrades,
        With the life-long love of comrades.

Of course, it would be an oversimplification to represent Whitman as a sheer and simple optimist. "There Was a Child Went Forth" does not omit from its chant the "sense of what is real, the thought if after all it should prove unreal,/ The doubts of day-time and the doubts of night-time, the curious whether and how,/ Whether that which appears so is so, or is it all flashes and specks?" Again, his reaction to "science" as expressed in "The Learn'd Astronomer" was a "tired and sick" retreat, a romantic gaze at the stars through the "mystical moist night-air." A similar reaction to the factual emphasis of science occurs in Emily Dickinson's lines: " 'Arcturus' is his other name—/ I'd rather call him 'Star.'/ It's very mean of Science/ To go and interfere!" However, the universality that Whitman sought in America's varied geography Emily Dickinson achieved in a secluded little world encompassed by her garden. He strove for great breadth of vision; she isolated an atom of experience and probed it to the depths. He thirsted for publicity, and even printed fictitious newspaper accounts of enthusiastic response to his work; she believed "publication is the auction of the mind" and saw but seven of her seventeen hundred poems published during her lifetime.

Emily Dickinson (1830-1886) was a recluse who spent all her days in her "father's house" at Amherst, a rural town in Massachusetts. Among the early experiences that shattered this quiet world were an adolescent rejection of her father's dour Puritanism, the stern religious instruction she received at Mount Holyoke Female Seminary, and the premature death of a young law student to whom she had become strongly attached. These experiences she sublimated in perfectly chiseled lyrics which reveal a child's delight in nature's commonplaces as well as an adult's anxieties about the meaning of existence. There is a magnificent hot-cold intensity in her poems which is perfectly described by her famous definition of poetry: "If I read a book and it makes my whole body so cold no fire can ever warm me, I know that is poetry. If I feel physically as if the top of my head were taken off, I know that is poetry. These are the only ways I know. Is there any other way?"

Combining Whitman's idealism and Dickinson's skepticism and terse poetic diction, Edwin Arlington Robinson (1869-1935) in his shorter poems portrayed the ordinary lives of his fellow New England townsmen. Miniver Cheevy, Richard Cory, and other characters of his fictitious Tilbury Town echo the grim discouragement, materialism, and drive towards power that he found in contemporary America. His sonnet "Credo" contains his characteristic images of darkness and light that symbolize Robinson's strangely paradoxical philosophy of life: one must face the despair and annihilation that end every life, "The black and awful chaos of the night," but at the same time move ahead with a blind trust in the "coming glory of the Light." It must not be forgotten that Robinson, Whitman, and Dickinson witnessed somewhat the same forces at work about them — the new science, the passion for wealth and the unjust exploitation of the poor, the disturbing new philosophies of doubt and determinism. Whitman more or less turned away from them and placed his hope in an idealized democracy; Robinson faced the chaos like a Roman stoic; and Emily Dickinson reduced these new forces to the age-old philosophical problem of evil, pitted her own childlike faith against it, and universalized this charged conflict of opposites in her poetry.

One's-Self I Sing

WALT WHITMAN

One's-self I sing, a simple separate person,
Yet utter the word Democratic, the word En-Masse.

Of physiology from top to toe I sing,
Not physiognomy alone nor brain alone is worthy for the
   Muse, I say the Form complete is worthier far,
The Female equally with the Male I sing.

Of Life immense in passion, pulse, and power,
Cheerful, for freest action form'd under the laws divine,
The Modern Man I sing.

> *Do especially Questions 1, 48, 50, 52, 135, and 145. Consult
> the Model Poem on page 31.*

Miracles

WALT WHITMAN

Why, who makes much of a miracle?
As to me I know of nothing else but miracles,
Whether I walk the streets of Manhattan,
Or dart my sight over the roofs of houses toward the sky,
Or wade with naked feet along the beach just in the edge
   of the water,   5
Or stand under trees in the woods,
Or talk by day with anyone I love, or sleep in the bed at
   night with anyone I love,
Or sit at table at dinner with the rest,
Or look at strangers opposite me riding in the car,

The poems on the following pages are selected from *Leaves of Grass* by Walt Whitman, copyright 1924 by Doubleday & Company, Inc. and are reprinted with their
permission: "One's-Self I Sing," "Miracles," "When I Heard the Learn'd Astronomer," "Wood Odors," "Bivouac on a Mountain Side," "There Was a Child Went
Forth," "On the Beach at Night," "A Child Said What Is the Grass?"

Or watch honeybees busy around the hive of a summer
    forenoon,   10
Or animals feeding in the fields,
Or birds, or the wonderfulness of insects in the air,
Or the wonderfulness of the sundown, or of stars shining
    so quiet and bright,
Or the exquisite delicate thin curve of the new moon
    in spring;
These with the rest, one and all, are to me miracles,   15
The whole referring, yet each distinct and in its place.

To me every hour of the light and dark is a miracle,
Every cubic inch of space is a miracle,
Every square yard of the surface of the earth is spread
    with the same,
Every foot of the interior swarms with the same.   20

To me the sea is a continual miracle,
The fishes that swim — the rocks — the motion of the
    waves — the ships with men in them,
What stranger miracles are there?

---

*Do especially Questions 1, 11, 44, 50, 64, 66, 137, 146, 149, and
150. Consult the Model Poem on page 31.*

When I Heard the Learn'd Astronomer

WALT WHITMAN

When I heard the learn'd astronomer,
When the proofs, the figures, were ranged in columns
    before me,
When I was shown the charts and diagrams, to add,
    divide, and measure them,
When I sitting heard the astronomer where he lectured
    with much applause in the lecture-room,
How soon unaccountable I became tired and sick,
Till rising and gliding out I wander'd off by myself,
In the mystical moist night-air, and from time to time,
Look'd up in perfect silence at the stars.

Do especially Questions 12-14, 32, 46, 47, 145, 146, and 149. Consult the Model Poem on page 31.

Wood Odors

WALT WHITMAN

Morning after a night-rain
The fresh-cool summer-scent
Odors of pine and oak
The shade.

Wandering the negligent paths   5
— the soothing silence,
The stillness and the veiled
The myriad living columns of the temple
The holy Sabbath morning

Incense and songs of birds   10
in deep recesses
But most the delicate
smells fitting the soul
The sky aloft, seen through
the tree-tops   15
All the young growth &
green maturity of May
White laurel-blossoms within reach .
wood-pinks below — overhead stately tulip-
trees with yellow cup-shaped   20
flowers.

The meow
meo-o-ow of the cat-bird,
cluck of robin, gurgle
of thrush delicious   25

Over and under these, in the
silence, delicate wood-odors
Birds flitting through the trees
Tangles of old grape-vines.

Do especially Questions 34, 52, 59, 60, and 64. Consult the Model Poem on page 31.

Bivouac on a Mountain Side

WALT WHITMAN

I see before me now a traveling army halting,
Below a fertile valley spread, with barns and the
orchards of summer,
Behind, the terraced sides of a mountain, abrupt, in
places rising high,
Broken, with rocks, with clinging cedars, with tall
shapes dingily seen,
The numerous camp-fires scatter'd near and far, some
away up on the mountain,
The shadowy forms of men and horses, looming, large-
sized, flickering,
And over all the sky—the sky! far, far out of reach,
studded, breaking out, the eternal stars.

Do especially Questions 11, 50, 52, 64, 68, and 140. Consult the Model Poem on page 31.

There Was a Child Went Forth

WALT WHITMAN

There was a child went forth every day,
And the first object he look'd upon, that object he
became,
And that object became part of him for the day or a
certain part of the day,
Or for many years or stretching cycles of years.

The early lilacs became part of this child,   5
And grass and white and red morning-glories, and white
and red clover, and the song of the phoebe-bird,

And the Third-month lambs and the sow's pink-faint
    litter, and the mare's foal and the cow's calf,
And the noisy brood of the barnyard or by the mire of
    the pond-side,
And the fish suspending themselves so curiously below
    there, and the beautiful curious liquid,
And the water-plants with their graceful flat heads, all
    became part of him.   10

The field-sprouts of Fourth-month and Fifth-month
    became part of him,
Winter-grain sprouts and those of the light-yellow corn,
    and the esculent roots of the garden,
And the apple-trees cover'd with blossoms and the fruit
    afterward, and wood-berries, and the commonest
    weeds by the road,
And the old drunkard staggering home from the
    outhouse of the tavern whence he had lately risen,
And the schoolmistress that pass'd on her way to the
    school,   15
And the friendly boys that pass'd, and the quarrelsome
    boys,
And the tidy and fresh-cheek'd girls, and the barefoot
    Negro boy and girl,
And all the changes of city and country wherever he
    went.

His own parents, he that had father'd him and she that
    had conceiv'd him in her womb and birth'd him,
They gave this child more of themselves than that,   20
They gave him afterward every day, they became part
    of him.

The mother at home quietly placing the dishes on the
    supper-table,
The mother with mild words—clean her cap and gown,
    a wholesome odor falling off her person and clothes
    as she walks by,

The father, strong, self-sufficient, manly, mean, anger'd,
    unjust,
The blow, the quick loud word, the tight bargain, the
    crafty lure,   25
The family usages, the language, the company, the
    furniture, the yearning and swelling heart,
Affection that will not be gainsay'd, the sense of what is
    real, the thought if after all it should prove unreal,
The doubts of day-time and the doubts of night-time,
    the curious whether and how,
Whether that which appears so is so, or is it all flashes
    and specks?
Men and women crowding fast in the streets, if they
    are not flashes and specks what are they?   30
The streets themselves and the façades of houses, and
    goods in the windows,
Vehicles, teams, the heavy-plank'd wharves, the huge
    crossing at the ferries,
The village on the highland seen from afar at sunset,
    the river between,
Shadows, aureola and mist, the light falling on roofs
    and gables of white or brown two miles off,
The schooner near by sleepily dropping down the tide,
    the little boat slack-tow'd astern,   35
The hurrying tumbling waves, quick-broken crests,
    slapping,
The strata of color'd clouds, the long bar of maroon-tint
    away solitary by itself, the spread of purity it lies
    motionless in,
The horizon's edge, the flying sea-crow, the fragrance
    of salt marsh and shore mud,
These became part of that child who went forth every
    day, and who now goes, and will always go forth every
    day.

---

*Do especially Questions 1, 11, 32, 33, 49, 50, 64, 66, 68, 137,
146, and 157. Consult the Model Poem on page 31.*

On the Beach at Night

WALT WHITMAN

On the beach at night,
Stands a child with her father,
Watching the east, the autumn sky.

Up through the darkness,
While ravening clouds, the burial clouds, in black
    masses spreading,   5
Lower sullen and fast athwart and down the sky,
Amid a transparent clear belt of ether yet left in the east,
Ascends large and calm the lord-star Jupiter,
And nigh at hand, only a very little above,
Swim the delicate sisters the Pleiades.[1]   10

From the beach the child holding the hand of her father,
Those burial clouds that lower victorious soon to devour
    all,
Watching, silently weeps.

Weep not, child,
Weep not, my darling,   15
With these kisses let me remove your tears,
The ravening clouds shall not long be victorious;
They shall not long possess the sky, they devour the
    stars only in apparition,
Jupiter shall emerge, be patient, watch again another
    night, the Pleiades shall emerge,
They are immortal, all those stars both silvery and
    golden shall shine out again,   20
The great stars and the little ones shall shine out again,
    they endure,
The vast immortal suns and the long-enduring pensive
    moons shall again shine.

[1]PLEIADES (ple′ə dēz″) — The cluster of stars called "The Seven Sisters."

Then dearest child mournest thou only for Jupiter?
Considerest thou alone the burial of the stars?

Something there is,   25
(With my lips soothing thee, adding I whisper,
I give thee the first suggestion, the problem and
    indirection,)
Something there is more immortal even than the stars,
(Many the burials, many the days and nights, passing
    away,)
Something that shall endure longer even than lustrous
    Jupiter,   30
Longer than sun or any revolving satellite,
Or the radiant sisters the Pleiades.

---

*Do especially Questions 12-14, 21, 35, 44, 59, 60, 61, 64, 137,
146, and 157. Consult the Model Poem on page 31.*

A Child Said
What Is the Grass?

(From *Song of Myself*)

WALT WHITMAN

A child said *What is the grass?* fetching it to me with
    full hands;
How could I answer the child? I do not know what it
    is any more than he.

I guess it must be the flag of my disposition, out of
    hopeful green stuff woven.

Or I guess it is the handkerchief of the Lord,
A scented gift and remembrancer designedly dropt,   5
Bearing the owner's name someway in the corners, that
    we may see and remark, and say *Whose?*

Or I guess the grass is itself a child, the produced babe
of the vegetation.

Or I guess it is a uniform hieroglyphic,
And it means, Sprouting alike in broad zones and
narrow zones,
Growing among black folks as among white,   10
Kanuck, Tuckahoe, Congressman, Cuff, I give them
the same, I receive them the same.

And now it seems to me the beautiful uncut hair of
graves.

Tenderly will I use you curling grass,
It may be you transpire from the breasts of young men,
It may be if I had known them I would have loved
them,   15
It may be you are from old people, or from offspring
taken soon out of their mothers' laps,
And here you are the mothers' laps.

This grass is very dark to be from the white heads of
old mothers,
Darker than the colorless beards of old men,
Dark to come from under the faint red roofs of mouths. 20

O I perceive after all so many uttering tongues,[1]
And I perceive they do not come from the roofs of
mouths for nothing.

I wish I could translate the hints about the dead young
men and women,
And the hints about old men and mothers, and the
offspring taken soon out of their laps.

[1]Probable interpretation: the grass seems too dark to have been nourished
by the red mouths of decaying corpses under the grass — but the tongue-
shaped blade of grass nevertheless speaks symbolically to me about
those corpses.

What do you think has become of the young and old
   men?   25
And what do you think has become of the women and
   children?

They are alive and well somewhere;
The smallest sprout shows there is really no death,
And if ever there was it[2] led forward life, and does not
   wait at the end to arrest it,
And ceas'd the moment life appear'd.   30

All goes onward and outward, nothing collapses,
And to die is different from what any one supposed,
   and luckier.

[2]Death.

Do especially Questions 12-14, 32, 33, 34, 45, 47, 51, 57, 63, 137, 146, 147, and 157. Consult the Model Poem on page 31.

WALT WHITMAN *1819-1892*

Born in Long Island, New York, the second of nine children, Walt Whitman by his fourteenth year obtained a job on the press of the *Long Island Star* and had begun to write. Brooklyn, New Orleans, and Chicago were the scenes of his early career as newspaper columnist and editor; Washington was the city in which he worked among the wounded during the war; and Camden, New Jersey, was the scene of his final years. He printed his own first edition of *Leaves of Grass* in 1855, and by 1892 it had grown from a mere twelve poems — including "There Was a Child Went Forth" and "Song of Myself" — to a ninth edition that contained the complete body of his poetry. The changes in any poem from one edition to another are an instructive study of the developing poet — he gradually removed passages that early critics judged obscene and crude, and strove for more compressed iambic lines. The first four poems presented here show his general Transcendentalist themes of self and nature; the next represents his war poetry; the last three, perhaps his greatest short lyrics, catch the fresh wondering view of a child.

Selected Poems

EMILY DICKINSON

985[1]

The Missing All—prevented Me
From missing minor Things.
If nothing larger than a World's
Departure from a Hinge—
Or Sun's extinction, be observed—
'Twas not so large that I
Could lift my Forehead from my work
For Curiosity.

1755

To make a prairie it takes a clover and one bee,
One clover, and a bee,
And revery.
The revery alone will do,
If bees are few.

824

The Wind begun to rock the Grass
With threatening Tunes and low—
He threw a Menace at the Earth—
A Menace at the Sky.

[1]The untitled poems of Emily Dickinson are identified here by the numbers given them in the Thomas H. Johnson edition of her collected poems.

The Leaves unhooked themselves from Trees —   5
And started all abroad
The Dust did scoop itself like Hands
And threw away the Road.

The Wagons quickened on the Streets
The Thunder hurried slow —   10
The Lightning showed a Yellow Beak
And then a livid Claw.

The Birds put up the Bars to Nests —
The Cattle fled to Barns —
There came one drop of Giant Rain   15
And then as if the Hands

That held the Dams had parted hold
The Waters Wrecked the Sky,
But overlooked my Father's House —
Just quartering a Tree —   20

1129

Tell all the Truth but tell it slant —
Success in Circuit lies
Too bright for our infirm Delight
The Truth's superb surprise
As Lightning to the Children eased
With explanation kind
The Truth must dazzle gradually
Or every man be blind —

1349

I'd rather recollect a setting
Than own a rising sun
Though one is beautiful forgetting —
And true the other one.

Because in going is a Drama
Staying cannot confer
To die divinely once a Twilight —
Than wane is easier —

Do especially the following Questions:
Poem 985: 1, 45, 49, 50, 63, 67, 135, 146, 147
Poem 1755: 1, 11, 49, 50, 63, 146
Poem 824: 32, 34, 44, 52, 58, 63, 64, 66, 69, 135, 146
Poem 1129: 32, 47, 52, 53, 59, 60, 146, 149
Poem 1349: 1, 12-14, 48, 59, 60, 135, 146, 149

341

After great pain, a formal feeling comes —
The Nerves sit ceremonious, like Tombs —
The stiff Heart questions was it He, that bore,
And Yesterday, or Centuries before?

The Feet, mechanical, go round —   5
Of Ground, or Air, or Ought —
A Wooden way
Regardless grown,
A Quartz contentment, like a stone —

This is the Hour of Lead —   10
Remembered, if outlived,
As Freezing persons, recollect the Snow —
First — Chill — then Stupor — then the letting go —

949

Under the Light, yet under,
Under the Grass and the Dirt,
Under the Beetle's Cellar
Under the Clover's Root,

Further than Arm could stretch   5
Were it Giant long,
Further than Sunshine could
Were the Day Year long,

Over the Light, yet over,
Over the Arc of the Bird —   10
Over the Comet's chimney —
Over the Cubit's Head,

Further than Guess can gallop
Further than Riddle ride —
Oh for a Disc[1] to the Distance   15
Between Ourselves and the Dead!

[1]Perhaps a "discus" to throw through this distance.

1078

The Bustle in a House
The Morning after Death
Is solemnest of industries
Enacted upon Earth —

The Sweeping up the Heart
And putting Love away
We shall not want to use again
Until Eternity.

1732

My life closed twice before its close;
It yet remains to see
If Immortality unveil
A third event to me

So huge, so hopeless to conceive
As these that twice befell.
Parting is all we know of heaven,
And all we need of hell.

> *Do especially the following Questions:*
> Poem 341: 34, 44, 48, 57, 63, 64, 135, 145, 146, 148, 157
> Poem 949: 46, 52, 58, 64, 65, 66, 71, 137, 146
> Poem 1078: 46, 52, 59, 60, 64, 65, 70, 137, 149
> Poem 1732: 12-14, 44, 49, 59, 60, 135, 146, 148

338

I know that He exists.
Somewhere — in Silence —
He has hid his rare life
From our gross eyes.

'Tis an instant's play.   5
'Tis a fond Ambush —
Just to make Bliss
Earn her own surprise!

But — should the play
Prove piercing earnest —   10
Should the glee — glaze —
In Death's — stiff — stare —

Would not the fun
Look too expensive!
Would not the jest —   15
Have crawled too far!

1090

I am afraid to own a Body —
I am afraid to own a Soul —
Profound — precarious Property —
Possession, not optional —

Double Estate — entailed[1] at pleasure
Upon an unsuspecting Heir —
Duke in a moment of Deathlessness
And God, for a Frontier.

[1]Goods settled on a person and his descendants which cannot be sold.

1052

I never saw a Moor—
I never saw the Sea—
Yet know I how the Heather[1] looks
And what a Billow be.

I never spoke with God
Nor visited in Heaven—
Yet certain am I of the spot
As if the Checks[2] were given—

[1]A wild plant growing in a "moor" or extensive area of waste ground.
[2]Probably, railroad tickets.

Do especially the following Questions:
Poem 338: 11, 32, 34, 45, 47, 59, 60, 64, 65, 137, 146, 149, 150
Poem 1090: 46, 52, 58, 64, 65, 146, 149
Poem 1052: 12-14, 33, 44, 48, 58, 61, 63, 137, 144, 145, 146, 149

EMILY DICKINSON   *1830-1886*

In a letter in 1862 to T. W. Higginson, who was later to act as her first editor, Emily Dickinson answered cryptically a few of his questions about her life: "You asked how old I was? I made no verse, but one or two, until this winter, sir. I had a terror since September, I could tell to none; and so I sing, as the boy does of the burying ground, because I am afraid. You inquire about my books. For poets, I have Keats, and Mr. and Mrs. Browning. For prose, Mr. Ruskin, Sir Thomas Browne, and the Revelations. I went to school, but in your manner of the phrase had no education. When a little girl, I had a friend who taught me Immortality; but venturing too near, himself, he never returned. Soon after my tutor died, and for several years my lexicon was my only companion. Then I found one more, but he was not contented I be his scholar, so he left the land. You ask of my companions. Hills, sir, and the sundown, and a dog large as myself, that my father bought me. They are better than beings because they know, but do not tell; and the noise in the pool at noon excels my piano. I have a brother and sister; my mother does not care for thought, and father, too busy with his briefs to notice what we do . . . . They are religious, except me . . . ."

War Is Kind

STEPHEN CRANE

Do not weep, maiden, for war is kind.
Because your lover threw wild hands toward the sky
And the affrighted steed ran on alone,
Do not weep.
War is kind.   5

   Hoarse, booming drums of the regiment,
   Little souls who thirst for fight,
   These men were born to drill and die.
   The unexplained glory flies above them,
   Great is the battle-god, great, and his kingdom —   10
   A field where a thousand corpses lie.

Do not weep, babe, for war is kind.
Because your father tumbled in the yellow trenches,
Raged at his breast, gulped and died,
Do not weep.
War is kind.   15

   Swift blazing flag of the regiment,
   Eagle with crest of red and gold,
   These men were born to drill and die.
   Point for them the virtue of slaughter,   20
   Make plain to them the excellence of killing
   And a field where a thousand corpses lie.

Mother whose heart hung humble as a button
On the bright splendid shroud of your son,
Do not weep.
War is kind.   25

---

*Do especially Questions 1, 11, 44, 45, 46, 59f, 59h, 62, 63, 71,
and 157. Consult the Model Poem on page 31.*

The following poems are reprinted from *The Collected Poems of Stephen Crane*,
courtesy of Alfred A. Knopf, Inc.

The Wayfarer

STEPHEN CRANE

The wayfarer,
Perceiving the pathway to truth,
Was struck with astonishment.
It was thickly grown with weeds.
"Ha," he said,   5
"I see that none has passed here
In a long time."
Later he saw that each weed
Was a singular knife.
"Well," he mumbled at last,   10
"Doubtless there are other roads."

Do especially Questions 1, 11, 32, 61, and 148. Consult the
Model Poem on page 31.

A Man Said to the Universe

STEPHEN CRANE

A man said to the universe:
"Sir, I exist!"
"However," replied the universe,
"The fact has not created in me
A sense of obligation."

Do especially Questions 1, 32, and 61. Consult the Model
Poem on page 31.

The Trees in the Garden

STEPHEN CRANE

The trees in the garden rained flowers.
Children ran there joyously.
They gathered the flowers

25

Each to himself.
Now there were some   5
Who gathered great heaps—
Having opportunity and skill—
Until, behold, only chance blossoms
Remained for the feeble.
Then a little spindling tutor   10
Ran importantly to the father, crying:
"Pray, come hither!
See this unjust thing in your garden!"
But when the father had surveyed
He admonished the tutor: 15
"Not so, small sage!
This thing is just.
For, look you,
Are not they who possess the flowers
Stronger, bolder, shrewder   20
Than they who have none?
Why should the strong—
The beautiful strong—
Why should they not have the flowers?"
Upon reflection, the tutor bowed to the ground. 25
"My lord," he said,
"The stars are displaced
By this towering wisdom."

Do especially Questions 1, 11, and 32. Consult the Model Poem on page 31.

STEPHEN CRANE   *1871-1900*

For biographical information about Crane, see page 174.

Credo

EDWIN ARLINGTON ROBINSON

I cannot find my way: there is no star
In all the shrouded heavens anywhere;
And there is not a whisper in the air

"Credo" reprinted from *The Children of the Night* (1897) by Edwin Arlington Robinson, with the permission of Charles Scribner's Sons.

Of any living voice but one so far
That I can hear it only as a bar   5
Of lost, imperial music, played when fair
And angel fingers wove, and unaware,
Dead leaves to garlands where no roses are.

No, there is not a glimmer, nor a call,
For one that welcomes, welcomes when he fears,   10
The black and awful chaos of the night;
For through it all—above, beyond it all—
I know the far-sent message of the years,
I feel the coming glory of the Light.

Do especially Questions 12-14, 33, 44, 48, 58, 61, 63, 137, and 157. Consult the Model Poem on page 31.

Mr. Flood's Party

EDWIN ARLINGTON ROBINSON

Old Eben Flood, climbing alone one night
Over the hill between the town below
And the forsaken upland hermitage
That held as much as he should ever know
On earth again of home, paused warily.   5
The road was his with not a native near;
And Eben, having leisure, said aloud,
For no man else in Tilbury Town to hear:

"Well, Mr. Flood, we have the harvest moon
Again, and we may not have many more;   10
The bird is on the wing, the poet says,
And you and I have said it here before.
Drink to the bird." He raised up to the light
The jug that he had gone so far to fill,
And answered huskily: "Well, Mr. Flood,   15
Since you propose it, I believe I will."

Alone, as if enduring to the end
A valiant armor of scarred hopes outworn,
He stood there in the middle of the road
Like Roland's ghost winding[1] a silent horn.   20
Below him, in the town among the trees,
Where friends of other days had honored him,
A phantom salutation of the dead
Rang thinly till old Eben's eyes were dim.

Then, as a mother lays her sleeping child   25
Down tenderly, fearing it may awake,
He set the jug down slowly at his feet
With trembling care, knowing that most things break;
And only when assured that on firm earth
It stood, as the uncertain lives of men   30
Assuredly did not, he paced away,
And with his hand extended paused again:

"Well, Mr. Flood, we have not met like this
In a long time; and many a change has come
To both of us, I fear, since last it was   35
We had a drop together. Welcome home!"
Convivially returning with himself,
Again he raised the jug up to the light;
And with an acquiescent quaver said:
"Well, Mr. Flood, if you insist, I might.   40

"Only a very little, Mr. Flood—
For auld lang syne. No more, sir; that will do."
So, for the time, apparently it did,
And Eben evidently thought so too;
For soon amid the silver loneliness   45
Of night he lifted up his voice and sang,
Secure, with only two moons listening,
Until the whole harmonious landscape rang—

"For auld lang syne." The weary throat gave out,
The last word wavered, and the song being done,   50
[1]Blowing.

He raised again the jug regretfully
And shook his head, and was again alone.
There was not much that was ahead of him,
And there was nothing in the town below—
Where strangers would have shut the many doors   55
That many friends had opened long ago.

---

*Do especially Questions 45, 48, 58, 63, 72, 74, 76, 89, 90, 91,
96, 100, 103, 111, 112, and 117. Consult the Model Poem on
page 31.*

Miniver Cheevy

EDWIN ARLINGTON ROBINSON

Miniver Cheevy, child of scorn,
    Grew lean while he assailed the seasons;
He wept that he was ever born,
    And he had reasons.

Miniver loved the days of old   5
    When swords were bright and steeds were prancing;
The vision of a warrior bold
    Would set him dancing.

Miniver sighed for what was not,
    And dreamed, and rested from his labors;   10
He dreamed of Thebes and Camelot,
    And Priam's neighbors.

Miniver mourned the ripe renown
    That made so many a name so fragrant;
He mourned Romance, now on the town,   15
    And Art, a vagrant.

Miniver loved the Medici,[1]
   Albeit he had never seen one;
He would have sinned incessantly
   Could he have been one.   20

Miniver cursed the commonplace
   And eyed a khaki suit with loathing;
He missed the medieval grace
   Of iron clothing.

Miniver scorned the gold he sought,   25
   But sore annoyed was he without it;
Miniver thought, and thought, and thought,
   And thought about it.

Miniver Cheevy, born too late,
   Scratched his head and kept on thinking;   30
Miniver coughed, and called it fate,
   And kept on drinking.

[1]MEDICI (med'ə chi) — Famous Renaissance Italian family.

Do especially Questions 15-20, 32, 34, 48, 59, 60, 63, 66, 72, 74, 76, 89, 103, 110, 111, 112, 117, and 145. Consult the Model Poem on page 31.

Richard Cory

EDWIN ARLINGTON ROBINSON

Whenever Richard Cory went down town,
   We people on the pavement looked at him:
He was a gentleman from sole to crown,
   Clean favored, and imperially slim.

"Richard Cory" from *The Children of the Night* (1897) by Edwin Arlington Robinson, with the permission of Charles Scribner's Sons.

And he was always quietly arrayed,   5
   And he was always human when he talked;
But still he fluttered pulses when he said,
   "Good morning," and he glittered when he walked.

And he was rich—yes, richer than a king—
   And admirably schooled in every grace: 10
In fine, we thought that he was everything
   To make us wish that we were in his place.

So on we worked, and waited for the light,
   And went without the meat, and cursed the bread;
And Richard Cory, one calm summer night,   15
   Went home and put a bullet through his head.

MODEL POEM

Richard Cory approached from the Seven Views of the *Dictionary of Questions*

FIRST VIEW

1. What is my first impression of the work as a total unit? My first reaction was one of surprise, and then of curiosity. I was surprised at what happened in the poem, and curious about why it happened. The poem is easy to read and, except for the surprise ending, seems rather simple.

SECOND VIEW

2. Under which type . . . would I classify the work from a first reading? The work is obviously a poem, but I am confused about whether it is a narrative or lyric poem. Although the poem tells a story, and could therefore be narrative, mood and emotional states seem to be more important. We are not told why Richard Cory kills himself. Perhaps the first stanzas of the poem have some special meaning. Everything seems to be leading up to the last line. Even though the suicide comes as a surprise, I was not completely unprepared for it, for it is natural to suspect that there must be a "tragic flaw" in a person described as so admirable. The poem must be a lyric.

THIRD VIEW

11. What is the theme of the work? I think the theme may be "money doesn't bring happiness." Somehow the statement seems too simple; I may be able to express it more exactly after I have answered other questions.

16. First, who is the central character? The central character is Richard Cory, but the narrator (and the people like him for whom he is speaking) is also central to the poem. The narrator seems just as bewildered by Richard Cory's act as I was.

17. Next, what of major importance happened to him? Richard Cory, a man who apparently had everything to live for, takes his own life.

20. What new or significant vision of the world did I grasp through the eyes of the central character? Richard Cory must have been in great despair, but he kept it hidden from public view. Whatever it was that made him take his life must have been so overwhelming that money, position, health, admiration—none of these were important enough to make him want to live. Richard Cory's real life must have been quite different from the one the townspeople saw. His view of the world must have included a great deal of pride, because it must have been pride that made him commit suicide. That is, he refused to face life under what he considered unbearable circumstances, and apparently, if he couldn't live his life out in precisely the manner he wished, he would not live it at all. The people who had real suffering, the townspeople who envied him, complained, but they faced up to the requirements of their lives.

FOURTH VIEW

32. What in the work is the dominant physical viewpoint and the mental viewpoint? The poem is told from the point of view of a narrator who is one of the "people" whose lives were so unlike Richard Cory's. The mental viewpoint is one of irony. I recall that the last stanza has two lines describing the hard life of the townspeople, and then the straightforward statement of Cory's death. Also, Cory kills himself "one calm summer night," a night least given to thoughts of death, when everybody else was relaxed.

34. Does the poet use stanza divisions to mark changes in feelings and viewpoints, or does the theme develop independently of such divisions? The change in feeling is the abrupt one in the last stanza. Each division, however, seems to intensify something that has been mentioned in the preceding stanza and to elaborate in some other detail what Richard was like. I can describe this effect better in the following manner:

First stanza: Richard Cory is identified; the townspeople envy and admire him. He is described as a gentleman "clean favored and imperially slim."

Second stanza: More details of Cory's distinction and splendor; even though he is "imperial" he is "human" when he talks; he dresses with taste and has very good manners; he must have been handsome because he can flutter pulses even with a simple "good morning"; "he glittered when he walked" picks up the suggestion of royalty in "imperial" and "arrayed."

Third stanza: Cory is "richer than a king"; again the suggestion of royalty and exclusiveness; he is "admirably schooled in every grace," which repeats the idea of the previous stanza in which Cory is said to be "human," that is, pleasant, gentle, not aloof; the last two lines state the obvious envy of the people, but also suggest that something unpleasant is going to happen: "In fine, we thought that he was everything/To make us wish that we were in his place." The verb tense suggests a change of feeling is about to come.

Fourth stanza: The first two lines describe the condition of the common people; the last two are a simple statement of Cory's suicide. The contrast between these two pairs of lines is striking and sums up the whole effect of the act, the difference between the two classes, and the theme of the poem. The theme is not simply that money does not bring happiness, but that it probably promotes unhappiness, or, more specifically, it reduces the tolerance for unhappiness, and thus makes the rich man fragile, susceptible, and more prone to misery than poverty does. I think that is closer to the theme than my answer in Question 11 of the Third View.

FIFTH VIEW

63. How does the imagery of the poem contribute to the shaping of the theme? Does the imagery unify the poem or merely enrich it as an ornament? My analysis of each stanza in Question 34 partly answers this question. Throughout the poem the image of royalty is developed. The use of words and phrases such as "imperially slim," "arrayed," "glittered," "richer than a king" are selected to enhance the image and provide a contrast with the common people. The line "And went without the meat, and cursed the bread" aptly provokes the picture of the poor, who have not even the luxury of meat, and whose necessities are inferior; it also points up the emphasis on material things: the people have few material things; Cory has everything. The people are also "waiting for the light"; they are in one kind of darkness, looking forward to better times — Cory is in another kind of darkness, even though he "glitters," and without hope altogether. This hopelessness is even more ironic when I recall that Cory is described in the first stanza as "clean favored" which suggests impeccableness and that fortune had indulged him. In the first two lines of the poem, the image is deceptively simple: *Whenever* Richard Cory went . . . "suggests that he went to that part of town seldom; "We people . . . looked at him" suggests the eyes of envy and admiration focused on him. I think now that the entire effect, all the things I took for granted, were very carefully worked out. The words have clear meanings and even clearer connotations.

SIXTH VIEW

146. How does my understanding of the present work ... contribute to further understanding of life in general?
This poem makes me think about how little one can know of another's life, how different are the worlds people live in, and how the inner recesses of the human heart can be kept secluded almost forever. It also makes me think of how meaningless are the trappings of a person's life. The people "on the pavement" saw only the material things because they were concerned, in their own lives, about them, and therefore were perplexed by Cory's action. Perhaps some trifle made Cory commit suicide; perhaps something deeply significant. We don't know. Nor does it seem important to know the facts; it is only important to know that the "people" endured their hardships; Cory did not, and they lived in entirely different worlds.

SEVENTH VIEW

147. What is my final evaluation of the work? How does the work clarify, support, or contradict my own concept of what the "Good Life" is? This poem makes me think a good deal about what, for me, the "Good Life" would be. I am generally accustomed to thinking of the "Good Life" as one completely free of anxiety about material things. I have usually assumed that if one had all the comforts of material things, happiness and the rest would naturally follow. This poem contradicts that theory altogether. While I am still certain that a life spent in grasping for basic necessities is no life at all, now I am wondering what a life full of material luxury and nothing else is worth. There must be something else that brings fulfillment. I am not sure what this "something else" is, but I am sure it is not just money or "success."

Flammonde

EDWIN ARLINGTON ROBINSON

The man Flammonde, from God knows where,
With firm address and foreign air,
With news of nations in his talk
And something royal in his walk,
With glint of iron in his eyes,   5
But never doubt, nor yet surprise,
Appeared, and stayed, and held his head
As one by king accredited.

Erect, with his alert repose
About him, and about his clothes,   10
He pictured all tradition hears
Of what we owe to fifty years.
His cleansing heritage of taste
Paraded neither want nor waste;
And what he needed for his fee   15
To live, he borrowed graciously.

He never told us what he was,
Or what mischance, or other cause,
Had banished him from better days
To play the Prince of Castaways.   20
Meanwhile he played surpassing well
A part, for most, unplayable;
In fine, one pauses, half afraid
To say for certain that he played.

For that, one may as well forego   25
Conviction as to yes or no;
Nor can I say just how intense
Would then have been the difference
To several, who, having striven
In vain to get what he was given,   30
Would see the stranger taken on
By friends not easy to be won.

Moreover, many a malcontent
He soothed and found munificent;
His courtesy beguiled and foiled   35
Suspicion that his years were soiled;
His mien distinguished any crowd,
His credit strengthened when he bowed;
And women, young and old, were fond
Of looking at the man Flammonde.   40

There was a woman in our town
On whom the fashion was to frown;
But while our talk renewed the tinge
Of a long-faded scarlet fringe,

The man Flammonde saw none of that,   45
And what he saw we wondered at—
That none of us, in her distress,
Could hide or find our littleness.

There was a boy that all agreed
Had shut within him the rare seed   50
Of learning. We could understand,
But none of us could lift a hand.
The man Flammonde appraised the youth,
And told a few of us the truth;
And thereby, for a little gold,   55
A flowered future was unrolled.

There were two citizens who fought
For years and years, and over nought;
They made life awkward for their friends,
And shortened their own dividends.   60
The man Flammonde said what was wrong
Should be made right; nor was it long
Before they were again in line,
And had each other in to dine.

And these I mention are but four   65
Of many out of many more.
So much for them. But what of him—
So firm in every look and limb?
What small satanic sort of kink
Was in his brain? What broken link   70
Withheld him from the destinies
That came so near to being his?

What was he, when we came to sift
His meaning, and to note the drift
Of incommunicable ways   75
That make us ponder while we praise?
Why was it that his charm revealed
Somehow the surface of a shield?
What was it that we never caught?
What was he, and what was he not?   80

How much it was of him we met
We cannot ever know; nor yet
Shall all he gave us quite atone
For what was his, and his alone;
Nor need we now, since he knew best,   85
Nourish an ethical unrest:
Rarely at once will nature give
The power to be Flammonde and live.

We cannot know how much we learn
From those who never will return,   90
Until a flash of unforeseen
Remembrance falls on what has been.
We've each a darkening hill to climb;
And this is why, from time to time
In Tilbury Town, we look beyond   95
Horizons for the man Flammonde.

---

*Do especially Questions 2, 11, 12-14, 32, 66, 70, 147, and 157.
Consult the Model Poem on page 31.*

Karma*

EDWIN ARLINGTON ROBINSON

Christmas was in the air and all was well
With him, but for a few confusing flaws
In divers of God's images. Because
A friend of his would neither buy nor sell,
Was he to answer for the axe that fell?   5
He pondered; and the reason for it was,
Partly, a slowly freezing Santa Claus
Upon the corner, with his beard and bell.

°In Hinduism and Buddhism, the whole ethical consequence of a person's
acts that fix his lot or future existence.

Acknowledging an improvident surprise,
He magnified a fancy that he wished   10
The friend whom he had wrecked were here again.
Not sure of that, he found a compromise;
And from the fullness of his heart he fished
A dime for Jesus who had died for men.

Do especially Questions 11, 44, 64, 65, 70, 74, 76, 89, 90, 102, 103, 111, 112, 117, 138, 145, and 146. Consult the Model Poem on page 31.

EDWIN ARLINGTON ROBINSON   *1869-1935*

It was not until the 1920's that Edwin Arlington Robinson received public recognition as a poet, with three successive Pulitzer prizes. "Credo," "Richard Cory," and many of his other short lyrics, however, date before 1900. Among his poems chosen here, "Credo" appears first as an introduction; "Mr. Flood's Party" introduces Tilbury Town; the next three poems portray some of its inhabitants. Robinson has expressed his attitude towards the art of poetry in eight lines of blank verse:

> To get at the eternal strength of things,
> And fearlessly to make strong songs of it,
> Is, to my mind, the mission of that man
> The world would call a poet. He may sing
> But roughly, and withal ungraciously;
> But if he touch to life the one right chord
> Wherein God's music slumbers, and awake
> To truth one drowsed ambition, he sings well.

From "Octave I" from *The Children of the Night* by Edwin Arlington Robinson (Charles Scribner's Sons, 1896).

PROBLEM QUESTIONS

1. The New York *Times* of 1855 greeted Walt Whitman's *Leaves of Grass* with this review: "His poems differ from prose only in the lines being cut into length instead of continuously printed. Considered as prose, then, we find a poverty of thought, paraded forth with a hubbub of stray words and accompanied with a vehement self-assertion...." Defend Whitman in the following manner: first, frame your own definition of poetry that will not

exclude the eight selected poems from its scope; secondly, try to explain his diction and self-assertion in terms of his poetic credo as expressed in the introduction to this unit.

2. Compare your own definition of poetry as you have stated it in answering the preceding question on Walt Whitman with Emily Dickinson's definition. How would you now revise your definition to include the emotional effect that poetry creates in a responsive reader?

3. Using specific poems as examples, demonstrate Whitman's striving for "great breadth of vision" and Emily Dickinson's efforts to "isolate an atom of experience." Also, compare the attitude toward nature and the use of figurative language of the two poets as expressed, for example, in "A Child Said What Is the Grass?" and "The Wind Begun to Rock the Grass" (824).

4. Stephen Crane's poetry reveals his hatred of sentiment, his search for truth, and his bitter disillusionment. Point out these characteristics in the poems in this unit. Select one of them as an example of exquisite irony.

5. Much of Robinson's work is concerned with tragedy and moral conflict. His psychological portraits show man frustrated, obsessed by failure, tortured by his own character. Discuss these statements in relation to one of the character portrayals in the unit. Compare also Robinson's ironic humor with Crane's.

Unit Two

GROWTH OF THE DEMOCRATIC IDEA

The great intellectual upheaval that was exciting Europeans in the latter half of the nineteenth century and the first decade of the twentieth was equally as stimulating to Americans. The most important of the revolutionary ideas that caused this upheaval was in the area of natural science, the biological and evolutionary theories of Darwin who had discovered evidence pointing to the gradual development and evolution of the different species of life. Of necessity this new understanding of the world had a monumental and lasting effect on theology. Consequently, there arose in America fictional, nonfictional, and poetic responses to evolution — some in opposition, some in agreement, others trying to establish a synthesis between science and religion.

Other ideas that gripped the thinking of Americans during this period were sequels to ideas held in pre-war days: social reform; the rediscovery of the past; an interest in folklore; a delight in regional differences. Other ideas were rebellions against long-established notions; a changed attitude toward language is one example. The works of Americans in this unit are a select representation of the manifestations of these ideas during the period.

What did Americans believe was the sum total of the democratic idea? What was the essence of the Republic? There is no better symbol of these ideals than Abraham Lincoln. According to one literary historian, "In Lincoln the people of the United States could finally see themselves, each for himself and all together. . . . Virtually the Gettysburg Speech is one of the great American poems, having its use and acceptation far beyond American shores. It curiously incarnates the claims, assurances, and pretenses of republican institutions, of democratic procedure, of the rule of the people, and it directly implies that popular government can come into being and can then 'perish from the earth.'" Not only in terms of the ideal of the Republic was Lincoln "everyman"; he was also an aspect of many of the other ideas, mentioned earlier, that attracted Americans: the interest in folklore—Lincoln's stories, tales, and jokes were widely circulated; the changed attitude toward language—no longer awed by the genteel Old World rhythms of Irving and Poe, Americans delighted in the emergence of *American* English, and the language patterns of Lincoln "ranged from the plainest of street vernacular to hoary and archaic Anglo-Saxon terms."

As Lincoln represented the synthesis of the folk medium and classical rhetoric, the democratic idea and pioneer individualism, so William James (1842-1910), a product of an entirely different world, represented a synthesis. While the intellectual harmony of Lincoln was unpremeditated, William James's attempt to reduce the conflict between religion and science, individualism and bureaucracy and other apparent dichotomies, was conscious and consistent. James was always persuaded that ideas must be subject to continuous examination, and that their value lay in their applicability to the practical world of action. It was this position, called pragmatism, that led him to assert that any aspect of religion was "true" if it provided the necessary spiritual satisfaction—thus the believer had no real quarrel with the scientist, and the scientist could deny the believer "absolute" truth, but not faith. In relation to the conflict between the individual and an increasingly complex society, James, who hated all moral, civil, and intellectual impositions, believed that the mind and energy of man could be successfully employed to shape the future according to the most desirable of human needs and wants. The selection in this unit from "The Moral Equivalent of War" is a fine example of the pragmatism and rational synthesis for which William James is well known.

Unlike Lincoln in every respect except brilliance and wit, Henry Adams (1838-1918) voiced skepticism and disillusion at the trends in America, and indeed, in the entire universe. A descendant of Presidents John and John Quincy Adams, he was an historian with literary interests. Adams knew what Hawthorne, Melville, and others knew: that "American literature must be a reinterpretation of the eternal issues in human experience in terms of life in contemporary America." At the Paris Exposition of 1900, Adams found a huge dynamo and dreamed of himself "flying in the Gallery of Machines . . . his historical neck broken by the sudden eruption of forces totally new." Here was a symbol of the infinite, directionless, scientific forces that man was unleashing in his new doctrines. Haunted by the tragedy of his sister's death and his wife's suicide, Adams turned from his early professorship of medieval history at Harvard and devoted himself to a life of writing and travel. Published posthumously in 1918, *The Education of Henry Adams* interprets thirteenth-century Europe as "the point of history when man held the highest idea of himself as a unit in a unified universe"; analyzes his early education at Harvard; and traces Darwinism and other intellectual influences on his life. Although *Mont-Saint-Michel and Chartres* and *The Education* are more famous, Adams spent most of his life on a nine-volume *History of the United States During the Administrations of Jefferson and Madison,* an analysis of the mysterious historical forces shaping modern America—interesting to readers today as a documented prophecy that the two great powers of the future would be Russia and the United States.

Another representative of American thought during this period was Mark Twain (1835-1910). More generally associated with the Lincolnesque outlook on life—a mixture of irony, raw humor, and confidence—Twain, in his later years outstripped Henry Adams in skepticism and cosmic disillusion. Probably Mark Twain, more than anyone else, articulated for the masses acceptable attitudes about Darwinism, politics, morality, frontier life, expansion, Europeans, the American language, regionalism, and "realism."

Life on the Mississippi, from which two selections are presented in this unit, and *Roughing It* are the more famous of his nonfictional works. The discipline of an apprentice river-boat pilot, the majestic sweep of the Mississippi River, the strong and picturesque American idiom, the stamp of regionalism on every character, the self-indulgent morality underlined by a strong sense of justice and egalitarianism—all are characteristics of Americana of which Twain has come to be a symbol.

Considered in its entirety, the prose of American writers and thinkers during this period is a clear indication of the direction in which American thought, action, and character was to move.

Farewell Address at Springfield, Illinois

ABRAHAM LINCOLN

My friends: No one, not in my situation, can appreciate my feeling of sadness at this parting. To this place, and the kindness of these people, I owe everything. Here I have lived a quarter of a century, and have passed from a young to an old man. Here my children have been born, and one is buried. I now leave, not knowing when or whether ever I may return, with a task before me greater than that which rested upon Washington. Without the assistance of that Divine Being who ever attended him, I cannot succeed. With that assistance, I cannot fail. Trusting in Him who can go with me, and remain with you, and be everywhere for good, let us confidently hope that all will yet be well. To His care commending you, as I hope in your prayers you will commend me, I bid you an affectionate farewell.

Do especially Questions 1, 11, 12, 44, 46, 48, 49, 52, 133, and 137.

The Gettysburg Address

ABRAHAM LINCOLN

Four score and seven years ago our fathers brought forth on this continent a new nation, conceived in liberty and dedicated to the proposition that all men are created equal.

Now we are engaged in a great civil war, testing whether that nation, or any nation so conceived and so dedicated, can long endure. We are met on a great battlefield of that war. We have come to dedicate a portion of that field as a final resting place for those who here gave their lives that that nation might live. It is altogether fitting and proper that we should do this.

But in a larger sense we cannot dedicate, we cannot consecrate, we cannot hallow this ground. The brave men, living and dead, who struggled here, have consecrated it far above our poor power to add or detract. The world will little note nor long remember what we say here, but it can never forget what they did here. It is for us, the living, rather, to be dedicated here to the unfinished work which they who fought here have thus far so nobly advanced. It is rather for us to be here dedicated to the great task remaining before us — that from these honored dead we take increased devotion to that cause for which they gave the last full measure of devotion; that we here highly resolve that these dead shall not have died in vain; that this nation, under God, shall have a new birth of freedom; and that government of the people, by the people, for the people, shall not perish from the earth.

Do especially Questions 12-14, 31, 46, 49, 51, 52, 145, and 146.

Second Inaugural Address

ABRAHAM LINCOLN

Fellow-Countrymen:

At this second appearing to take the oath of the presidential office, there is less occasion for an extended address than there was at the first. Then a statement, somewhat in detail, of a course to be pursued, seemed fitting and proper. Now, at the expiration of four years, during which public declarations have been constantly called forth on every point and phase of the great contest which still absorbs the attention and engrosses the energies of the nation, little that is new could be presented. The progress of our arms, upon which all else chiefly depends, is as well known to the public as to myself; and it is, I trust, reasonably satisfactory and encouraging to all. With high hope for the future, no prediction in regard to it is ventured.

On the occasion corresponding to this four years ago, all thoughts were anxiously directed to an impending civil war. All dreaded it—all sought to avert it. While the inaugural address was being delivered from this place, devoted altogether to saving the Union without war, insurgent agents were in the city seeking to destroy it without war—seeking to dissolve the Union, and divide effects, by negotiation. Both parties deprecated° war; but one of them would make war rather than let the nation survive; and the other would accept war rather than let it perish. And the war came.

One-eighth of the whole population were colored slaves, not distributed generally over the Union, but localized in the southern part of it. These slaves constituted a peculiar and powerful interest. All knew that this interest was, somehow, the cause of the war. To strengthen, perpetuate, and extend this interest was the object for which the insurgents would rend the Union, even by war; while the government claimed no right to do more than to restrict the territorial enlargement of it.[1]

---

[1]Before the outbreak of war Lincoln said he had no right "to interfere with the institution of slavery in the states where it exists." However, he felt that Congress should legally ban its extension to new territories.

Neither party expected for the war the magnitude or the duration which it has already attained. Neither anticipated that the cause of the conflict might cease[2] with, or even before, the conflict itself should cease. Each looked for an easier triumph and a result less fundamental and astounding. Both read the same Bible, and pray to the same God; and each invokes His aid against the other. It may seem strange that any man should dare to ask a just God's assistance in wringing their bread from the sweat of other men's faces; but let us judge not, that we be not judged. The prayers of both could not be answered—that of neither has been answered fully.

The Almighty has his own purposes. "Woe unto the world because of offenses! for it must needs be that offenses come; but woe to that man by whom the offense cometh."[3] If we shall suppose that American slavery is one of those offenses which, in the providence of God, must needs come, but which, having continued through His appointed time, He now wills to remove, and that He gives to both North and South this terrible war, as the woe due to those by whom the offense came, shall we discern therein any departure from those divine attributes which the believers in a living God always ascribe to Him? Fondly do we hope—fervently do we pray—that this mighty scourge of war may speedily pass away. Yet, if God wills that it continue until all the wealth piled by the bondman's two hundred and fifty years of unrequited toil shall be sunk, and until every drop of blood drawn with the lash shall be paid by another drawn with the sword, as was said three thousand years ago, so still it must be said, "The judgments of the Lord are true and righteous altogether."[4]

With malice toward none; with charity for all; with firmness in the right, as God gives us to see the right, let us strive on to finish the work we are in; to bind up the nation's wounds; to care for him who shall have borne the battle, and for his widow and his orphan—to do all which may

[2]Slavery was abolished by the Emancipation Proclamation on January 1, 1863.
[3]This quotation is from Matthew 18:7.
[4]This quotation is from Psalms 19:9.

achieve and cherish a just and lasting peace among ourselves, and with all nations.

Do especially Questions 11, 12-14, 26, 27, 28, 29, 30, 31, 48, 49, 51, 52, 53, 137, and 146.

ABRAHAM LINCOLN *1809-1865*

Abraham Lincoln, born February 12, 1809, near Hodgenville,
Kentucky, stands today one of the great men, not only of the nation
but of the world. The story of his humble birth, his struggle with
poverty, his intellectual curiosity that could not be satisfied, his
slow rise to political power with its culmination in the highest
office in the United States—these are facts known to every American; yet each retelling seems but to burnish more brightly the
fame of this unusual man. When Lincoln was seven years of age,
his father moved from Kentucky to Indiana, where the family lived
until Lincoln was twenty-one. Later they moved to Illinois, with
which state he was ever after associated.

In 1831 Lincoln began to study law and in 1834 was elected to
the Illinois legislature. During the succeeding years the slavery
question became involved with nearly every phase of politics. In
1858, Lincoln accepted the Republican nomination for United
States Senator, and in the Lincoln-Douglas debates during the
campaign that followed he had many opportunities to put before
the public his ideas of union and of slavery. Defeated by Douglas
for the senatorship, he had nevertheless made himself so popular
that he was nominated for president by the Republican party in its
National Convention at Chicago two years later. The facts of his
life from this time on are a part of history and are well known. His
many letters and speeches reveal Lincoln's nobility of mind, his
compassion, and straightforward thought and ideals. He has become the American who, not even Washington excepted, is closest
to the nation's heart and love.

Farewell to the Army of Northern Virginia

ROBERT E. LEE

HEADQUARTERS, ARMY OF NORTHERN VIRGINIA
April 10, 1865

GENERAL ORDER No. 9

After four years of arduous service marked by unsurpassed courage and fortitude, the Army of Northern Virginia has been compelled to yield to overwhelming numbers and resources.

I need not tell the survivors of so many hard-fought battles who have remained steadfast to the last that I have consented to this result from no distrust of them; but feeling that valor and devotion could accomplish nothing that would compensate for the loss that must have attended the continuance of the contest, I determined to avoid the useless sacrifice of those whose past services have endeared them to their countrymen. By the terms of the agreement, officers and men can return to their homes and remain until exchanged.

You may take with you the satisfaction that proceeds from the consciousness of duty faithfully performed, and I earnestly pray that a merciful God will extend to you His blessing and protection.

With an unceasing admiration of your constancy and devotion to your country, and a grateful remembrance of your kind and generous consideration of myself, I bid you all an affectionate farewell.

R. E. LEE, *General*

Do especially Questions 44, 45, 46, 49, 52, 133, and 147.

ROBERT E. LEE   1807-1870

Robert E. Lee was related by both birth and marriage to the leading families of Virginia. His father, "Light Horse Harry" Lee, had been governor of Virginia, and two Lees, Richard and Francis, were signers of the Declaration of Independence.

In 1829 Lee graduated with distinction from the United States Military Academy at West Point. He served in the Mexican War, and in April, 1861, at the outbreak of the Civil War, was offered command of the Federal forces. That brilliant offer Lee declined with a heavy heart. He resigned his commission in the United States Army and went to Richmond to place his services at the disposal of Virginia.

Lee regarded slavery as an evil, and in common with many of the land-owners of Virginia, had liberated his slaves. Yet he considered that it would be a greater evil to attempt to eradicate slavery by force. He believed in the advantages of the Union, but he also believed in the rights of the states to secede if they wished. One of the great generals of all time, he showed his greatness in the way he accepted the result of the war. After his surrender he set himself to heal the wounds of his people, and though impoverished by the war, he refused a commercial offer to write his account of the great events in which he had taken a leading part. He accepted the presidency of Washington College (afterwards Washington and Lee University) and there he spent his last years teaching, by precept and example, his concepts of American citizenship.

The Moral Equivalent of War*

WILLIAM JAMES

The war against war is going to be no holiday excursion or camping party. The military feelings are too deeply grounded to abdicate their place among our ideals until better substitutes are offered than the glory and shame that come to nations as well as to individuals from the ups and downs of politics and the vicissitudes° of trade. There is something highly paradoxical° in the modern man's relation to war. Ask all our millions, north and south, whether they

*This essay was written for the Association for International Conciliation and was also published in *McClure's Magazine*, August, 1910.

would vote now (were such a thing possible) to have our war for the Union expunged° from history, and the record of a peaceful transition to the present time substituted for that of its marches and battles, and probably hardly a handful of eccentrics would say yes. Those ancestors, those efforts, those memories and legends, are the most ideal part of what we now own together, a sacred spiritual possession worth more than all the blood poured out. Yet ask those same people whether they would be willing in cold blood to start another civil war now to gain another similar possession, and not one man or woman would vote for the proposition. In modern eyes, precious though wars may be, they must not be waged solely for the sake of the ideal harvest. Only when forced upon one, only when an enemy's injustice leaves us no alternative, is a war now thought permissible.

It was not thus in ancient times. The earlier men were hunting men, and to hunt a neighboring tribe, kill the males, loot the village, and possess the females, was the most profitable, as well as the most exciting, way of living. Thus were the more martial tribes selected, and in chiefs and peoples a pure pugnacity° and love of glory came to mingle with the more fundamental appetite for plunder.

Modern war is so expensive that we feel trade to be a better avenue to plunder; but modern man inherits all the innate pugnacity and all the love of glory of his ancestors. Showing war's irrationality and horror is of no effect upon him. The horrors make the fascination. War is the *strong* life; it is life *in extremis;* war-taxes are the only ones men never hesitate to pay, as the budgets of all nations show us.

History is a bath of blood. *The Iliad* is one long recital of how Diomedes and Ajax, Sarpedon and Hector *killed.* No detail of the wounds they made is spared us, and the Greek mind fed upon the story. Greek history is a panorama of jingoism° and imperialism — war for war's sake, all the citizens being warriors. It is horrible reading, because of the irrationality of it all — save for the purpose of making "history" — and the history is that of the utter ruin of a civilization in intellectual respects perhaps the highest the earth has ever seen.

Those wars were purely piratical.° Pride, gold, women, slaves, excitement, were their only motives. In the Peloponnesian War,[1] for example, the Athenians ask the inhabitants of Melos (the island where the "Venus of Milo" was found), hitherto neutral, to own their lordship. The envoys meet, and hold a debate which Thucydides[2] gives in full, and which, for sweet reasonableness of form, would have satisfied Matthew Arnold.[3] "The powerful exact what they can," said the Athenians, "and the weak grant what they must." When the Meleans say that sooner than be slaves they will appeal to the gods, the Athenians reply: "Of the gods we believe and of men we know that, by a law of their nature, wherever they can rule they will. This law was not made by us, and we are not the first to have acted upon it; we did but inherit it, and we know that you and all mankind, if you were as strong as we are, would do as we do. So much for the gods; we have told you why we expect to stand as high in their good opinion as you." Well, the Meleans still refused, and their town was taken. "The Athenians," Thucydides quietly says, "thereupon put to death all who were of military age and made slaves of the women and children. They then colonized the island, sending thither five hundred settlers of their own."

Alexander's[4] career was piracy pure and simple, nothing but an orgy of power and plunder, made romantic by the character of the hero. There was no rational principle in it, and the moment he died his generals and governors attacked one another. The cruelty of those times is incredible. When Rome finally conquered Greece, Paulus Æmilius was told by the Roman Senate to reward his soldiers for their toil by "giving" them the old kingdom of Epirus. They sacked seventy cities and carried off a hundred and

---

[1]The war between Athens and Sparta (431-404 B.C.) which resulted in the leadership of Greece passing from Athens to Sparta.
[2]The greatest historian of ancient times; author of *The History of the Peloponnesian War.*
[3]English poet and classical scholar (1822-1888) who believed culture — "the best that has been thought and said in the world" — the only cure for the dissatisfactions he found in England in his day.
[4]King of Macedonia (356, 336-323 B.C.) and conqueror of the East.

fifty thousand inhabitants as slaves. How many they killed I know not; but in Etolia they killed all the senators, five hundred and fifty in number. Brutus[5] was "the noblest Roman of them all," but to reanimate his soldiers on the eve of Philippi he similarly promises to give them the cities of Sparta and Thessalonica to ravage, if they win the fight.

Such was the gory nurse that trained societies to cohesiveness.° We inherit the warlike type; and for most of the capacities of heroism that the human race is full of we have to thank this cruel history. Dead men tell no tales, and if there were any tribes of other type than this they have left no survivors. Our ancestors have bred pugnacity into our bone and marrow, and thousands of years of peace won't breed it out of us. The popular imagination fairly fattens on the thought of wars. Let public opinion once reach a certain fighting pitch, and no ruler can withstand it. In the Boer War[6] both governments began with bluff but couldn't stay there, the military tension was too much for them. In 1898 our people had read the word "war" in letters three inches high for three months in every newspaper. The pliant politician McKinley[7] was swept away by their eagerness, and our squalid war with Spain became a necessity.

At the present day, civilized opinion is a curious mental mixture. The military instincts and ideals are as strong as ever, but are confronted by reflective criticisms which sorely curb their ancient freedom. Innumerable writers are showing up the bestial side of military service. Pure loot and mastery seem no longer morally avowable motives, and pretexts must be found for attributing them solely to the enemy. England and we, our army and navy authorities repeat without ceasing, arm solely for "peace," Germany and Japan it is who are bent on loot and glory. "Peace" in

[5]Marcus Brutus, the friend of Caesar who joined the conspirators against Caesar because he made himself a dictator. The quotation is from Shakespeare's play, *Julius Caesar*.
[6]A dispute between England and the Transvaal Republic (1899-1902) which resulted in the founding of the Union of South Africa.
[7]William McKinley (1843-1901), twenty-fifth President of the United States, who was forced by political pressure to intervene in a Cuban insurrection against Spain.

military mouths today is a synonym for "war expected."
The word has become a pure provocative, and no government wishing peace sincerely should allow it ever to be
printed in a newspaper. Every up-to-date dictionary should
say that "peace" and "war" mean the same thing, now *in
posse*, now *in actu*.[8] It may even reasonably be said that
the intensely sharp competitive *preparation* for war by the
nations *is the real war*, permanent, unceasing; and that the
battles are only a sort of public verification of the mastery
gained during the "peace"-interval.

It is plain that on this subject civilized man has developed a sort of double personality. If we take European
nations, no legitimate interest of any one of them would
seem to justify the tremendous destructions which a war to
compass it would necessarily entail. It would seem as
though common sense and reason ought to find a way to
reach agreement in every conflict of honest interests. I
myself think it our bounden duty to believe in such international rationality as possible. But, as things stand, I see
how desperately hard it is to bring the peace-party and the
war-party together, and I believe that the difficulty is due to
certain deficiencies in the program of pacificism° which set
the militarist imagination strongly, and to a certain extent
justifiably, against it. In the whole discussion both sides are
on imaginative and sentimental ground. It is but one utopia°
against another, and everything one says must be abstract
and hypothetical.° Subject to this criticism and caution, I
will try to characterize in abstract strokes the opposite
imaginative forces, and point out what to my own very
fallible mind seems the best utopian hypothesis, the most
promising line of conciliation.

In my remarks, pacificist though I am, I will refuse to
speak of the bestial side of the war-*régime* (already done
justice to by many writers) and consider only the higher
aspects of militaristic sentiment. Patriotism no one thinks
discreditable; nor does anyone deny that war is the romance of history. But inordinate ambitions are the soul of
every patriotism, and the possibility of violent death the

[8]IN POSSE . . . IN ACTU — In *capacity*, now in *actuality*.

soul of all romance. The militarily patriotic and romantic-
minded everywhere, and especially the professional military class, refuse to admit for a moment that war may be a
transitory phenomenon in social evolution. The notion of a
sheep's paradise like that revolts, they say, our higher
imagination. Where then would be the steeps° of life? If
war had ever stopped, we should have to re-invent it, on
this view, to redeem life from flat degeneration.

Reflective apologists for war at the present day all take it
religiously. It is a sort of sacrament. Its profits are to the
vanquished as well as to the victor; and quite apart from any
question of profit, it is an absolute good, we are told, for it is
human nature at its highest dynamic. Its "horrors" are a
cheap price to pay for rescue from the only alternative
supposed, of a world of clerks and teachers, of co-education
and zo-ophily,⁹ of "consumer's leagues" and "associated
charities," of industrialism unlimited, and femininism una-
bashed. No scorn, no hardness, no valor any more! Fie
upon such a cattleyard of a planet!

So far as the central essence of this feeling goes, no
healthy minded person, it seems to me, can help to some
degree partaking of it. Militarism is the great preserver of
our ideals of hardihood, and human life with no use for
hardihood would be contemptible. Without risks or prizes
for the darer, history would be insipid indeed; and there is a
type of military character which everyone feels that the race
should never cease to breed, for everyone is sensitive to its
superiority. The duty is incumbent on mankind, of keeping
military characters in stock—of keeping them, if not for use,
then as ends in themselves and as pure pieces of perfection,
—so that Roosevelt's weaklings and mollycoddles¹⁰ may not
end by making everything else disappear from the face of
nature.

This natural sort of feeling forms, I think, the innermost
soul of army-writings. Without any exception known to me,

⁹Love of animals.
¹⁰Theodore Roosevelt, President of the United States, 1901-1909, believed in a strong, well-armed America as a guarantor of world peace. He
considered those of his associates who did not agree with him "weaklings
and mollycoddles."

militarist authors take a highly mystical view of their subject, and regard war as a biological or sociological necessity,
uncontrolled by ordinary psychological checks and motives. When the time of development is ripe the war must
come, reason or no reason, for the justifications pleaded are
invariably fictitious. War is, in short, a permanent human
obligation. General Homer Lea, in his book *The Valor of
Ignorance,* plants himself squarely on this ground. Readiness for war is for him the essence of nationality, and ability
in it the supreme measure of the health of nations. . . .

Having said thus much in preparation, I will now confess
my own utopia. I devoutly believe in the reign of peace
and in the gradual advent of some sort of a social balance.
The fatalistic view of the war-function is to me nonsense,
for I know that war-making is due to definite motives and
subject to prudential checks and reasonable criticisms, just
like any other form of enterprise. And when whole nations
are the armies, and the science of destruction vies in
intellectual refinement with the sciences of production, I
see that war becomes absurd and impossible from its own
monstrosity. Extravagant ambitions will have to be replaced by reasonable claims, and nations must make common cause against them. I see no reason why all this
should not apply to yellow as well as to white countries, and
I look forward to a future when acts of war shall be formally
outlawed as between civilized peoples.

All these beliefs of mine put me squarely into the anti-
militarist party. But I do not believe that peace either
ought to be or will be permanent on this globe, unless the
states pacifically organized preserve some of the old elements of army-discipline. A permanently successful peace-
economy cannot be a simple pleasure-economy. In the
more or less socialistic future towards which mankind
seems drifting we must still subject ourselves collectively
to those severities which answer to our real position upon
this only partly hospitable globe. We must make new
energies and hardihoods continue the manliness to which
the military mind so faithfully clings. Martial virtues must
be the enduring cement; intrepidity, contempt of softness,

surrender of private interest, obedience to command, must still remain the rock upon which states are built—unless, indeed, we wish for dangerous reactions against common-wealths fit only for contempt, and liable to invite attack whenever a centre of crystallization for military-minded enterprise gets formed anywhere in their neighborhood.

The war-party is assuredly right in affirming and reaffirm-ing that the martial virtues, although originally gained by the race through war, are absolute and permanent human goods. Patriotic pride and ambition in their military form are, after all, only specifications of a more general competi-tive passion. They are its first form, but that is no reason for supposing them to be its last form. Men now are proud of belonging to a conquering nation, and without a murmur they lay down their persons and their wealth, if by so doing they may fend off subjection. But who can be sure that *other aspects of one's country* may not, with time and education and suggestion enough, come to be regarded with similarly effective feelings of pride and shame? Why should men not some day feel that it is worth a blood-tax to belong to a collectivity superior in *any* ideal respect? Why should they not blush with indignant shame if the com-munity that owns them is vile in any way whatsoever? Individuals, daily more numerous, now feel this civic passion. It is only a question of blowing on the spark till the whole population gets incandescent, and on the ruins of the old morals of military honor, a stable system of morals of civic honor builds itself up. What the whole community comes to believe in grasps the individual as in a vise. The war-function has grasped us so far; but constructive inter-ests may some day seem no less imperative, and impose on the individual a hardly lighter burden.

Let me illustrate my idea more concretely. There is nothing to make one indignant in the mere fact that life is hard, that men should toil and suffer pain. The planetary conditions once for all are such, and we can stand it. But that so many men, by mere accidents of birth and oppor-tunity, should have a life of *nothing else* but toil and pain and hardness and inferiority imposed upon them, should have *no* vacation, while others natively no more deserving never get any taste of this campaigning life at all — *this* is capable of arousing indignation in reflective minds. It may end by seeming shameful to all of us that some of us have nothing but campaigning, and others nothing but unmanly ease. If now — and this is my idea — there were, instead of military conscription a conscription of the whole youthful population to form for a certain number of years a part of the army enlisted against *Nature*, the injustice would tend to be evened out, and numerous other goods to the commonwealth would follow. The military ideals of hardihood and discipline would be wrought into the growing fibre of the people; no one would remain blind as the luxurious classes now are blind, to man's relations to the globe he lives on, and to the permanently sour and hard foundations of his higher life. To coal and iron mines, to freight trains, to fishing fleets in December, to dishwashing, clothes-washing, and window-washing, to road-building and tunnel-making, to foundries and stoke-holes, and to the frames of skyscrapers, would our gilded youths be drafted off, according to their choice, to get the childishness knocked out of them, and to come back into society with healthier sympathies and soberer ideas. They would have paid their blood-tax, done their own part in the immemorial human warfare against nature; they would tread the earth more proudly, the women would value them more highly, they would be better fathers and teachers of the following generation.

Such a conscription, with the state of public opinion that would have required it, and the many moral fruits it would bear, would preserve in the midst of a pacific civilization the manly virtues which the military party is so afraid of seeing disappear in peace. We should get toughness without callousness, authority with as little criminal cruelty as possible, and painful work done cheerily because the duty is temporary, and threatens not, as now, to degrade the whole remainder of one's life. I spoke of the "moral equivalent" of war. So far, war has been the only force that can discipline a whole community, and until an equivalent discipline is organized, I believe that war must have its way. But I have no serious doubt that the ordinary prides and shames of social man, once developed to a certain intensity, are capable of organizing such a moral equivalent as I have sketched, or some other just as effective for preserving manliness of type. It is but a question of time, of skillful propagandism, and of opinion-making men seizing historic opportunities.

Do especially Questions 1, 11, 12-14, 26-31, 47, 53, 145, and 150. Consult the Model Essay in Volume One.

WILLIAM JAMES   *1842-1910*

Born of a wealthy family in New York City, James was educated by private tutors both at home and in Europe. He abandoned a career in painting to study medicine at the Harvard Medical School, but never practiced. In 1872 he began a long period of teaching at Harvard where he became interested in problems of psychology and philosophy. His *Principles of Psychology,* although somewhat outdated by later discoveries, remains a classic school text on the subject. From middle life through his last years he wrote many articles and books on various aspects of religion and philosophy. His brilliant expositional style is especially evident in his "The Moral Equivalent of War" in which he expresses his hatred of war and proposes the conscription of youth for projects of manual labor—a plan resembling in some respects our modern Peace Corps.

FROM *The Education of Henry Adams*

HENRY ADAMS

...While at Wenlock,[1] he received a letter from President Eliot inviting him to take an Assistant Professorship of History, to be created shortly at Harvard College. After waiting ten or a dozen years for someone to show conscious-

---

[1]Wenlock Abbey, a monastery in England.

From *The Education of Henry Adams,* Copyright 1946 by Charles F. Adams. Reprinted by permission of the publisher, Houghton Mifflin Company, and Constable & Co., Ltd.

ness of his existence, even a *Terebratula*[2] would be pleased and grateful for a compliment which implied that the new President of Harvard College wanted his help; but Adams knew nothing about history, and much less about teaching, while he knew more than enough about Harvard College; and wrote at once to thank President Eliot, with much regret that the honor should be above his powers. His mind was full of other matters. The summer, from which he had expected only amusement and social relations with new people, had ended in the most intimate personal tragedy,[3] and the most terrific political convulsion[4] he had ever known or was likely to know. He had failed in every object of his trip. The Quarterlies had refused his best essay. He had made no acquaintances and hardly picked up the old ones. He sailed from Liverpool, on September 1, to begin again where he had started two years before, but with no longer a hope of attaching himself to a President or a party or a press. He was a free lance and no other career stood in sight or mind. To that point education had brought him.

Yet he found, on reaching home, that he had not done quite so badly as he feared. His article on the Session in the July *North American* had made a success. Though he could not quite see what partisan object it served, he heard with flattered astonishment that it had been reprinted by the Democratic National Committee and circulated as a campaign document by the hundred thousand copies. He was henceforth in oppositon, do what he might; and a Massachusetts Democrat, say what he pleased; while his only reward or return for this partisan service consisted in being formally answered by Senator Timothy Howe, of Wisconsin, in a Republican campaign document, presumed to be also freely circulated, in which the Senator, besides refuting his opinions, did him the honor—most unusual and picturesque in a Senator's rhetoric—of likening him to a begonia.

[2] A species of mollusc, simpler than a clam, more complex than a coral.
[3] Adams' sister had died.
[4] The outbreak of the Franco-Prussian War.

The begonia is, or then was, a plant of such senatorial qualities as to make the simile, in intention, most flattering. Far from charming in its refinement, the begonia was remarkable for curious and showy foliage; it was conspicuous; it seemed to have no useful purpose; and it insisted on standing always in the most prominent positions. Adams would have greatly liked to be a begonia in Washington, for this was rather his ideal of the successful statesman, and he thought about it still more when the *Westminster Review* for October brought him his article on the Gold Conspiracy, which was also instantly pirated on a great scale. Piratical he was himself henceforth driven to be, and he asked only to be pirated, for he was sure not to be paid; but the honors of piracy resemble the colors of the begonia; they are showy but not useful. Here was a *tour de force*° he had never dreamed himself equal to performing: two long, dry, quarterly, thirty-or-forty-page articles, appearing in quick succession, and pirated for audiences running well into the hundred thousands; and not one person, man or woman, offering him so much as a congratulation, except to call him a begonia.

Had this been all, life might have gone on very happily as before, but the ways of America to a young person of literary and political tastes were such as the so-called evolution of civilized man had not before evolved. No sooner had Adams made at Washington what he modestly hoped was a sufficient success, than his whole family set on him to drag him away. For the first time since 1861 his father interposed; his mother entreated; and his brother Charles argued and urged that he should come to Harvard College. Charles had views of further joint operations in a new field. He said that Henry had done at Washington all he could possibly do; that his position there wanted solidity; that he was, after all, an adventurer; that a few years in Cambridge would give him personal weight; that his chief function was not to be that of teacher, but that of editing the *North American Review* which was to be coupled with the profes-. sorship, and would lead to the daily press. In short, that he needed the university more than the university needed him.

Henry knew the university well enough to know that the department of history was controlled by one of the most astute and ideal administrators in the world—Professor Gurney—and that it was Gurney who had established the new professorship, and had cast his net over Adams to carry the double load of medieval history and the *Review*. He could see no relation whatever between himself and a professorship. He sought education; he did not sell it. He knew no history; he knew only a few historians; his ignorance was mischievous because it was literary, accidental, indifferent. On the other hand he knew Gurney, and felt much influenced by his advice. One cannot take one's self quite seriously in such matters; it could not much affect the sum of solar energies whether one went on dancing with girls in Washington, or began talking to boys at Cambridge. The good people who thought it did matter had a sort of right to guide. One could not reject their advice; still less disregard their wishes.

The sum of the matter was that Henry went out to Cambridge and had a few words with President Eliot which seemed to him almost as American as the talk about diplomacy with his father ten years before. "But, Mr. President," urged Adams, "I know nothing about Medieval History." With the courteous manner and bland smile so familiar for the next generation of Americans, Mr. Eliot mildly but firmly replied, "If you will point out to me anyone who knows more, Mr. Adams, I will appoint him." The answer was neither logical nor convincing, but Adams could not meet it without overstepping his privileges. He could not say that, under the circumstances, the appointment of any professor at all seemed to him unnecessary.

So, at twenty-four hours' notice, he broke his life in halves again in order to begin a new education, on lines he had not chosen, in subjects for which he cared less than nothing; in a place he did not love, and before a future which repelled. Thousands of men have to do the same thing, but his case was peculiar because he had no need to do it. He did it because his best and wisest friends urged it, and he never could make up his mind whether they were right or not. To him this kind of education was always false. For himself he had no doubts. He thought it a mistake; but his opinion did not prove that it was one, since, in all probability, whatever he did would be more or less a mistake. He had reached cross-roads of education which all led astray. What he could gain at Harvard College he did not know, but in any case it was nothing he wanted. What he lost at Washington he could partly see, but in any case it was not fortune. Grant's administration wrecked men by thousands, but profited few. Perhaps Mr. Fish[5] was the solitary exception. One might search the whole list of Congress, Judiciary, and Executive during the twenty-five years 1870 to 1895, and find little but damaged reputation. The period was poor in purpose and barren in results.

Henry Adams, if not the rose, lived as near it as any politician, and knew, more or less, all the men in any way prominent at Washington, or knew all about them. Among them, in his opinion, the best equipped, the most active-minded, and most industrious was Abram Hewitt,[6] who sat in Congress for a dozen years, between 1874 and 1886, sometimes leading the House and always wielding influence second to none. With nobody did Adams form closer or longer relations than with Mr. Hewitt, whom he regarded as the most useful public man in Washington; and he was the more struck by Hewitt's saying, at the end of his laborious career as legislator, that he left behind him no permanent result except the Act consolidating the Surveys. Adams knew no other man who had done so much, unless Mr. Sherman's[7] legislation is accepted as an instance of success. Hewitt's nearest rival would probably have been Senator Pendleton[8] who stood father to civil service reform in 1882, an attempt to correct a vice that should never have

[5]Hamilton Fish, Secretary of State under President Grant.
[6]Abram Stevens Hewitt, New York industrialist and Democratic Representative to Congress.
[7]James Schoolcraft Sherman served (1887-91, 1893-1909) as a Republican in Congress and headed the House Committee on Indian Affairs for fourteen years.
[8]George Hunt Pendleton, United States Senator from Ohio (1879-1883). He was responsible for legislation introducing competitive examinations in the Civil Service.

been allowed to be born. These were the men who succeeded.

The press stood in much the same light. No editor, no political writer, and no public administrator achieved enough good reputation to preserve his memory for twenty years. A number of them achieved bad reputations, or damaged good ones that had been gained in the Civil War. On the whole, even for Senators, diplomats, and Cabinet officers, the period was wearisome and stale.

None of Adams' generation profited by public activity unless it were William C. Whitney,[9] and even he could not be induced to return to it. Such ambitions as these were out of one's reach, but supposing one tried for what was feasible, attached one's self closely to the Garfields, Arthurs, Frelinghuysens, Blaines, Bayards, or Whitneys, who happened to hold office; and supposing one asked for the mission to Belgium or Portugal, and obtained it; supposing one served a term as Assistant Secretary or Chief of Bureau; or, finally, supposing one had gone as sub-editor on the New York *Tribune* or *Times* — how much more education would one have gained than by going to Harvard College? These questions seemed better worth an answer than most of the questions on examination papers at college or in the civil service; all the more because one never found an answer to them, then or afterwards, and because, to his mind, the value of American society altogether was mixed up with the value of Washington.

At first, the simple beginner, struggling with principles, wanted to throw off responsibility on the American people, whose bare and toiling shoulders had to carry the load of every social or political stupidity; but the American people had no more to do with it than with the customs of Peking. American character might perhaps account for it, but what accounted for American character? All Boston, all New England, and respectable New York, including Charles Francis Adams the father and Charles Francis Adams the

[9]William Collins Whitney, Secretary of the Navy under President Grover Cleveland (1885-1889) secured legislation for the making of armor-plated war vessels.

son, agreed that Washington was no place for a respectable young man. All Washington, including Presidents, Cabinet officers, Judiciary, Senators, Congressmen, and clerks, expressed the same opinion, and conspired to drive away every young man who happened to be there, or tried to approach. Not one young man of promise remained in the Government service. All drifted into opposition. The Government did not want them in Washington. Adams' case was perhaps the strongest because he thought he had done well. He was forced to guess it, since he knew no one who would have risked so extravagant a step as that of encouraging a young man in a literary career, or even in a political one; society forbade it, as well as residence in a political capital; but Harvard College must have seen some hope for him, since it made him professor against his will; even the publishers and editors of the *North American Review* must have felt a certain amount of confidence in him, since they put the *Review* in his hands. After all, the *Review* was the first literary power in America, even though it paid almost as little in gold as the United States Treasury. The degree of Harvard College might bear a value as ephemeral° as the commission of a President of the United States; but the government of the college, measured by money alone, and patronage, was a matter of more importance than that of some branches of the national service. In social position, the college was the superior of them all put together. In knowledge, she could assert no superiority, since the Government made no claims, and prided itself on ignorance. The service of Harvard College was distinctly honorable; perhaps the most honorable in America; and if Harvard College thought Henry Adams worthy employing at four dollars a day, why should Washington decline his services when he asked nothing? Why should he be dragged from a career he liked in a place he loved, into a career he detested, in a place and climate he shunned? Was it enough to satisfy him that all America should call Washington barren and dangerous? What made Washington more dangerous than New York?

The American character showed singular limitations

which sometimes drove the student of civilized man to despair. Crushed by his own ignorance — lost in the darkness of his own gropings — the scholar finds himself jostled of a sudden by a crowd of men who seem to him ignorant that there is a thing called ignorance; who have forgotten how to amuse themselves; who cannot even understand that they are bored. The American thought of himself as a restless, pushing, energetic, ingenious person, always awake and trying to get ahead of his neighbors. Perhaps this idea of the national character might be correct for New York or Chicago; it was not correct for Washington. There the American showed himself, four times in five, as a quiet, peaceful, shy figure, rather in the mould of Abraham Lincoln, somewhat sad, sometimes pathetic, once tragic; or like Grant, inarticulate, uncertain, distrustful of himself, still more distrustful of others, and awed by money. That the American, by temperament, worked to excess, was true; work and whiskey were his stimulants; work was a form of vice; but he never cared much for money or power after he earned them. The amusement of the pursuit was all the amusement he got from it; he had no use for wealth. Jim Fisk alone seemed to know what he wanted; Jay Gould never did.[10] At Washington one met mostly such true Americans, but if one wanted to know them better, one went to study them in Europe. Bored, patient, helpless; pathetically dependent on his wife and daughters; indulgent to excess; mostly a modest, decent, excellent, valuable citizen; the American was to be met at every railway station in Europe, carefully explaining to every listener that the happiest day of his life would be the day he should land on the pier at New York. He was ashamed to be amused; his mind no longer answered to the stimulus of variety; he could not face a new thought. All his immense strength, his intense nervous energy, his keen analytic perceptions, were oriented in one direction, and he could not change it.

[10]James Fisk, American financier, in 1866 established a brokerage house in New York City. With Jay Gould, another capitalist, and Daniel Drew, Fisk conducted the famous struggle with Cornelius Vanderbilt for control of the Erie Railroad. Later Fisk and Gould unscrupulously manipulated Erie stock so as to wreck the railroad and secure millions for themselves.

Congress was full of such men; in the Senate, Sumner[11] was almost the only exception; in the Executive, Grant and Boutwell[12] were varieties of the type—political specimens —pathetic in their helplessness to do anything with power when it came to them. They knew not how to amuse themselves; they could not conceive how other people were amused. Work, whiskey, and cards were life. The atmosphere of political Washington was theirs—or was supposed by the outside world to be in their control—and this was the reason why the outside world judged that Washington was fatal even for a young man of thirty-two, who had passed through the whole variety of temptations, in every capital of Europe, for a dozen years; who never played cards, and who loathed whiskey....

[11]Charles Sumner, outspoken Senator from Massachusetts, who violently opposed Grant's scheme to annex Santo Domingo.
[12]George Sewall Boutwell, Secretary of the Treasury (1869-1873) was considered one of President Grant's many poor appointments. He neglected many important problems to advance his chief concern to reduce the national debt.

Do especially Questions 1, 11, 12-14, 26-31, 48, 49, 52, 53, 135, 145, 146, 147, and 150. Consult the Model Essay in Volume One.

HENRY ADAMS   *1838-1918*

Henry Adams' great-grandfather was the nation's second president, his grandfather was its sixth president, and his father was a famous diplomat and foreign minister. Reared in a tolerant religious atmosphere, he soon drifted into what he characterized in *The Education of Henry Adams* as his chief "weaknesses": "The habit of doubt; of distrusting his own judgment and of totally rejecting the judgment of the world; the tendency to regard every question as open; the hesitation to act except as a choice of evils; the shirking of responsibility; the love of line, form, quality; the horror of ennui;° the passion for companionship and the antipathy to society...." These weaknesses made him a lifelong skeptic. Following his stay at Harvard, which he recounts in the passage in this volume, he went to Washington to write history and to seek friends among the political leaders of his day. "So far as [I] had a function in life," he wrote, "it was as stable-companion to statesmen." In the succeeding years he traveled widely and completed his nine-volume *History of the United States During the Administrations of Jefferson and Madison.* Later works, particularly *The Education of Henry Adams,* continued to expound his unique theory of history as a dynamic Force.

FROM *Life on the Mississippi*

MARK TWAIN

A BOY'S AMBITION

When I was a boy, there was but one permanent ambition among my comrades in our village on the west bank of the Mississippi River. That was, to be a steamboatman. We had transient ambitions of other sorts, but they were only transient. When a circus came and went, it left us all burning to become clowns; the first Negro minstrel show that ever came to our section left us all suffering to try that kind of life; now and then we had a hope that, if we lived and were good, God would permit us to be pirates. These ambitions faded out, each in its turn; but the ambition to be a steamboatman always remained.

Once a day a cheap, gaudy packet° arrived upward from St. Louis, and another downward from Keokuk. Before these events, the day was glorious with expectancy; after them, the day was a dead and empty thing. Not only the boys, but the whole village, felt this. After all these years I can picture that old time to myself now, just as it was then: the white town drowsing in the sunshine of a summer's morning; the streets empty, or pretty nearly so; one or two clerks sitting in front of the Water Street stores, with their splint-bottomed chairs tilted back against the walls, chins on breasts, hats slouched over their faces, asleep — with shingle-shavings enough around to show what broke them down; a sow and a litter of pigs loafing along the sidewalk, doing a good business in watermelon rinds and seeds; two or three lonely little freight piles scattered about the "levee"; a pile of "skids" on the slope of the stone-paved

"A Boy's Ambition" and "A Daring Deed," from *Life on the Mississippi* by Mark Twain. Reprinted by permission of Harper & Row, Publishers.

wharf, and the fragrant town drunkard asleep in the shadow
of them; two or three wood flats at the head of the wharf, but
nobody to listen to the peaceful lapping of the wavelets
against them; the great Mississippi, the majestic, the magnificent Mississippi, rolling its mile-wide tide along, shining in the sun; the dense forest away on the other side; the
"point" above the town, and the "point" below, bounding
the river-glimpse and turning it into a sort of sea, and withal
a very still and brilliant and lonely one.

Presently a film of dark smoke appears above one of those
remote "points"; instantly a Negro drayman, famous for his
quick eye and prodigious voice, lifts up the cry, "S-t-e-a-m-
boat a-comin'!" and the scene changes! The town drunkard
stirs, the clerks wake up, a furious clatter of drays follows,
every house and store pours out a human contribution, and
all in a twinkling the dead town is alive and moving. Drays,
carts, men, boys, all go hurrying from many quarters to a
common center, the wharf. Assembled there, the people
fasten their eyes upon the coming boat as upon a wonder
they are seeing for the first time. And the boat *is* rather a
handsome sight, too. She is long and sharp and trim and
pretty; she has two tall, fancy-topped chimneys, with a
gilded device of some kind swung between them; a fanciful
pilot-house, all glass and "gingerbread," perched on top of
the "texas"[1] deck behind them; the paddle-boxes are gorgeous with a picture or with gilded rays above the boat's
name; the boiler-deck, the hurricane-deck, and the texas
deck are fenced and ornamented with clean white railings;
there is a flag gallantly flying from the jack-staff; the furnace
doors are open and the fires glaring bravely; the upper
decks are black with passengers; the captain stands by the
big bell, calm, imposing, the envy of all; great volumes of
the blackest smoke are rolling and tumbling out of the
chimneys—a husbanded grandeur created with a bit of
pitch-pine just before arriving at a town; the crew are
grouped on the forecastle; the broad stage is run far out over
the port bow, and an envied deck-hand stands pictur-
esquely on the end of it with a coil of rope in his hand; the

[1]The *texas* was a structure on the top deck containing the officers' quarters.
The cabins on steamboats were named after states of the union. The
officers' cabin was the *texas* because it was the largest.

pent stream is screaming through the gauge-cocks; the captain lifts his hand, a bell rings, the wheels stop; then they turn back, churning the water to foam, and the steamer is at rest. Then such a scramble as there is to get aboard, and to get ashore, and to take in freight and to discharge freight, all at one and the same time; and such a yelling and cursing as the mates facilitate it all with! Ten minutes later the steamer is under way again, with no flag on the jack-staff and no black smoke issuing from the chimneys. After ten more minutes the town is dead again, and the town drunkard asleep by the skids once more.

My father was a justice of the peace, and I supposed he possessed the power of life and death over all men, and could hang anybody that offended him. This was distinction enough for me as a general thing; but the desire to be a steamboatman kept intruding, nevertheless. I first wanted to be a cabinboy, so that I could come out with a white apron on and shake a table-cloth over the side, where all my old comrades could see me; later I thought I would rather be the deck-hand who stood on the end of the stage-plank with the coil of rope in his hand, because he was particularly conspicuous. But these were only day-dreams — they were too heavenly to be contemplated as real possibilities.

By and by one of our boys went away. He was not heard of for a long time. At last he turned up as apprentice engineer or "striker" on a steamboat. This thing shook the bottom out of all my Sunday-school teachings. That boy had been notoriously worldly, and I just the reverse; yet he was exalted to this eminence, and I left in obscurity and misery. There was nothing generous about this fellow in his greatness. He would always manage to have a rusty bolt to scrub while his boat tarried at our town, and he would sit on the inside guard and scrub it, where we all could see him and envy him and loathe him. And whenever his boat was laid up he would come home and swell around the town in his blackest and greasiest clothes, so that nobody could help remembering that he was a steamboatman; and he used all sorts of steamboat technicalities in his talk, as if he were so used to them that he forgot common people could not understand them. He would speak of the "labboard" side of a horse in an easy, natural way that would make one wish he was dead. And he was always talking about "St. Looy" like an old citizen; he would refer casually to occasions when he was "coming down Fourth Street," or when he was "passing by the Planter's House," or when there was a fire and he took a turn on the brakes of "the old Big Missouri"; and then he would go on and lie about how many towns the size of ours were burned down there that day. Two or three of the boys had long been persons of consideration among us because they had been to St. Louis once and had a vague general knowledge of its wonders, but the day of their glory was over now. They lapsed into a humble silence, and learned to disappear when the ruthless "cub"-engineer approached. This fellow had money, too, and hair-oil. Also an ignorant silver watch and a showy brass watch-chain. He wore a leather belt and used no suspenders. If ever a youth was cordially admired and hated by his comrades, this one was. No girl could withstand his charms. He "cut out" every boy in the village. When his boat blew up at last, it diffused a tranquil contentment among us such as we had not known for months. But when he came home the next week, alive, renowned, and appeared in church all battered up and bandaged, a shining hero, stared at and wondered over by everybody, it seemed to us that the partiality of Providence for an undeserving reptile had reached a point where it was open to criticism.

This creature's career could produce but one result, and it speedily followed. Boy after boy managed to get on the river. The minister's son became an engineer. The doctor's and the postmaster's sons became "mud clerks"; the wholesale liquor dealer's son became a barkeeper on a boat; four sons of the chief merchant, and two sons of the county judge, became pilots. Pilot was the grandest position of all. The pilot, even in those days of trivial wages, had a princely salary — from a hundred and fifty to two hundred and fifty dollars a month, and no board to pay. Two months of his wages would pay a preacher's salary for a year. Now some of us were left disconsolate. We could not get on the river — at least our parents would not let us.

So, by and by, I ran away. I said I would never come home again till I was a pilot and could come in glory. But somehow I could not manage it. I went meekly aboard a few of the boats that lay packed together like sardines at the long St. Louis wharf, and humbly inquired for the pilots, but got only a cold shoulder and short words from mates and clerks. I had to make the best of this sort of treatment for the time being, but I had comforting day-dreams of a future when I should be a great and honored pilot, with plenty of money, and could kill some of these mates and clerks and pay for them.

A DARING DEED

When I returned to the pilot-house St. Louis was gone, and I was lost. Here was a piece of river which was all down in my book, but I could make neither head nor tail of it: you understand, it was turned around. I had seen it when coming up-stream, but I had never faced about to see how it looked when it was behind me. My heart broke again, for it was plain that I had got to learn this troublesome river *both ways.*

The pilot-house was full of pilots, going down to "look at the river." What is called the "upper river" (the two hundred miles between St. Louis and Cairo, where the Ohio comes in) was low; and the Mississippi changes its channel so constantly that the pilots used to always find it necessary to run down to Cairo to take a fresh look, when their boats were to lie in port a week; that is, when the water was at a low stage. A deal of this "looking at the river" was done by poor fellows who seldom had a berth, and whose only hope of getting one lay in their being always freshly posted and therefore ready to drop into the shoes of some reputable pilot, for a single trip, on account of such pilot's sudden illness, or some other necessity. And a good many of them constantly ran up and down inspecting the river, not because they ever really hoped to get a berth, but because (they being guests of the boat) it was cheaper to "look at the river" than stay ashore and pay board. In time these fellows grew dainty in their tastes, and only infested boats that had an established reputation for setting good tables. All visiting pilots were useful, for they were always ready and willing, winter or summer, night or day, to go out in the yawl and help buoy the channel or assist the boat's pilots in any way they could. They were likewise welcomed because all pilots are tireless talkers, when gathered together, and as they talk only about the river they are always understood and are always interesting. Your true pilot cares nothing about anything on earth but the river, and his pride in his occupation surpasses the pride of kings.

We had a fine company of these river inspectors along this trip. There were eight or ten, and there was abundance of room for them in our great pilot-house. Two or three of them wore polished silk hats, elaborate shirt-fronts, diamond breastpins, kid gloves, and patent-leather boots. They were choice in their English, and bore themselves with a dignity proper to men of solid means and prodigious reputation as pilots. The others were more or less loosely clad, and wore upon their heads tall felt cones that were suggestive of the days of the Commonwealth.

I was a cipher in this august company, and felt subdued, not to say torpid. I was not even of sufficient consequence to assist at the wheel when it was necessary to put the tiller hard down in a hurry; the guest that stood nearest did that when occasion required—and this was pretty much all the time, because of the crookedness of the channel and the scant water. I stood in a corner; and the talk I listened to took the hope all out of me. One visitor said to another:

"Jim, how did you run Plum Point, coming up?"

"It was in the night, there, and I ran it the way one of the boys on the *Diana* told me; started out about fifty yards above the woodpile on the false point, and held on the cabin under Plum Point till I raised the reef—quarter less twain—then straightened up for the middle bar till I got well abreast the old one-limbed cottonwood in the bend, then got my stern on the cottonwood, and head on the low place above the point, and came through a-booming—nine and a half."

"Pretty square crossing, an't it?"

"Yes, but the upper bar's working down fast."

Another pilot spoke up and said:

"I had better water than that, and ran it lower down; started out from the false point—mark twain—raised the second reef abreast the big snag in the bend, and had quarter less twain."

One of the gorgeous ones remarked:

"I don't want to find fault with your leadsmen, but that's a good deal of water for Plum Point, it seems to me."

There was an approving nod all around as this quiet snub dropped on the boaster and "settled" him. And so they went on talk-talk-talking. Meantime, the thing that was running in my mind was, "Now, if my ears hear aright, I have not only to get the names of all the towns and islands and bends, and so on, by heart, but I must even get up a warm personal acquaintanceship with every old snag and one-limbed cottonwood and obscure wood-pile that ornaments the banks of this river for twelve hundred miles; and more than that, I must actually know where these things are in the dark, unless these guests are gifted with eyes that can pierce through two miles of solid blackness. I wish the piloting business was in Jericho and I had never thought of it."

At dusk Mr. Bixby[2] tapped the big bell three times (the signal to land), and the captain emerged from his drawing-room in the forward end of the "texas," and looked up inquiringly. Mr. Bixby said:

"We will lay up here all night, captain."

"Very well, sir."

That was all. The boat came to shore and was tied up for the night. It seemed to me a fine thing that the pilot could do as he pleased, without asking so grand a captain's permission. I took my supper and went immediately to bed, discouraged by my day's observations and experiences. My late voyage's note-booking was but a confusion of meaningless names. It had tangled me all up in a knot every time I had looked at it in the daytime. I now hoped for respite in sleep; but no, it reveled all through my head till sunrise again, a frantic and tireless nightmare.

[2]The pilot who was teaching the author to become a pilot.

Next morning I felt pretty rusty and low-spirited. We went booming along, taking a good many chances, for we were anxious to "get out of the river" (as getting out to Cairo was called) before night should overtake us. But Mr. Bixby's partner, the other pilot, presently grounded the boat, and we lost so much time getting her off that it was plain the darkness would overtake us a good long way above the mouth. This was a great misfortune, especially to certain of our visiting pilots, whose boats would have to wait for their return, no matter how long that might be. It sobered the pilot-house talk a good deal. Coming up-stream, pilots did not mind low water or any kind of darkness; nothing stopped them but fog. But down-stream work was different; a boat was too nearly helpless, with a stiff current pushing behind her; so it was not customary to run down-stream at night in low water.

There seemed to be one small hope, however: if we could get through the intricate and dangerous Hat Island crossing before night, we could venture the rest, for we would have plainer sailing and better water. But it would be insanity to attempt Hat Island at night. So there was a deal of looking at watches all the rest of the day, and a constant ciphering upon the speed we were making; Hat Island was the eternal subject; sometimes hope was high and sometimes we were delayed in a bad crossing, and down it went again. For hours all hands lay under the burden of this suppressed excitement; it was even communicated to me, and I got to feeling so solicitous about Hat Island, and under such an awful pressure of responsibility, that I wished I might have five minutes on shore to draw a good, full, relieving breath, and start over again. We were standing no regular watches. Each of our pilots ran such portions of the river as he had run when coming up-stream, because of his greater familiarity with it; but both remained in the pilot-house constantly.

An hour before sunset Mr. Bixby took the wheel, and Mr. W. stepped aside. For the next thirty minutes every man held his watch in his hand and was restless, silent, and uneasy. At last somebody said, with a doomful sigh:

"Well, yonder's Hat Island—and we can't make it."

All the watches closed with a snap, everybody sighed and muttered something about its being "too bad, too bad — ah, if we could *only* have got here half an hour sooner!" and the place was thick with the atmosphere of disappointment. Some started to go out, but loitered, hearing no bell-tap to land. The sun dipped behind the horizon, the boat went on. Inquiring looks passed from one guest to another; and one who had his hand on the door-knob and had turned it, waited, then presently took away his hand and let the knob turn back again. We bore steadily down the bend. More looks were exchanged, and nods of surprised admiration — but no words. Insensibly the men drew together behind Mr. Bixby, as the sky darkened and one or two dim stars came out. The dead silence and sense of waiting became oppressive. Mr. Bixby pulled the cord, and two deep, mellow notes from the big bell floated off on the night. Then a pause, and one more note was struck. The watchman's voice followed, from the hurricane-deck:

"Labboard lead, there! Stabboard lead!"

The cries of the leadsmen began to rise out of the distance, and were gruffly repeated by the word-passers on the hurricane-deck.

"M-a-r-k three! M-a-r-k three! Quarter-less-three! Half twain! Quarter twain! Ma-r-k twain! Quarter-less —"

Mr. Bixby pulled two bell-ropes, and was answered by faint jinglings far below in the engine-room, and our speed slackened. The steam began to whistle through the gauge-cocks. The cries of the leadsmen went on — and it is a weird sound, always, in the night. Every pilot in the lot was watching now, with fixed eyes, and talking under his breath. Nobody was calm and easy but Mr. Bixby. He would put his wheel down and stand on a spoke, and as the steamer swung into her (to me) utterly invisible marks — for we seemed to be in the midst of a wide and gloomy sea — he would meet and fasten her there. Out of the murmur of half-audible talk, one caught a coherent sentence now and then — such as:

"There; she's over the first reef all right!"

After a pause, another subdued voice:

"Her stern's coming down just *exactly* right, by *George!*"

"Now she's in the marks; over she goes!"

Somebody else muttered:

"Oh, it was done beautiful — *beautiful!*"

Now the engines were stopped altogether, and we drifted with the current. Not that I could see the boat drift, for I could not, the stars being all gone by this time. This drifting was the dismalest work; it held one's heart still. Presently I discovered a blacker gloom than that which surrounded us. It was the head of the island. We were closing right down upon it. We entered its deeper shadow, and so imminent seemed the peril that I was likely to suffocate; and I had the strongest impulse to do *something*, anything, to save the vessel. But still Mr. Bixby stood by his wheel, silent, intent as a cat, and all the pilots stood shoulder to shoulder at his back.

"She'll not make it!" somebody whispered.

The water grew shoaler and shoaler, by the leadsman's cries, till it was down to:

"Eight-and-a-half! E-i-g-h-t feet! E-i-g-h-t feet! Seven-and—"

Mr. Bixby said warningly through his speaking-tube to the engineer:

"Stand by, now!"

"Ay, ay, sir!"

"Seven-and-a-half! Seven feet! *Six*-and—"

We touched bottom! Instantly, Mr. Bixby set a lot of bells ringing, shouted through the tube, "*Now*, let her have it — every ounce you've got!" then to his partner, "Put her hard down! snatch her! snatch her!" The boat rasped and ground her way through the sand, hung upon the apex of disaster a single tremendous instant, and then over she went! And such a shout as went up at Mr. Bixby's back never loosened the roof of a pilot-house before!

There was no more trouble after that. Mr. Bixby was a hero that night; and it was some little time, too, before his exploit ceased to be talked about by river-men.

Fully to realize the marvelous precision required in laying the great steamer in her marks in that murky waste of water, one should know that not only must she pick her intricate way through snags and blind reefs, and then shave the head of the island so closely as to brush the overhanging foliage with her stern, but at one place she must pass almost within arm's reach of a sunken and invisible wreck that would snatch the hull timbers from under her if she should strike it, and destroy a quarter of a million dollars' worth of steamboat and cargo in five minutes, and maybe a hundred and fifty human lives into the bargain.

The last remark I heard that night was a compliment to Mr. Bixby, uttered in soliloquy and with unction by one of our guests. He said:

"By the Shadow of Death, but he's a lightning pilot!"

Do especially Questions 1, 2, 11, 44, 48, 49, 52, 76, 77, 78, 79, 81, 134, 135, 136, 146, and 148. Consult the Model Essay in Volume One.

MARK TWAIN   (SAMUEL LANGHORNE CLEMENS)
1835-1910

More than a hundred years have passed since the birth of Sam Clemens in the frontier town of Florida, Missouri. He grew up in the town of Hannibal, which he immortalized as the home of Tom Sawyer and Huckleberry Finn. After his father died, Sam worked on his brother's newspaper and later became a steamboat pilot on the Mississippi River. Around the beginning of the Civil War young Sam became a prospector in Nevada. With the failure of his get-rich-quick scheme he turned to writing for some of the western papers. In 1859 he first used his pseudonym, Mark Twain, which means "two fathoms deep," and from then on his real name was all but forgotten. "The Celebrated Jumping Frog of Calaveras County" is the story that brought him fame. Twain traveled widely, writing and lecturing on his experiences. His timeless and exuberant stories have given the world a vivid record of the era in which he lived. His *Life on the Mississippi* is a mixture of reminiscence, history, and travelogue. It springs from intimate knowledge of small-town life deep in the interior of America—and of the colorful pageantry of steamboat travel.

PROBLEM QUESTIONS

1. "Lincoln's style has all the qualities of his mind: flexibility, directness, humanity. It is always applied art, never for an instant unfaithful to the business in hand, seldom if ever overlaying the direct thought with mere rhetorical decoration. It is the simple clear logic of the lawyer, and behind the mellow cadences is a brooding sadness which was to be with him to the end." Exemplify by quotations from Lincoln's works. Compare the brief address by Lee to one of Lincoln's. What similar personal qualities of both writers are revealed in the speeches?

2. Comment upon the following statement by James in the light of present-day thinking: "Only when forced upon one, only when an enemy's injustice leaves us no alternative, is a war now thought permissible." Discuss James's remarks about the militarists' idea that war is a biological or sociological necessity—is war still an "absolute good" or "human nature at its highest dynamic"? Explain in your own terms what James offers as a substitute for war—a "stable system of morals of civic honor." What form has his "moral equivalent of war" taken in the present day?

3. When Senator Howe likened Henry Adams to a begonia, why was Adams not offended? Explain how he applied the characteristics of the begonia to a statesman. Summarize the reasons why Adams believed his education had been a failure—that is, why did he feel that the world of law and order that he sought was disintegrating? Compare his analyses of the American people and of the leadership in Washington with your own ideas of modern American life.

4. How did Twain make use of "local color" to show the exact feeling of the old-time river-boat days? Mention some of the descriptive passages or colorful expressions he used that reveal his exuberant style or sense of humor. If you have read Twain's famous story "The Celebrated Jumping Frog of Calaveras County," compare the techniques he used in writing fiction with those he used in nonfiction.

5. Through the writers represented in this unit, trace the theme of "the growth of the democratic idea." Which authors express concepts that are still important in the American way of life? Which is most optimistic in outlook? Which most pessimistic? Which seems most "American"?

Unit Three

THE TRIUMPH
OF REGIONALISM

The nationalism that produced two shattering World Wars in the present century had its beginnings during the nineteenth century. What, people asked, distinguished an American from an Englishman, or an Irish immigrant in Boston from his brother back home, or a French-speaking New Orleans Creole from his relatives in France? Whatever differences there were could perhaps be listed under the diverse folk-ideas, customs, and myths among nations. There was a time when almost everyone's education consisted of the attitudes, the ideals, and the customs handed down from generation to generation by word of mouth. Before the era of widespread formal education with its use of traditional books and methods, the games, dances, proverbs, and folklore of a nation set it apart from all others. In music, for example, Russian peasant dances provided nineteenth-century composers like Rimski-Korsakov and Moussorgsky with material quite distinct from Grieg's Norwegian or Brahm's Hungarian or Dvořák's and Smetana's Slavonic dances. America during the same period developed its own square dances as distinctive variations of the English country dance; in the South, the sentimental ballads of Stephen Foster and the widely popular minstrel shows prepared America for an interest in the genuinely native Negro spirituals, for the harmonies and rhythms that later crystallized in modern Blues and Jazz; and composers like Edward MacDowell experimented with Indian melodies and tried unsuccessfully to break with European traditions.

81

In short, after a period of conscious identification with their various motherlands, Americans, by the nineteenth century, had adapted their various cultures to the New World and become fiercely regionalistic. Old World values were modified or rejected. A vigorous search for and pride in native, regional characteristics took place, and this regionalistic pride was reflected in the growing body of literature. The most fertile sources of native material proved to be the Negro and Creole lore of the South and the tall tales and cowboy ballads of the expanding West —all material composed by whole groups or anonymous individuals, passed on orally from generation to generation, and apparently farthest removed from Old World literary influences. Spirituals are spontaneous outcries, born of the hardships and trials of an enslaved race. The cowboy ballads of the West conjure up a picture of men singing around a campfire after interminable hours of lonely hard work. They sing of Paul Bunyan, of dying heroes and lovers, and of badmen like Jesse James. The same rough lonely heroes, though somewhat more sentimentalized, appear in Bret Harte's "The Luck of Roaring Camp" and other tales of the primitive mining camps. It was not until the appearance of Hamlin Garland and Frank Norris that the pioneer-farmer was presented with more realism as a victim of nature and of land-speculators.

The success of the local-color movement in America was no accident. Harte, Twain, and Garland in the West, Miss Freeman and Miss Jewett in rural New England—these short story writers were supported by powerful critic-apologists. There were strong defenses of the whole regionalist movement. "Why should the Western artists and poets look away to Greece and Rome and Persia for themes?" Hamlin Garland wrote in his *Crumbling Idols*. "I have met Western people who were writing blank-verse tragedies of the Middle Ages and painting pictures of sirens and cherubs, and still considered themselves Western artists and Western writers.... They were poets of books, not of life.... It is a settled conviction with me that each locality must produce its own literary record, each special phase of life utter its own voice.... The sun of truth strikes each part of the earth at a little different angle; it is this angle which gives life and infinite variety to literature." William Dean Howells, too, championed the movement and proclaimed that "no language is ever old on the lips of those who speak it, no matter how decrepit it drops from the pen. We have only to leave our studies, editorial and other, and go into the shops and fields. . . ." Like Garland, Howells wanted the characters of American literature to speak "true American, with all the varying Tennessean, Philadelphian, Bostonian, and New York accents. . . ."

The Luck of Roaring Camp

BRET HARTE

There was commotion in Roaring Camp. It could not have been a fight, for in 1850 that was not novel enough to have called together the entire settlement. The ditches and claims were not only deserted, but "Tuttle's grocery" had contributed its gamblers, who, it will be remembered, calmly continued their game the day that French Pete and Kanaka Joe shot each other to death over the bar in the front room. The whole camp was collected before a rude cabin on the outer edge of the clearing. Conversation was carried on in a low tone, but the name of a woman was frequently repeated. It was a name familiar enough in the camp — "Cherokee Sal."

Perhaps the less said of her the better. She was a coarse, and it is to be feared, a very sinful woman. But at that time she was the only woman in Roaring Camp, and was just then lying in sore extremity, when she most needed the ministration of her own sex. Dissolute, abandoned, and irreclaimable, she was yet suffering a martyrdom hard enough to bear even when veiled by sympathizing woman-hood, but now terrible in her loneliness. The primal curse

"The Luck of Roaring Camp" by Bret Harte, reprinted by permission of Houghton Mifflin Company.

had come to her in that original isolation which must have made the punishment of the first transgression so dreadful. It was, perhaps, part of the expiation° of her sin, that, at a moment when she most lacked her sex's intuitive tenderness and care, she met only the half-contemptuous faces of her masculine associates. Yet a few of the spectators were, I think, touched by her sufferings. Sandy Tipton thought it was "rough on Sal," and, in the contemplation of her condition, for a moment rose superior to the fact that he had an ace and two bowers in his sleeve.

It will be seen, also, that the situation was novel. Deaths were by no means uncommon in Roaring Camp, but a birth was a new thing. People had been dismissed from the camp effectively, finally, and with no possibility of return; but this was the first time that anybody had been introduced *ab initio.*° Hence the excitement.

"You go in there, Stumpy," said a prominent citizen known as "Kentuck," addressing one of the loungers. "Go in there, and see what you kin do. You've had experience in them things."

Perhaps there was a fitness in the selection. Stumpy, in other climes, had been the putative° head of two families; in fact, it was owing to some legal informality in these proceedings that Roaring Camp—a city of refuge—was indebted to his company. The crowd approved the choice, and Stumpy was wise enough to bow to the majority. The door closed upon the extempore° surgeon and midwife, and Roaring Camp sat down outside, smoked its pipe, and awaited the issue.

The assemblage numbered about a hundred men. One or two of these were actual fugitives from justice, some were criminal, and all were reckless. Physically, they exhibited no indication of their past lives and character. The greatest scamp had a Raphael face, with a profusion of blond hair; Oakhurst, a gambler, had the melancholy air and intellectual abstraction of a Hamlet, the coolest and most courageous man was scarcely over five feet in height, with a soft voice and an embarrassed, timid manner. The term "roughs" applied to them was a distinction rather than a definition. Perhaps in the minor details of fingers, toes, ears, etc., the camp may have been deficient, but these slight omissions did not detract from their aggregate force. The strongest man had but three fingers on his right hand; the best shot had but one eye.

Such was the physical aspect of the men that were dispersed around the cabin. The camp lay in a triangular valley, between two hills and a river. The only outlet was a steep trail over the summit of a hill that faced the cabin, now illuminated by the rising moon. The suffering woman might have seen it from the rude bunk whereon she lay—seen it winding like a silver thread until it was lost in the stars above.

A fire of withered pine boughs added sociability to the gathering. By degrees the natural levity of Roaring Camp returned. Bets were freely offered and taken regarding the result. Three to five that "Sal would get through with it"; even, that the child would survive; side bets as to the sex and complexion of the coming stranger. In the midst of an excited discussion an exclamation came from those nearest the door, and the camp stopped to listen. Above the swaying and moaning of the pines, the swift rush of the river, and the crackling of the fire rose a sharp, querulous cry—a cry unlike anything heard before in the camp. The pines stopped moaning, the river ceased to rush, and the fire to crackle. It seemed as if Nature had stopped to listen too.

The camp rose to its feet as one man! It was proposed to explode a barrel of gun-powder, but, in consideration of the situation of the mother, better counsels prevailed, and only a few revolvers were discharged; for, whether owing to the rude surgery of the camp, or some other reason, Cherokee Sal was sinking fast. Within an hour she had climbed, as it were, that rugged road that led to the stars, and so passed out of Roaring Camp, its sin and shame forever. I do not think that the announcement disturbed them much, except in speculation as to the fate of the child. "Can he live now?" was asked of Stumpy. The answer was doubtful. The only other being of Cherokee Sal's sex and maternal condition in the settlement was a donkey. There was some conjecture as to fitness, but the experiment was tried. It was less problematical than the ancient treatment of Romulus and Remus, and apparently as successful.

When these details were completed, which exhausted another hour, the door was opened, and the anxious crowd, who had already formed themselves into a queue, entered in single file. Beside the low bunk or shelf, on which the figure of the mother was starkly outlined below the blankets, stood a pine table. On this a candle-box was placed, and within it, swathed in staring red flannel, lay the last arrival at Roaring Camp. Beside the candle-box was placed a hat. Its use was soon indicated. "Gentlemen," said Stumpy, with a singular mixture of authority and *ex officio*° complacency—"Gentlemen will please pass in at the front door, round the table, and out at the back door. Them as wishes to contribute anything toward the orphan will find a hat handy." The first man entered with his hat on; he uncovered, however, as he looked about him, and so, unconsciously, set an example to the next. In such communities good and bad actions are catching. As the procession filed in, comments were audible—criticisms addressed, perhaps, rather to Stumpy, in the character of showman—"Is that him?" "Mighty small specimen"; "Hasn't more'n got the color"; "Ain't bigger nor a derringer."° The contributions were as characteristic: A silver tobacco box; a doubloon; a navy revolver, silver mounted; a gold specimen; a very beautifully embroidered lady's handkerchief (from Oakhurst the gambler); a diamond breastpin, a diamond ring (suggested by the pin, with the remark from the giver that he "saw that pin and went two diamonds better"); a slung shot; a Bible (contributor not detected); a golden spur; a silver teaspoon (the initials, I regret to say, were not the giver's); a pair of surgeon's shears; a lancet; a Bank of England note for £5; and about $200 in loose gold and silver coin. During these proceedings Stumpy maintained a silence as impassive as the dead on his left—a gravity as inscrutable as that of the newly-born on his right. Only one incident occurred to break the monotony of the curious procession. As Kentuck bent over the candle-box half curiously, the child turned, and, in a spasm of pain, caught at his groping finger, and held it fast for a moment. Kentuck looked foolish and embarrassed. Something like a blush tried to assert itself in his weather-beaten cheek. "The d—d little cuss!" he said, as he extricated his finger, with, perhaps, more tenderness and care than he might have been deemed capable of showing. He held that finger a little apart from its fellows as he went out, and examined it curiously. The examination provoked the same original remark in regard to the child. In fact, he seemed to enjoy repeating it. "He rastled with my finger," he remarked to Tipton, holding up the member, "the d—d little cuss!"

It was four o'clock before the camp sought repose. A light burnt in the cabin where the watchers sat, for Stumpy did not go to bed that night. Nor did Kentuck. He drank quite freely and related with great gusto his experience, invariably ending with his characteristic condemnation of the newcomer. It seemed to relieve him of any unjust implication of sentiment, and Kentuck had the weaknesses of the nobler sex. When everybody else had gone to bed, he walked down to the river, and whistled reflectingly. Then he walked up the gulch, past the cabin, still whistling with demonstrative unconcern. At a large redwood tree he paused and retraced his steps, and again passed the cabin. Halfway down to the river's bank he again paused, and then returned and knocked at the door. It was opened by Stumpy. "How goes it?" said Kentuck, looking past Stumpy toward the candle-box. "All serene," replied Stumpy. "Anything up?" "Nothing." There was a pause—an embarrassing one—Stumpy still holding the door. Then Kentuck had recourse to his finger, which he held up to Stumpy. "Rastled with it,—the d—d little cuss," he said, and retired.

The next day Cherokee Sal had such rude sepulture° as Roaring Camp afforded. After her body had been committed to the hillside, there was a formal meeting of the camp to discuss what should be done with her infant. A resolution to adopt it was unanimous and enthusiastic. But an animated discussion in regard to the manner and feasibility of providing for its wants at once sprung up. It was remarkable that the argument partook of none of those fierce personalities with which discussions were usually conducted at Roaring Camp. Tipton proposed that they should send the child to Red Dog—a distance of forty miles—where female attention could be procured. But the unlucky suggestion met with fierce and unanimous opposition. It was evident that no plan which entailed parting from their new acquisition would for a moment be entertained. "Besides," said Tom Ryder, "them fellows at Red Dog would swap it, and ring in somebody else on us." A disbelief in the honesty of other camps prevailed at Roaring Camp as in other places.

The introduction of a female nurse in the camp also met with objection. It was argued that no decent woman could be prevailed to accept Roaring Camp as her home, and the speaker urged that "they didn't want any more of the other kind." This unkind allusion to the defunct mother, harsh as it may seem, was the first spasm of propriety—the first symptom of the camp's regeneration. Stumpy advanced nothing. Perhaps he felt a certain delicacy in interfering with the selection of a possible successor in office. But when questioned, he averred stoutly that he and "Jinny"—the mammal before alluded to—could manage to rear the child. There was something original, independent, and heroic about the plan that pleased the camp. Stumpy was retained. Certain articles were sent for to Sacramento. "Mind," said the treasurer, as he pressed a bag of gold-dust into the expressman's hand, "the best that can be got—lace, you know, and filigree-work and frills—d—n the cost!"

Strange to say, the child thrived. Perhaps the invigorating climate of the mountain camp was compensation for material deficiencies. Nature took the foundling to her broader breast. In that rare atmosphere of the Sierra foothills—that air pungent with balsamic odor, that ethereal cordial,° at once bracing and exhilarating, he may have found food and nourishment, or a subtle chemistry that transmuted donkeys' milk to lime and phosphorus. Stumpy inclined to the belief that it was the latter and good nursing.

"Me and that donkey," he would say, "has been father and mother to him! Don't you," he would add, apostrophizing the helpless bundle before him, "never go back on us."

By the time he was a month old, the necessity of giving him a name became apparent. He had generally been known as "the Kid," "Stumpy's boy," "the Cayote" (an allusion to his vocal powers) and even by Kentuck's endearing diminutive of "the d—d little cuss." But these were felt to be vague and unsatisfactory, and were at last dismissed under another influence. Gamblers and adventurers are generally superstitious, and Oakhurst one day declared that the baby had brought "the luck" to Roaring Camp. It was certain that of late they had been successful. "Luck" was the name agreed upon, with the prefix of Tommy for greater convenience. No allusion was made to the mother, and the father was unknown. "It's better," said the philosophical Oakhurst, "to take a fresh deal all round. Call him Luck, and start him fair." A day was accordingly set apart for the christening. What was meant by this ceremony the reader may imagine, who has already gathered some idea of the reckless irreverence of Roaring Camp. The master of ceremonies was one "Boston," a noted wag, and the occasion seemed to promise the greatest facetiousness.° This ingenious satirist had spent two days in preparing a burlesque of the church service, with pointed local allusions. The choir was properly trained, and Sandy Tipton was to stand godfather. But after the procession had marched to the grove with music and banners, and the child had been deposited before a mock altar, Stumpy stepped before the expectant crowd. "It ain't my style to spoil fun, boys," said the little man, stoutly, eyeing the faces around him, "but it strikes me that this thing ain't exactly on the squar. It's playing it pretty low down on this yer baby to ring in fun on him that he ain't goin' to understand. And ef there's going to be any godfathers round, I'd like to see who's got any better rights than me." A silence followed Stumpy's speech. To the credit of all humorists be it said that the first man to acknowledge its justice was the satirist, thus stopped of his fun. "But," said Stumpy, quickly, following up his advantage, "we're here for a christening, and we'll have it. I proclaim you Thomas Luck, according to the laws of the United States and the State of California, so help me God." It was the first time that the name of the Deity had been uttered otherwise but profanely in the camp. The form of christening was perhaps even more ludicrous than the satirist had conceived; but strangely enough, nobody saw it and nobody laughed. "Tommy" was christened as seriously as he would have been under a Christian roof, and cried and was comforted in as orthodox fashion.

And so the work of regeneration began in Roaring Camp. Almost imperceptibly a change came over the settlement. The cabin assigned to "Tommy Luck"—or "The Luck," as he was more frequently called—first showed signs of improvement. It was kept scrupulously clean and whitewashed. Then it was boarded, clothed, and papered. The rosewood cradle—packed eighty miles by mule—had, in Stumpy's way of putting it, "sorter killed the rest of the furniture." So the rehabilitation of the cabin became a necessity. The men who were in the habit of lounging in at Stumpy's to see "how The Luck got on" seemed to appreciate the change, and, in self-defense, the rival establishment of "Tuttle's grocery" bestirred itself, and imported a carpet and mirrors. The reflections of the latter on the appearance of Roaring Camp tended to produce stricter habits of personal cleanliness. Again Stumpy imposed a kind of quarantine upon those who aspired to the honor and privilege of holding "The Luck." It was a cruel mortification to Kentuck—who, in the carelessness of a large nature and the habits of frontier life, had begun to regard all garments as a second cuticle, which, like a snake's, only sloughed off through decay—to be debarred this privilege from certain prudential reasons. Yet such was the subtle influence of innovation that he thereafter appeared regularly every afternoon in a clean shirt, and face still shining from his ablutions. Nor were moral and social sanitary laws neglected. "Tommy," who was supposed to spend his whole existence in a persistent attempt to repose, must not be disturbed by noise. The shouting and yelling which had gained the camp its infelicitous° title were not permitted within hearing distance of Stumpy's. The men conversed in whispers, or smoked with Indian gravity. Profanity was tacitly given up in these sacred precincts, and throughout the camp a popular form of expletive, known as "D—n the luck!" and "Curse the luck!" was abandoned, as having a new personal bearing. Vocal music was not interdicted, being supposed to have a soothing, tranquilizing quality, and one song, sung by "Man-o'-War Jack," an English sailor from Her Majesty's Australian colonies, was quite popular as a lullaby. It was a lugubrious recital of the exploits of "the *Arethusa,* Seventy-four," in a muffled minor, ending with a prolonged dying fall at the burden of each verse, "On b-o-o-o-ard of the *Arethusa.*" It was a fine sight to see Jack holding The Luck, rocking from side to side as if with the motion of a ship, and crooning forth this naval ditty. Either through the peculiar rocking of Jack or the length of his song—it contained ninety stanzas, and was continued with conscientious deliberation to the bitter end—the lullaby generally had the desired effect. At such times the men would lie at full length under the trees, in the soft summer twilight, smoking their pipes and drinking in the melodious utterances. An indistinct idea that this was pastoral happiness pervaded the camp. "This 'ere kind o' think," said the Cockney Simmons, meditatively reclining on his elbow, "is 'evingly." It reminded him of Greenwich.

On the long summer days The Luck was usually carried to the gulch, from whence the golden store of Roaring Camp was taken. There, on a blanket spread over pine boughs, he would lie while the men were working in the ditches below. Latterly, there was a rude attempt to decorate this bower with flowers and sweet-smelling shrubs, and generally someone would bring him a cluster of wild honey-suckles, azaleas, or the painted blossoms of Las Mariposas. The men had suddenly awakened to the fact that there were beauty and significance in these trifles, which they had so long trodden carelessly beneath their feet. A flake of glittering mica, a fragment of variegated quartz, a bright pebble from the bed of the creek, became beautiful to eyes thus cleared and strengthened, and were invariably put aside for "The Luck." It was wonderful how many treasures the woods and hillsides yielded that "would do for Tommy." Surrounded by playthings such as never child out of fairyland had before, it is to be hoped that Tommy was content. He appeared to be serenely happy, albeit there was an infantine gravity about him, a contemplative light in his round gray eyes, that sometimes worried Stumpy. He was always tractable and quiet, and it is recorded that once, having crept beyond his "corral" — a hedge of tessellated pine boughs, which surrounded his bed — he dropped over the bank on his head in the soft earth, and remained with his mottled legs in the air in that position for at least five minutes with unflinching gravity. He was extricated without a murmur. I hesitate to record the many other instances of his sagacity, which rest, unfortunately, upon the statements of prejudiced friends. Some of them were not without a tinge of superstition. "I crep' up the bank just now," said Kentuck one day, in a breathless state of excitement, "and dern my skin if he wasn't a-talking to a jaybird as was a-sittin on his lap. There they was, just as free and sociable as anything you please, a-jawin at each other just like two cherrybums." Howbeit, whether creeping over the pine boughs or lying lazily on his back, blinking at the leaves above him, to him the birds sang, the squirrels chattered, and the flowers bloomed. Nature was his nurse and playfellow. For him she would let slip between the leaves golden shafts of sunlight that fell just within his grasp; she would send wandering breezes to visit him with the balm of bay and resinous gums; to him the tall redwoods nodded familiarly and sleepily, the bumblebees buzzed, and the rooks cawed a slumbrous accompaniment.

Such was the golden summer of Roaring Camp. They were "flush times" — and the Luck was with them. The claims had yielded enormously. The camp was jealous of its privileges and looked suspiciously on strangers. No encouragement was given to immigration, and, to make their seclusion more perfect, the land on either side of the mountain wall that surrounded the camp they duly pre-empted. This, and a reputation for singular proficiency with the revolver, kept the reserve of Roaring Camp invio-late. The expressman — their only connecting link with the surrounding world — sometimes told wonderful stories of the camp. He would say, "They've a street up there in 'Roaring,' that would lay over any street up there in Red Dog. They've got vines and flowers round their houses, and they wash themselves twice a day. But they're mighty rough on strangers, and they worship an Ingin baby."

With the prosperity of the camp came a desire for further improvement. It was proposed to build a hotel in the following spring, and to invite one or two decent families to reside there for the sake of "The Luck," who might perhaps profit by female companionship. The sacrifice that this concession to the sex cost these men, who were fiercely skeptical in regard to its general virtue and usefulness, can only be accounted for by their affection for Tommy. A few still held out. But the resolve could not be carried into effect for three months, and the minority meekly yielded in the hope that something might turn up to prevent it. And it did.

The winter of '51 will long be remembered in the foot-hills. The snow lay deep on the sierras, and every moun-tain creek became a river, and every river a lake. Each gorge and gulch was transformed into a tumultuous water-course that descended the hillsides, tearing down giant trees and scattering its drift and debris along the plain. Red Dog had been twice under water, and Roaring Camp had been forewarned. "Water put the gold into them gulches," said Stumpy; "it's been here once and will be here again!" And that night the North Fork suddenly leaped over its banks, and swept up the triangular valley of Roaring Camp.

In the confusion of rushing water, crashing trees, and crackling timber, and the darkness which seemed to flow with the water and blot out the fair valley, but little could be done to collect the scattered camp. When the morning broke, the cabin of Stumpy nearest the river-bank was gone. Higher up the gulch they found the body of its unlucky owner; but the pride—the hope—the joy—the Luck—of Roaring Camp had disappeared. They were returning with sad hearts, when a shout from the bank recalled them.

It was a relief-boat from down the river. They had picked up, they said, a man and an infant, nearly exhausted, about two miles below. Did anybody know them, and did they belong here?

It needed but a glance to show them Kentuck lying there, cruelly crushed and bruised, but still holding The Luck of Roaring Camp in his arms. As they bent over the strangely assorted pair, they saw that the child was cold and pulseless. "He is dead," said one. Kentuck opened his eyes. "Dead?" he repeated feebly. "Yes, my man, and you are dying too." A smile lit the eyes of the expiring Kentuck. "Dying!" he repeated, "he's a-taking me with him—tell the boys I've got the Luck with me now"; and the strong man, clinging to the frail babe as a drowning man is said to cling to a straw, drifted away into the shadowy river that flows forever to the unknown sea.

Do especially Questions 1, 11, 15, 16, 17, 19, 74, 75, 76, 77, 80, 87, 90, and 95. Consult the Model Short Story in Volume One.

FRANCIS BRET HARTE   *1836-1902*

As a young man in California, Bret Harte passed rapidly from one job to another—express messenger, printer, teacher, drug store clerk, miner, and journalist—and found these experiences useful material for later short stories. When they appeared in 1870, "Tennessee's Partner," "The Luck of Roaring Camp," and "The Outcasts of Poker Flat" won the acclaim of American audiences back East. The Western locales of the stories, the blunt, rough characters, and the crude language had the appeal of freshness and novelty.

Under the Lion's Paw

HAMLIN GARLAND

It was the last of autumn and first day of winter coming together. All day long the plowmen on their prairie farms had moved to and fro in their wide level fields through the falling snow, which melted as it fell, wetting them to the skin—all day, notwithstanding the frequent squalls of snow, the dripping, desolate clouds, and the muck of the furrows, black and tenacious as tar.

Under their dripping harness the horses swung to and fro silently, with that marvelous uncomplaining patience which marks the horse. All day the wild geese, honking wildly as they sprawled sidewise down the wind, seemed to be fleeing from an enemy behind, and with neck out-thrust and wings extended, sailed down the wind, soon lost to sight.

Yet the plowman behind his plow, though the snow lay on his ragged greatcoat, and the cold, clinging mud rose on his heavy boots, fettering him like gyves,° whistled in the very beard of the gale. As day passed, the snow, ceasing to melt, lay along the plowed land and lodged in the depth of the stubble, till on each slow round the last furrow stood out black and shining as jet between the plowed land and the gray stubble.

When night began to fall, and the geese, flying low, began to alight invisibly in the near cornfield, Stephen Council was still at work "finishing a land." He rode on his sulky plow[1] when going with the wind, but walked when facing it. Sitting bent and cold but cheery under his slouch hat, he talked encouragingly to his four-in-hand.

"Come round there, boys!—Round agin! We got t' finish this land. Come in there, Dan! *Stiddy*, Kate,—stiddy! None o'y'r tantrums, Kittie. It's purty tuff, but got a be

---

[1]A plow with wheels and driver's seat attached.

"Under the Lion's Paw" from *Main-Travelled Roads* by Hamlin Garland, reprinted by permission of Constance Garland Doyle and Isabel Garland Lord.

did. *Tchk! tchk!* Step along, Pete! Don't let Kate git y'r singletree[2] on the wheel. *Once* more!"

They seemed to know what he meant and that this was the last round, for they worked with greater vigor than before.

"Once more, boys, an' then, sez I, oats an' a nice warm stall, an' sleep f'r all."

By the time the last furrow was turned on the land, it was too dark to see the house, and the snow was changing to rain again. The tired and hungry man could see the light from the kitchen shining through the leafless hedge, and he lifted a great shout, "Supper f'r a half a dozen!"

It was nearly eight o'clock by the time he had finished his chores and started for supper. He was picking his way carefully through the mud, when the tall form of a man loomed up before him with a premonitory° cough.

"Waddy ye want?" was the rather startled question of the farmer.

"Well, ye see," began the stranger in a deprecating tone, "we'd like t' git in f'r the night. We've tried every house f'r the last two miles, but they hadn't any room f'r us. My wife's jest about sick, 'n' the children are cold and hungry—"

"Oh, y' want 'o stay all night, eh?"

"Yes, sir, it 'ud be a great accom—"

"Waal, I don't make it a practice t' turn anybuddy 'way hungry, not on sech nights as this. Drive right in. We ain't got much, but sech as it is—"

But the stranger had disappeared. And soon his steaming, weary team, with drooping heads and swinging single-trees, moved past the well to the block beside the path. Council stood at the side of the schooner[3] and helped the children out—two little half-sleeping children—and then a small woman with a babe in her arms.

"There ye go!" he shouted jovially to the children. "*Now* we're all right! Run right along to the house there an' tell Ma'm Council you wants sumpthin' t' eat. Right this way, Mis'—keep right off t' the right there. I'll go an'

2A swinging bar to which the straps of a harness are fastened.
3A covered wagon.

git a lantern. Come," he said to the dazed and silent group at his side.

"Mother," he shouted, as he neared the fragrant and warmly-lighted kitchen, "here are some wayfarers an' folks who need sumpthin' t' eat an' a place t' snooze." He ended by pushing them all in.

Mrs. Council, a large, jolly, rather coarse-looking woman, took the children in her arms. "Come right in, you little rabbits. 'Most asleep, hey? Now here's a drink o' milk f'r each o' ye. I'll have s'm tea in a minute. Take off y'r things and set up t' the fire."

While she set the children to drinking milk, Council got out his lantern and went out to the barn to help the stranger about his team, where his loud, hearty voice could be heard as it came and went between the haymow and the stalls.

The woman came to light as a small, timid, and discouraged-looking woman, but still pretty in a thin and sorrowful way.

"Land sakes! An' you've traveled all the way from Clear Lake t'day in this mud! Waal! waal! No wonder you're all tired out. Don't wait f'r the men, Mis'—" She hesitated, waiting for the name.

"Haskins."

"Mis' Haskins, set right up to the table an' take a good swig o' tea whilst I make y' s'm toast. It's green tea, an' it's good. I tell Council as I git older I don't seem to enjoy Young Hyson n'r Gunpowder.[4] I want the reel green tea jest as it comes off'n the vines. Seems t' have more heart in it, some way. Don't s'pose it has. Council says it's all in m' eye."

Going on in this easy way, she soon had the children filled with bread and milk and the woman thoroughly at home, eating some toast and sweet-melon pickles and sipping the tea.

"See the little rats!" she laughed at the children. "They're full as they can stick now, and they want to go to bed. Now, don't git up, Mis' Haskins; set right where you are an' let

[4]Brands of tea.

me look after 'em. I know all about young ones, though I'm all alone now. Jane went an' married last fall. But, as I tell Council, it's lucky we keep our health. Set right there, Mis' Haskins; I won't have you stir a finger."

It was an unmeasured pleasure to sit there in the warm, homely kitchen, the jovial chatter of the housewife driving out and holding at bay the growl of the impotent,° cheated wind.

The little woman's eyes filled with tears, which fell down upon the sleeping baby in her arms. The world was not so desolate and cold and hopeless, after all.

"Now I hope Council won't stop out there and talk politics all night. He's the greatest man to talk politics an' read the *Tribune*—How old is it?"

She broke off and peered down at the face of the babe.

"Two months 'n' five days," said the mother, with a mother's exactness.

"Ye don't say! I want 'o know! The dear little pudzy-wudzy!" she went on, stirring it up in the neighborhood of the ribs with her fat forefinger. "Pooty tough on 'oo to go gallivant'n cross lots this way—"

"Yes, that's so; a man can't lift a mountain," said Council, entering the door. "Mother, this is Mr. Haskins, from Kansas. He's been eat up 'n' drove out by grasshoppers."

"Glad t' see yeh!—Pa, empty that washbasin 'n' give him a chance t' wash."

Haskins was a tall man, with a thin, gloomy face. His hair was a reddish brown, like his coat, and seemed equally faded by the wind and sun; and his sallow face, though hard and set, was pathetic somehow. You would have felt that he had suffered much by the line of his mouth showing under his thin, yellow mustache.

"Hain't Ike got home yet, Sairy?"

"Hain't seen 'im."

"W-a-a-l, set right up, Mr. Haskins; wade right into what we've got; 'taint much, but we manage to live on it—she gits fat on it," laughed Council, pointing his thumb at his wife.

After supper, while the women put the children to bed, Haskins and Council talked on, seated near the huge cooking stove, the steam rising from their wet clothing. In the Western fashion Council told as much of his own life as he drew from his guest. He asked but few questions, but by and by the story of Haskins' struggles and defeat came out. The story was a terrible one; but he told it quietly, seated with his elbows on his knees, gazing most of the time at the hearth.

"I didn't like the looks of the country, anyhow," Haskins said, partly rising and glancing at his wife. "I was ust t' northern Ingyannie,[5] where we have lots o' timber 'n' lots o' rain, 'n' I didn't like the looks o' that dry prairie. What galled me the worst was goin' s' far away acrosst so much fine land layin' all through here vacant."

"And the 'hoppers eat ye four years, hand runnin', did they?"

"Eat! They wiped us out. They chawed everything that was green. They jest set around waitin' fr us t' die t' eat us, too. My God! I ust t' dream of 'em sittin' 'round on the bedpost, six feet long, workin' their jaws. They eat the fork handles. They got worse 'n' worse till they jest rolled on one another, piled up like snow in winter. Well, it ain't no use. If I was t' talk all winter, I couldn't tell nawthin'. But all the while I couldn't help thinkin' of all that land back here that nobuddy was usin' that I ought 'o had 'stead o' bein' out there in that cussed country."

"Waal, why didn't ye stop an' settle here?" asked Ike, who had come and was eating his supper.

"Fer the simple reason that you fellers wanted ten 'r fifteen dollars an acre fer the bare land, and I hadn't no money fer that kind o' thing."

"Yes, I do my own work," Mrs. Council was heard to say in the pause which followed. "I'm a gettin' purty heavy t' be on m' laigs all day, but we can't afford t' hire, so I keep rackin' around somehow, like a foundered horse. S' lame—I tell Council he can't tell how lame I am, f'r I'm

[5]Indiana.

jest as lame in one laig as t' other." And the good soul laughed at the joke on herself as she took a handful of flour and dusted the biscuit board to keep the dough from sticking.

"Well, I hain't *never* been very strong," said Mrs. Haskins. "Our folks was Canadians an' small-boned, and then since my last child I hain't got up again fairly. I don't like t' complain. Tim has about all he can bear now—but they was days this week when I jest wanted to lay right down an' die."

"Waal, now, I'll tell ye," said Council from his side of the stove, silencing everybody with his good-natured roar, "I'd go down and *see* Butler, *anyway*, if I was you. I guess he'd let you have his place purty cheap; the farm's all run down. He's ben anxious t' let t' somebuddy next year. It 'ud be a good chance fer you. Anyhow, you go to bed and sleep like a babe. I've got some plowin' t' do, anyhow, an' we'll see if somethin' can't be done about your case. Ike, you go out an' see if the horses is all right, an' I'll show the folks t' bed."

When the tired husband and wife were lying under the generous quilts of the spare bed, Haskins listened a moment to the wind in the eaves and then said, with a slow and solemn tone:

"There are people in this world who are good enough t' be angels, an' only haff t' die to *be* angels."

Jim Butler was one of those men called in the West "land poor."[6] Early in the history of Rock River he had come into the town and started in the grocery business in a small way, occupying a small building in a mean part of the town. At this period of his life he earned all he got and was up early and late, sorting beans, working over butter, and carting his goods to and from the station. But a change came over him at the end of the second year, when he sold a lot of land for four times what he paid for it. From that time forward he believed in land speculation as the surest way of getting rich. Every cent he could save or spare from his trade, he put into land at forced sale or

[6]Owning much unprofitable land; having all one's capital in land.

mortgages on land, which were "just as good as the wheat," he was accustomed to say.

Farm after farm fell into his hands, until he was recognized as one of the leading landowners of the county. His mortgages were scattered all over Cedar County; and as they slowly but surely fell in, he sought usually to retain the former owner as tenant.

He was not ready to foreclose;° indeed, he had the name of being one of the "easiest" men in the town. He let the debtor off again and again, extending the time whenever possible.

"I don't want y'r land," he said. "All I'm after is the int'rest on my money—that's all. Now, if y' want 'o stay on the farm, why, I'll give y' a good chance. I can't have the land lyin' vacant." And in many cases the owner remained as tenant.

In the meantime he had sold his store; he couldn't spend time in it; he was mainly occupied now with sitting around town on rainy days smoking and "gassin' with the boys," or in riding to and from his farms. In fishing time he fished a good deal. Doc Grimes, Ben Ashley, and Cal Cheatham were his cronies on these fishing excursions or hunting trips in the time of chickens or partridges. In winter they went to northern Wisconsin to shoot deer.

In spite of all these signs of easy life, Butler persisted in saying he "hadn't enough money to pay taxes on his land" and was careful to convey the impression that he was poor in spite of his twenty farms. At one time he was said to be worth fifty thousand dollars, but land had been a little slow of sale of late, so that he was not worth so much.

A fine farm, known as the Higley place, had fallen into his hands in the usual way the previous year, and he had not been able to find a tenant for it. Poor Higley, after working himself nearly to death on it in the attempt to lift the mortgage, had gone off to Dakota, leaving the farm and his curse to Butler.

This was the farm which Council advised Haskins to apply for, and the next day Council hitched up his team and drove down town to see Butler.

"You jest let *me* do the talkin'," he said. "We'll find him wearin' out his pants on some salt barrel somew'ers; and if he thought you *wanted* a place, he'd sock it to you hot and heavy. You jest keep quiet; I'll fix 'im."

Butler was seated in Ben Ashley's store telling fish yarns when Council sauntered in casually.

"Hello, But; lyin' agin, hey?"

"Hello, Steve! how goes it?"

"Oh, so-so. Too dang much rain these days. I thought it was goin' t' freeze up f'r good last night. Tight squeak if I get m' plowin' done. How's farmin' with *you* these days?"

"Bad. Plowin' ain't half done."

"It 'ud be a religious idee f'r you t' go out an' take a hand y'rself."

"I don't haff to," said Butler with a wink.

"Got anybody on the Higley place?"

"No. Know of anybody?"

"Waal, no; not eggsackly. I've got a relation back t' Michigan who's ben hot an' cold on the idee o' comin' West f'r some time. *Might* come if he could get a good layout. What do you talk on the farm?"

"Well, I d'know. I'll rent it on shares or I'll rent it money rent."

"Waal, how much money, say?"

"Well, say ten per cent on the price—two-fifty."

"Waal, that ain't bad. Wait on 'im till 'e thrashes?"

Haskins listened eagerly to this important question, but Council was coolly eating a dried apple which he had speared out of a barrel with his knife. Butler studied him carefully.

"Well, knocks me out of twenty-five dollars interest."

"My relation 'll need all he's got t' git his crops in," said Council in the same, indifferent way.

"Well, all right; *say* wait," concluded Butler.

"All right; this is the man. Haskins, this is Mr. Butler—no relation to Ben—the hardest-working man in Cedar County."

On the way home Haskins said: "I ain't much better

off. I'd like that farm; it's a good farm, but it's all run down, an' so 'm I. I could make a good farm of it if I had half a show. But I can't stock it n'r seed it."

"Waal, now, don't you worry," roared Council in his ear. "We'll pull y' through somehow till next harvest. He's agreed t' hire it plowed, an' you can earn a hundred dollars plowin', an' y' c'n git the seed o' me an' pay me back when y' can."

Haskins was silent with emotion, but at last he said, "I ain't got nothin' t' live on."

"Now, don't you worry 'bout that. You jest make your headquarters at ol' Steve Council's. Mother'll take a pile o' comfort in havin' y'r wife an' children 'round. Y' see, Jane's married off lately, an' Ike's away a good 'eal; so we'll be darn glad t' have y' stop with us this winter. Nex' spring we'll see if y' can't git a start agin." And he chirruped to the team, which sprang forward with the rumbling, clattering wagon.

"Say, looky here, Council, you can't do this. I never saw—" shouted Haskins in his neighbor's ear.

Council moved about uneasily in his seat and stopped his stammering gratitude by saying: "Hold on, now; don't make such a fuss over a little thing. When I see a man down, an' things all on top of 'm, I jest like t' kick 'em off an' help 'm up. That's the kind of religion I got, an' it's about the *only* kind."

They rode the rest of the way home in silence. And when the red light of the lamp shone out into the darkness of the cold and windy night, and he thought of this refuge for his children and wife, Haskins could have put his arm around the neck of his burly companion and squeezed him like a lover. But he contented himself with saying, "Steve Council, you'll git y'r pay f'r this some day."

"Don't want any pay. My religion ain't run on such business principles."

The wind was growing colder, and the ground was covered with a white frost as they turned into the gate of the Council farm, and the children came rushing out, shouting, "Papa's come!" They hardly looked like the same children who had sat at the table the night before. Their torpidity,° under the influence of sunshine and Mother Council, had given way to a sort of spasmodic° cheerfulness, as insects in winter revive when laid on the hearth.

Haskins worked like a fiend, and his wife, like the heroic woman that she was, bore also uncomplainingly the most terrible burdens. They rose early and toiled without intermission till the darkness fell on the plain, then tumbled into bed, every bone and muscle aching with fatigue, to rise with the sun next morning to the same round of the same ferocity of labor.

The eldest boy drove a team all through the spring, plowing and seeding, milked the cows, and did chores innumerable, in most ways taking the place of a man.

An infinitely pathetic but common figure — this boy on the American farm, where there is no law against child labor. To see him in his coarse clothing, his huge boots, and his ragged cap, as he staggered with a pail of water from the well or trudged in the cold and cheerless dawn out into the frosty field behind his team, gave the city-bred visitor a sharp pang of sympathetic pain. Yet Haskins loved his boy and would have saved him from this if he could, but he could not.

By June, the first year, the result of such Herculean° toil began to show on the farm. The yard was cleaned up and sown to grass, the garden plowed and planted, and the house mended.

Council had given them four of his cows.

"Take 'em an' run 'em on shares. I don't want 'o milk s' many. Ike's away s' much now, Sat'd'ys and Sundays, I can't stand the bother anyhow."

Other men, seeing the confidence of Council in the newcomer had sold him tools on time; and as he was really an able farmer, he soon had round him many evidences of his care and thrift. At the advice of Council he had taken the farm for three years, with the privilege of re-renting or buying at the end of the term.

"It's a good bargain, an' y' want 'o nail it," said Council. "If you have any kind ov a crop, you c'n pay y'r debts an' keep seed an' bread."

The new hope which now sprang up in the heart of Haskins and his wife grew great almost as a pain by the time the wide field of wheat began to wave and swirl in the winds of July. Day after day he would snatch a few moments after supper to go and look at it.

"Have ye seen the wheat t'day, Nettie?" he asked one night as he rose from supper.

"No, Tim, I ain't had time."

"Well, take time now. Let's go look at it."

She threw an old hat on her head—Tommy's hat—and, looking almost pretty in her thin, sad way, went out with her husband to the hedge.

"Ain't it grand, Nettie? Just look at it."

It was grand. Level, russet° here and there, heavy-headed, wide as a lake, and full of multitudinous whispers and gleams of wealth, it stretched away before the gazers like the fabled field of the cloth of gold.[7]

"Oh, I think—I *hope* we'll have a good crop, Tim; and oh, how good the people have been to us!"

"Yes; I don't know where we'd be t'day if it hadn't been f'r Council and his wife."

"They're the best people in the world," said the little woman, with a great sob of gratitude.

"We'll be in the field on Monday, sure," said Haskins, gripping the rail on the fence as if already at the work of the harvest.

The harvest came, bounteous, glorious; but the winds came and blew it into tangles, and the rain matted it here and there close to the ground, increasing the work of gathering it threefold.

Oh, how they toiled in those glorious days! Clothing dripping with sweat, arms aching, filled with briers, fingers raw and bleeding, backs broken with the weight of heavy

[7]A field near Calais where Henry VIII interviewed Francis I in 1520. The rich Renaissance pageantry of the scene gave the name "cloth of gold" to the field.

bundles, Haskins and his man toiled on. Tommy drove the harvester, while his father and a hired man bound on the machine. In this way they cut ten acres every day; and almost every night after supper, when the hand went to bed, Haskins returned to the field, shocking the bound grain in the light of the moon. Many a night he worked till his anxious wife came out at ten o'clock to call him in to rest and lunch.

At the same time she cooked for the men, took care of the children, washed and ironed, milked the cows at night, made the butter, and sometimes fed the horses and watered them while her husband kept at the shocking.

No slave in the Roman galleys could have toiled so frightfully and lived, for this man thought himself a free man and that he was working for his wife and babes.

When he sank into his bed with a deep groan of relief, too tired to change his grimy, dripping clothing, he felt that he was getting nearer and nearer to a home of his own and pushing the wolf of want a little farther from his door.

There is no despair so deep as the despair of a homeless man or woman. To roam the roads of the country or the streets of the city, to feel there is no rood° of ground on which the feet can rest, to halt weary and hungry outside lighted windows and hear laughter and song within— these are the hungers and rebellions that drive men to crime and women to shame.

It was the memory of this homelessness and the fear of its coming again that spurred Timothy Haskins and Nettie, his wife, to such ferocious labor during that first year.

"'M, yes; 'm, yes; first-rate," said Butler, as his eye took in the neat garden, the pigpen, and the well-filled barnyard. "You're gitt'n' quite a stock around yeh. Done well, eh?"

Haskins was showing Butler around the place. He had not seen it for a year, having spent the year in Washington and Boston with Ashley, his brother-in-law, who had been elected to Congress.

"Yes, I've laid out a good deal of money durin' the last three years. I've paid out three hundred dollars f'r fencin'."

"Um—h'm! I see. I see," said Butler while Haskins went on:

"The kitchen there cost two hundred; the barn ain't cost much in money, but I've put a lot o' time on it. I've dug a new well, and I—"

"Yes, yes, I see. You've done well. Stock worth a thousand dollars," said Butler, picking his teeth with a straw.

"About that," said Haskins modestly. "We begin to feel 's if we was gett'n' a home f'r ourselves, but we've worked hard. I tell you we begin to feel it, Mr. Butler, and we're goin' t' begin to ease up purty soon. We've been kind o' plannin' a trip back t' *her* folks after the fall plowin's done."

"*Eggs*-actly!" said Butler, who was evidently thinking of something else. "I suppose you've kind o' calc'lated on stayin' here three years more?"

"Well, yes. Fact is, I think I c'n buy the farm this fall if you'll give me a reasonable show."

"Um—m! What do you call a reasonable show?"

"Well, say a quarter down and three years' time."

Butler looked at the huge stacks of wheat which filled the yard, over which the chickens were fluttering and crawling, catching grasshoppers, and out of which the crickets were singing innumerably. He smiled in a peculiar way as he said: "Oh, I won't be hard on yeh. But what did you expect to pay f'r the place?"

"Why, about what you offered it for before, two thousand five hundred, or *possibly* three thousand dollars," he added quickly as he saw the owner shake his head.

"This farm is worth five thousand and five hundred dollars," said Butler in a careless and decided voice.

"*What!*" almost shrieked the astounded Haskins. "What's that? Five thousand? Why, that's double what you offered it for three years ago."

"Of course, and it's worth it. It was all run down then; now it's in good shape. You've laid out fifteen hundred dollars in improvements according to your own story."

"But *you* had nothin' t' do about that. It's my work an' my money."

"You bet it was; but it's my land."

"But what's to pay me for all my—"

"Ain't you had the use of 'em?" replied Butler, smiling calmly into his face.

Haskins was like a man struck on the head with a sandbag; he couldn't think; he stammered as he tried to say: "But—I never'd git the use—You'd rob me! More'n that: you agreed—you promised that I could buy or rent at the end of three years at—"

"That's all right. But I didn't say I'd let you carry off the improvements nor that I'd go on renting the farm at two-fifty. The land is doubled in value, it don't matter how; it don't enter into the question; an' now you can pay me five hundred dollars a year rent, or take it on your own terms at fifty-five hundred, or—git out."

He was turning away when Haskins, the sweat pouring from his face, fronted him, saying again:

"But *you've* done nothing to make it so. You hain't added a cent. I put it all there myself, expectin' to buy. I worked an' sweat to improve it. I was workin' for myself an' babes—"

"Well, why didn't you buy when I offered to sell? What y' kickin' about?"

"I'm kickin' about payin' you twice f'r my own things— my own fences, my own kitchen, my own garden."

Butler laughed. "You're too green t' eat, young feller. *Your* improvements! The law will sing another tune."

"But I trusted your word."

"Never trust anybody, my friend. Besides, I didn't promise not to do this thing. Why man, don't look at me like that. Don't take me for a thief. It's the law. The reg'lar thing. Everybody does it."

"I don't care if they do. It's stealin' jest the same. You take three thousand dollars of my money—the work o' my hands and my wife's." He broke down at this point. He was not a strong man mentally. He could face hardship, ceaseless toil, but he could not face the cold and sneering face of Butler.

"But I don't take it," said Butler coolly. "All you've got to do is to go on jest as you've been a-doin', or give me a thousand dollars down and a mortgage at ten per cent on the rest."

Haskins sat down blindly on a bundle of oats near by and with staring eyes and drooping head went over the situation. He was under the lion's paw. He felt a horrible numbness in his heart and limbs. He was hid in a mist, and there was no path out.

Butler walked about, looking at the huge stacks of grain and pulling now and again a few handfuls out, shelling the heads in his hands and blowing the chaff away. He hummed a little tune as he did so. He had an accommodating air of waiting.

Haskins was in the midst of the terrible toil of the last year. He was walking again in the rain and the mud behind his plow; he felt the dust and dirt of the threshing. The ferocious husking-time, with its cutting wind and biting, clinging snows, lay hard upon him. Then he thought of his wife, how she had cheerfully cooked and baked without holiday and without rest.

"Well, what do you think of it?" inquired the cool, mocking, insinuating voice of Butler.

"I think you're a thief and a liar!" shouted Haskins, leaping up. "A black-hearted houn'!" Butler's smile maddened him; with a sudden leap he caught a fork in his hands and whirled it in the air. "You'll never rob another man, damn ye!" he grated through his teeth, a look of pitiless ferocity in his accusing eyes.

Butler shrank and quivered, expecting the blow; stood, held hypnotized by the eyes of the man he had a moment before despised—a man transformed into an avenging demon. But in the deadly hush between the lift of the weapon and its fall there came a gush of faint, childish laughter; and then across the range of his vision, far away and dim, he saw the sun-bright head of his baby girl, as, with the pretty, tottering run of a two-year-old, she moved across the grass of the dooryard. His hands relaxed; the fork fell to the ground; his head lowered.

"Make out y'r deed an' mor'gage, an' git off'n my land, an' don't ye never cross my line again; if y' do, I'll kill ye."

Butler backed away from the man in wild haste, and climbing into his buggy with trembling limbs, drove off down the road, leaving Haskins seated dumbly on the sunny piles of sheaves, his head sunk into his hands.

Do especially Questions 73, 75, 77, 86, 103, 109, 111, and 137. Consult the Model Short Story in Volume One.

HAMLIN GARLAND   *1860-1940*

Working on the farm in summer and attending school in winter, Hamlin Garland as a young boy moved with his family from Wisconsin to Minnesota, next to Iowa, then to the Dakotas. When he returned from the East to this "Middle Border" many years later and discovered the crushing toil of the farmer, he began his propaganda crusade for land reform that dominates the theme of "The Lion's Paw" and other local-color tales in his collection *Main-Travelled Roads* (1894). His *Son of the Middle Border* (1917), a semi-fictional autobiography, emphasizes the American pioneer as the chief theme of his writings: "... to catch the dying echoes of their songs, to bask in the failing light of their faces."

The Courting of Sister Wisby

SARAH ORNE JEWETT

All the morning there had been an increasing temptation to take an out-door holiday, and early in the afternoon the temptation outgrew my power of resistance. A far-away pasture on the long southwestern slope of a high hill was persistently present to my mind, yet there seemed to be no particular reason why I should think of it. I was not sure that I wanted anything from the pasture, and there was no sign, except the temptation, that the pasture wanted anything of me. But I was on the farther side of as many as three fences before I stopped to think again where I was going, and why.

There is no use in trying to tell another person about that afternoon unless he distinctly remembers weather exactly like it. No number of details concerning an Arctic ice-blockade will give a single shiver to a child of the tropics. This was one of those perfect New England days in late summer, when the spirit of autumn takes a first stealthy flight, like a spy, through the ripening country-side, and, with feigned sympathy for those who droop with August heat, puts her cool cloak of bracing air about leaf and flower and human shoulders. Every living thing grows suddenly cheerful and strong; it is only when you catch sight of a horror-stricken little maple in swamp soil — a little maple that has second sight and foreknowledge of coming disaster to her race — only then does a distrust of autumn's friendliness dim your joyful satisfaction.

In midwinter there is always a day when one has the first foretaste of spring; in late August there is a morning when the air is for the first time autumn-like. Perhaps it is a hint to the squirrels to get in their first supplies for the winter hoards, or a reminder that summer will soon end, and everybody had better make the most of it. We are always looking forward to the passing and ending of winter, but when summer is here it seems as if summer must always last. As I went across the fields that day, I found myself half lamenting that the world must fade again, even that the best of her budding and bloom was only a preparation for another springtime, for an awakening beyond the coming winter's sleep.

The sun was slightly veiled; there was a chattering group of birds, which had gathered for a conference about their early migration. Yet, oddly enough, I heard the voice of a belated bobolink, and presently saw him rise from the grass and hover leisurely, while he sang a brief tune. He was much behind time if he were still a housekeeper; but as for the other birds who listened, they cared only for their own notes. An old crow went sagging by, and gave a croak at his despised neighbor, just as a black reviewer croaked at Keats[1] — so hard it is to be just to one's contemporaries. The bobolink was indeed singing out of season, and it was impossible to say whether he really belonged most to this summer or to the next. He might have been delayed on his northward journey; at any rate, he had a light heart now, to judge from his song, and I wished that I could ask him a few questions — how he liked being the last man among the bobolinks, and where he had taken singing lessons in the South.

Presently I left the lower fields, and took a path that led higher, where I could look beyond the village to the northern country mountainward. Here the sweet fern grew thick and fragrant, and I also found myself heedlessly treading on pennyroyal. Nearby, in a field corner, I long ago made a most comfortable seat by putting a stray piece of board and bit of rail across the angle of the fences. I have spent many a delightful hour there, in the shade and shelter of a young pitch-pine and a wild-cherry tree, with a lovely outlook toward the village, just far enough away beyond the green slopes and tall elms of the lower meadows. But that day I still had the feeling of being outward bound, and did not turn aside nor linger. The high pasture land grew more and more enticing.

I stopped to pick some blackberries that twinkled at me like beads among their dry vines, and two or three yellow-birds fluttered up from the leaves of a thistle and then came back again, as if they had complacently° discovered that I was only an overgrown yellow-bird, in strange disguise but perfectly harmless. They made me feel as if I were an intruder, though they did not offer to peck at me, and we parted company very soon. It was good to stand at last on the great shoulder of the hill. The wind was coming in from the sea, there was a fine fragrance from the pines, and the air grew sweeter every moment. I took new pleasure in the thought that, in a piece of wild pasture land like this, one

[1] A reference to the harsh criticism of Keats's poems by a reviewer in *Blackwood's Magazine*.

may get closest to Nature, and subsist upon what she gives
of her own free will. There have been no drudging, heavy-
shod ploughmen to overturn the soil, and vex it into yielding artificial crops. Here one has to take just what Nature is
pleased to give, whether one is a yellow-bird or a human
being. It is very good entertainment for a summer wayfarer,
and I am asking my reader now to share the winter provision which I harvested that day. Let us hope that the small
birds are also faring well after their fashion, but I give them
an anxious thought while the snow goes hurrying in long
waves across the buried fields, this windy winter night.

I next went farther down the hill, and got a drink of fresh
cool water from the brook, and pulled a tender sheaf of
sweet flag beside it. The mossy old fence just beyond was
the last barrier between me and the pasture which had sent
an invisible messenger earlier in the day, but I saw that
somebody else had come first to the rendezvous:° there was
a brown gingham cape-bonnet and a sprigged shoulder-
shawl bobbing up and down, a little way off among the
junipers. I had taken such uncommon pleasure in being
alone that I instantly felt a sense of disappointment; then a
warm glow of pleasant satisfaction rebuked my selfishness.
This could be no one but dear old Mrs. Goodsoe, the friend
of my childhood and fond dependence of my maturer years.
I had not seen her for many weeks, but here she was, out
on one of her famous campaigns for herbs, or perhaps just
returning from a blueberrying expedition. I approached
with care, so as not to startle the gingham bonnet; but she
heard the rustle of the bushes against my dress, and looked
up quickly, as she knelt, bending over the turf. In that
position she was hardly taller than the luxuriant junipers
themselves.

"I'm a-gittin' in my mulleins," she said briskly, "an' I've
been thinking o' you these twenty times since I come out o'
the house. I begun to believe you must ha' forgot me at
last."

"I have been away from home," I explained. "Why don't
you get in your pennyroyal too? There's a great plantation
of it beyond the next fence but one."

"Pennyr'yal!" repeated the dear old woman, with an air of compassion for inferior knowledge; "'tain't the right time, darlin'. Pennyr'yal's too rank now. But for mulleins this day is prime. I've got a dreadful graspin' fit for 'em this year; seems if I must be goin' to need 'em extry. I feel like the squirrels must when they know a hard winter's comin'." And Mrs. Goodsoe bent over her work again, while I stood by and watched her carefully cut the best full-grown leaves with a clumsy pair of scissors, which might have served through at least half a century for herb-gathering. They were fastened to her apron-strings by a long piece of list.°

"I'm going to take my jack-knife and help you," I suggested, with some fear of refusal. "I just passed a flourishing family of six or seven heads that must have been growing on purpose for you."

"Now be keerful, dear heart," was the anxious response; "choose 'em well. There's odds in mulleins same's there is in angels. Take a plant that's all run up to stalk, and there ain't but little goodness in the leaves. This one I'm at now must ha' been stepped on by some creatur and blighted of its bloom, and the leaves is han'some! When I was small I used to have a notion that Adam an' Eve must a took mulleins for their winter wear. Ain't they just like flannel, for all the world? I've had experience, and I know there's plenty of sickness might be saved to folks if they'd quit horseradish and such fiery, exasperating things, and use mullein drarves[2] in proper season. Now I shall spread these an' dry 'em nice on my spare floor in the garrit,[3] an' come to steam 'em for use along in the winter there'll be the vally[4] of the whole summer's goodness in 'em, sartin." And she snipped away with the dull scissors while I listened respectfully, and took great pains to have my part of the harvest present a good appearance.

"This is most too dry a head," she added presently, a little out of breath. "There! I can tell you there's

[2]Young shoots.
[3]Attic.
[4]Value.

win'rows[5] o' young doctors, bilin' over with book-larnin', that is truly ignorant of what to do for the sick, or how to p'int out those paths that well people foller toward sickness. Book-fools I call 'em, them young men, an' some on 'em never'll live to know much better, if they git to be Methuselahs.[6] In my time every middle-aged woman who had brought up a family had some proper ideas of dealin' with complaints. I won't say but there was some fools amongst *them,* but I'd rather take my chances, unless they'd forsook herbs and gone to dealin' with patent stuff. Now my mother really did sense the use of herbs and roots. I never see anybody that come up to her. She was a meek-looking woman, but very understandin' mother was."

"Then that's where you learned so much yourself, Mrs. Goodsoe," I ventured to say.

"Bless your heart, I don't hold a candle to her; 'tis but little I can recall of what she used to say. No, her l'arnin' died with her," said my friend, in a self-deprecating tone. "Why, there was as many as twenty kinds of roots alone that she used to keep by her, that I forgot the use of; an' I'm sure I shouldn't know where to find most of 'em, any. There was an herb"—*airb* she called it—"an herb called masterwort, that she used to get way from Pennsylvany; and she used to think everything of noble-liverwort, but I never could seem to get the right effects from it as she could. Though I don't know as she ever really did use masterwort where some-thin' else wouldn't a served. She had a cousin married out in Pennsylvany that used to take pains to get it to her every year or two, and so she felt 't was important to have it. Some set more by such things as come from a distance, but I rec'lect mother always used to maintain that folks was meant to be doctored with the stuff that grew right about 'em; 'twas sufficient, an' so ordered. That was before the whole population took to livin' on wheels, the way they do now. 'Twas never my idee that we was meant to know what's goin' on all over the world to once. There's goin' to be some sort of a set-back one o' these days, with these

[5]Windrows, stacks of drying hay.
[6]A Biblical figure said to have lived 969 years.

telegraphs an' things, an' letters comin' every hand's turn, and folks leavin' their proper work to answer 'em. I may not live to see it. 'Twas allowed to be difficult for folks to get about in old times, or to git word across the country, and they stood in their lot an' place, and weren't all just alike, either, same as pine-spills."[7]

We were kneeling side by side now, as if in penitence for the march of progress, but we laughed as we turned to look at each other.

"Do you think it did much good when everybody brewed a cracked quart mug of herb-tea?" I asked, walking away on my knees to a new mullein.

"I've always lifted my voice against the practice, far's I could," declared Mrs. Goodsoe; "an' I won't deal out none o' the herbs I save for no such nonsense. There was three houses along our road—I call no names—where you couldn't go into the livin' room without findin' a mess o' herb-tea drorin'[8] on the stove or side o' the fireplace, winter or summer, sick or well. One was thoroughwut, one would be camomile, and the other, like as not, yellow dock; but they all used to put in a little new rum to git out the goodness, or keep it from spilin'." (Mrs. Goodsoe favored me with a knowing smile.) "Land, how mother used to laugh! But poor creatures, they had to work hard, and I guess it never done 'em a mite o' harm; they was all good herbs. I wish you could hear the quawkin' there used to be when they was indulged with a real case o' sickness. Everybody would collect from far an' near; you'd see 'em coming along the road and across the pastures then; everybody clamorin' that nothin' would do no kind o' good but her choice o' teas or drarves to the feet. I wonder there was a babe lived to grow up in the whole lower part o' the town; an' if nothin' else 'peared to ail 'em, word was passed about that 'twas likely Mis' So-and-So's last young one was goin' to be foolish. Land, how they'd gather! I know one day the doctor come to Widder Peck's and the house was crammed so't he could scercely git inside the door; and he says, just

[7]Pine needles.
[8]Drawing, simmering.

as polite, 'Do send for some of the neighbors!' as if there wa'n't a soul to turn to, right or left. You'd ought to seen 'em begin to scatter."

"But don't you think the cars and telegraphs have given people more to interest them, Mrs. Goodsoe? Don't you believe people's lives were narrower then, and more taken up with little things?" I asked, unwisely, being a product of modern times.

"Not one mite, dear," said my companion stoutly. "There was as big thoughts then as there is now; these times was born o' them. The difference is in folks themselves; but now, instead o' doin' their own housekeepin' and watchin' their own neighbors—though that was carried to excess— they git word that a niece's child is ailin' the other side o' Massachusetts, and they drop everything and git on their best clothes, and off they jiggit in the cars. Tis a bad sign when folks wear out their best clothes faster 'n they do their everyday ones. The other side o' Massachusetts has got to look after itself by rights. An' besides that, Sunday-keepin's all gone out o' fashion. Some lays it to one thing an' some another, but some o' them old ministers that folks are all a-sighin' for did preach a lot o' stuff that wa'n't nothin' but chaff;° 'twa'n't the word o' God out o' either Old Testament or New. But everybody went to meetin' and heard it, and come home, and was set to fightin' with their next door neighbor over it. Now I'm a believer, and I try to live a Christian life, but I'd as soon hear a surveyor's book read out, figgers an' all, as try to get any simple truth out o' most sermons. It's them as is most to blame."

"What was the matter that day at Widow Peck's?" I hastened to ask, for I knew by experience that the good, clear-minded soul beside me was apt to grow unduly vexed and distressed when she contemplated the state of religious teaching.

"Why, there wa'n't nothin' the matter, only a gal o' Miss Peck's had met with a dis'pintment and had gone into screechin' fits. 'Twas a rovin' creatur' that had come along hayin' time, and he'd gone off an' forsook her betwixt two days; nobody ever knew what become of him. Them Pecks was 'Good Lord, anybody!' kind o' gals, and took up with whoever they could get. One of 'em married Heron, the Irishman; they lived in that little house that was burnt this summer, over on the edge o' the plains. He was a good-hearted creatur', with a laughin' eye and a clever word for everybody. He was the first Irishman that ever came this way, and we was all for gettin' a look at him, when he first used to go by. Mother's folks was what they call Scotch-Irish, though; there was an old race of 'em settled about here. They could foretell events, some on 'em, and had second sight. I know folks used to say mother's grand-mother had them gifts, but mother was never free to speak about it to us. She remembered her well, too."

"I suppose that you mean old Jim Heron, who was such a famous fiddler?" I asked with great interest, for I am always delighted to know more about that rustic hero, parochial Orpheus[9] that he must have been!

"Now, dear heart, I suppose you don't remember him, do you?" replied Mrs. Goodsoe, earnestly. "Fiddle! He'd about break your heart with them tunes of his, or else set your heels flying up the floor in a jig, though you was minister o' the First Parish and all wound up for a funeral prayer. I tell ye there ain't no tunes sounds like them used to. It used to seem to me summer nights when I was comin' along the plains road, and he set by the window playin', as if there was a bewitched human creatur' in that old red fiddle o' his. He could make it sound just like a woman's voice tellin' somethin' over and over, as if folks could help her out o' her sorrows if she could only make 'em under-stand. I've set by the stone wall and cried as if my heart was broke, and dear knows it wa'n't in them days. How he would twirl off them jigs and dance tunes! He used to make somethin' han'some out of 'em in fall an' winter, playin' at huskins and dancin' parties; but he was unstiddy by spells, as he got along in years, and never knew what it was to be forehanded.[10] Everybody felt bad when he died; you

---

[9]Orpheus, in Greek mythology, played the lyre so beautifully his music could spellbind beasts and move rocks.
[10]Prudent.

couldn't help likin' the creatur'. He'd got the gift—that's all
you could say about it.

"There was a Mis' Jerry Foss, that lived over by the brook
bridge, on the plains road, that had lost her husband early,
and was left with three child'n. She set the world by 'em,
and was a real pleasant, ambitious little woman, and was
workin' on as best she could with that little farm, when
there come a rage o' scarlet fever, and her boy and two girls
was swept off and laid dead within the same week. Every
one o' the neighbors did what they could, but she'd had no
sleep since they was taken sick, and after the funeral she set
there just like a piece o' marble, and would only shake her
head when you spoke to her. They all thought her reason
would go; and 'twould certain, if she couldn't have shed
tears. An' one o' the neighbors—'twas like mother's sense,
but it might have been somebody else—spoke o' Jim Heron.
Mother an' one or two o' the women that knew her best was
in the house with her. 'Twas right in the edge o' the woods
and some of us younger ones was over by the wall on the
other side of the road where there was a couple of old
willows—I remember just how the brook damp felt—and
we kept quiet's we could, and some other folks come along
down the road, and stood waitin' on the little bridge, hopin'
somebody'd come out, I suppose, and they'd git news.
Everybody was wrought up, and felt a good deal for her,
you know. By an' by Jim Heron come stealin' right out o'
the shadows an' set down on the doorstep, an' 'twas a good
while before we heard a sound; then, oh, dear me! 'twas
what the whole neighborhood felt for that mother all spoke
in the notes, an' they told me afterwards that Mis' Foss's
face changed in a minute, and she come right over an' got
into my mother's lap—she was a little woman—an' laid her
head down, and there she cried herself into a blessed sleep.
After a while one o' the other women stole out an' told the
folks, and we all went home. He only played that one tune.

"But there!" resumed Mrs. Goodsoe, after a silence,
during which my eyes were filled with tears. "His wife
always complained that the fiddle made her nervous. She

never 'peared to think nothin' o' poor Heron after she'd once got him."

"That's often the way," said I, with harsh cynicism, though I had no guilty person in my mind at the moment; and we went straying off, not very far apart, up through the pasture. Mrs. Goodsoe cautioned me that we must not get so far off that we could not get back the same day. The sunshine began to feel very hot on our backs, and we both turned toward the shade. We had already collected a large bundle of mullein leaves, which were carefully laid into a clean, calico apron, held together by the four corners, and proudly carried by me, though my companion regarded them with anxious eyes. We sat down together at the edge of the pine woods, and Mrs. Goodsoe proceeded to fan herself with her limp cape-bonnet.

"I declare, how hot it is! The east wind's all gone again," she said. "It felt so cool this forenoon that I overburdened myself with as thick a petticoat as any I've got. I'm despri't afeared of having a chill, now that I ain't so young as once. I hate to be housed up."

"It's only August, after all," I assured her unnecessarily, confirming my statement by taking two peaches out of my pocket, and laying them side by side on the brown pine needles between us.

"Dear sakes alive!" exclaimed the old lady, with evident pleasure. "Where did you get them, now? Doesn't anything taste twice better out-o'-doors? I ain't had such a peach for years. Do le's keep the stones, an' I'll plant 'em; it only takes four years for a peach pit to come to bearing, an' I guess I'm good for four years, 'thout I meet with some accident."

I could not help agreeing, or taking a fond look at the thin little figure, and her wrinkled brown face and kind, twinkling eyes. She looked as if she had properly dried herself, by mistake, with some of her mullein leaves, and was likely to keep her goodness, and to last the longer in consequence. There never was a truer, simple-hearted soul made out of the old-fashioned country dust than Mrs. Goodsoe. I thought, as I looked away from her across the wide country, that nobody was left in any of the farmhouses so original, so full of rural wisdom and reminiscence, so really able and dependable, as she. And nobody had made better use of her time in a world foolish enough to sometimes undervalue medicinal herbs.

When we had eaten our peaches we still sat under the pines, and I was not without pride when I had poked about in the ground with a little twig, and displayed to my crony a long fine root, bright yellow to the eye, and a wholesome bitter to the taste.

"Yis, dear, goldthread," she assented indulgently. "Seems to me there's more of it than anything except grass an' hardhack. Good for canker, but no better than two or three other things I can call to mind; but I always lay in a good wisp of it, for old times' sake. Now, I want to know why you should a bit it, and took away all the taste o' your nice peach? I was just thinkin' what a han'some entertainment we've had. I've got so I 'sociate certain things with certain folks, and goldthread was somethin' Lizy Wisby couldn't keep house without, no ways whatever. I believe she took so much it kind o' puckered her disposition."

"Lizy Wisby?" I repeated inquiringly.

"You knew her, if ever, by the name of Mis' Deacon Brimblecom," answered my friend, as if this were only a brief preface to further information, so I waited with respectful expectation. Mrs. Goodsoe had grown tired out in the sun, and a good story would be an excuse for sufficient rest. It was a most lovely place where we sat, half-way up the long hillside; for my part, I was perfectly contented and happy. "You've often heard of Deacon Brimblecom?" she asked, as if a great deal depended upon his being properly introduced.

"I remember him," said I. "They called him Deacon Brimfull, you know, and he used to go about with a witch-hazel branch to show people where to dig wells."

"That's the one," said Mrs. Goodsoe, laughing. "I didn't know's you could go so far back. I'm always divided between whether you can remember everything I can, or are only a babe in arms."

"I have a dim recollection of there being something strange about their marriage," I suggested, after a pause, which began to appear dangerous. I was so much afraid the subect would be changed.

"I can tell you all about it," I was quickly answered. "Deacon Brimblecom was very pious accordin' to his lights in his early years. He lived way back in the country then, and there come a rovin' preacher along, and set everybody up that way all by the ears. I've heard the old folks talk it over, but I forget most of his doctrine, except some of his followers was persuaded they could dwell among the angels while yet on airth, and this Deacon Brimfull, as you call him, felt sure he was called by the voice of a spirit bride. So he left a good, deservin' wife he had, an' four children, and built him a new house over to the other side of the land he'd had from his father. They didn't take much pains with the buildin', because they expected to be trans-lated[11] before long, and then the spirit brides and them folks was goin' to appear and divide up the airth amongst 'em, and the world's folks and onbelievers was goin' to serve 'em or be sent to torments. They had meetin's about in the schoolhouses, an' all sorts o' goin's on; some on 'em went crazy, but the deacon held on to what wits he had, an' by an' by the spirit bride didn't turn out to be much of a house-keeper an' he had always been used to good livin' so he sneaked home ag'in. One o' mother's sisters married up to Ash Hill, where it all took place; that's how I come to have the particulars."

"Then how did he come to find his Eliza Wisby?" I inquired. "Do tell me the whole story; you've got mullein leaves enough."

"There's all yesterday's at home, if I haven't," replied Mrs. Goodsoe. "The way he come a-courtin' o' Sister Wisby was this: she went a-courtin' o' him.

"There was a spell he lived to home, and then his poor wife died, and he had a spirit bride in good earnest, an' the child'n was placed about with his folks and hers, for they

[11]Called to heaven without dying.

was both out o' good families; and I don't know what come over him, but he had another pious fit that looked for all the world like the real thing. He hadn't no family cares, and he lived with his brother's folks, and turned his land in with theirs. He used to travel to every meetin' an' conference that was within reach of his old sorrel hoss's feeble legs; he j'ined the Christian Baptists that was just in their early prime, and he was a great exhorter, and got to be called deacon, though I guess he wa'n't deacon, 'less it was for a spare hand when deacon timber was scercer'n usual. An' one time there was a four-days' protracted meetin' to the church in the lower part of the town. 'Twas a real solemn time; somethin' more'n usual was goin' forward, an' they collected from the whole country round. Women folks liked it, an' the men too; it give 'em a change, an' they was quartered round free, same as conference folks now. Some on 'em, for a joke, sent Silas Brimblecom up to Lizy Wisby's, though she'd give out she couldn't accommodate nobody, because of expectin' her cousin's folks. Everybody knew 'twas a lie; she was amazin' close considerin' she had plenty to do with. There was a streak that wa'n't just right somewheres in Lizy's wits, I always thought. She was very kind in case o' sickness, I'll say that for her.

"You know where the house is, over there on what they call Windy Hill? There the deacon went, all unsuspectin', and 'stead o' Lizy's resentin' of him she put in her own hoss, and they come back together to evenin' meetin'. She was prominent among the sect herself, an' he bawled and talked, and she bawled and talked, an' took up more'n the time allotted in the exercises, just as if they was showin' off to each other what they was able to do at expoundin'. Everybody was laughin' at 'em after the meetin' broke up, and that next day an' the next, an' all through, they was constant, and seemed to be havin' a beautiful occasion. Lizy had always give out she scorned the men, but when she got a chance at a particular one 'twas altogether differ-ent, and the deacon seemed to please her somehow or 'nother, and—There! you don't want to listen to this old stuff that's past an' gone?"

"Oh, yes, I do," said I.

"I run on like a clock that's onset her striking hand," said Mrs. Goodsoe mildly. "Sometimes my kitchen timepiece goes on half the forenoon, and I says to myself the day before yisterday I would let it be a warnin', and keep it in mind for a check on my own speech. The next news that was heard was that the deacon an' Lizy—well, opinions differed which of 'em had spoke first, but them fools settled it before the protracted meetin' was over, and give away their hearts before he started for home. They considered 'twould be wise, though, considerin' their short acquaintance, to take one another on trial a spell; 'twas Lizy's notion, and she asked him why he wouldn't come over and stop with her till spring, and then, if they both continued to like, they could git married any time 'twas convenient. Lizy, she come and talked it over with mother, and mother disliked to offend her, but she spoke pretty plain; and Lizy felt hurt, an' thought they was showin' excellent judgment, so much harm come from hasty unions and folks comin' to a realizin' sense of each other's failin's when 'twas too late.

"So one day our folks saw Deacon Brimfull a-ridin' by with a gre't coopful of hens in the back o' his wagon, and bundles o' stuff tied on top and hitched to the exes underneath; and he riz a hymn just as he passed the house, and was speedin' the old sorrel with a willer switch. 'Twas most Thanksgivin' time, an' sooner'n she expected him. New Year's was the time she set; but he thought he'd come while the roads was fit for wheels. They was out to meetin' together Thanksgivin' Day, an' that used to be a gre't season for marryin'; so the young folks nudged each other, and some on 'em ventured to speak to the couple as they come down the aisle. Lizy carried it off real well; she wa'n't afraid o' what nobody said or thought, and so home they went. They'd got out her yaller sleigh and her hoss; she never would ride after the deacon's poor old creatur', and I believe it died long o' the winter from stiffenin' up.

"Yes," said Mrs. Goodsoe, emphatically, after we had silently considered the situation for a short space of time, "yes, there was consider'ble talk, now I tell you! The raskil boys pestered 'em just about to death for a while. They used to collect up there an' rap on the winders, and they'd turn out all the deacon's hens 'long at nine o'clock o' night, and chase 'em all over the dingle;[12] an' one night they even lugged the pig right out o' the sty, and shoved it into the back entry, an' run for their lives. They'd stuffed its mouth full o' somethin', so it couldn't squeal till it got there. There wa'n't a sign o' nobody to be seen when Lizy hasted out with the light, and she an' the deacon had to persuade the creatur' back as best they could; 'twas a cold night, and they said it took 'em till towards mornin'. You see the deacon was just the kind of a man that a hog wouldn't budge for; it takes a masterful man to deal with a hog. Well, there was no end to the works nor the talk, but Lizy left 'em pretty much alone. She did 'pear kind of dignified about it, I must say!"

"And then, were they married in the spring?"

"I was tryin' to remember whether it was just before Fast Day or just after," responded my friend, with a careful look at the sun, which was nearer the west than either of us had noticed. "I think likely 'twas along in the last o' April, any way some of us looked out o' the window one Monday mornin' early, and says, 'For goodness' sake! Lizy's sent the deacon home again!' His old sorrel havin' passed away, he was ridin' in Ezry Welsh's hoss-cart, with his hen-coop and more bundles than he had when he come, and looked as meechin' as ever you see. Ezry was drivin', and he let a glance fly swiftly round to see if any of us was lookin' out; an' then I declare if he didn't have the malice to turn right in towards the barn, where he see my oldest brother, Joshuay, an' says he real natural, 'Joshuay, just step out with your wrench. I believe I hear my kingbolt rattlin' kind o' loose.' Brother, he went out an' took in the sitooation, an' the deacon bowed kind of stiff. Joshuay was so full o' laugh, and Ezry Welsh, that they couldn't look one another in the face. There wa'n't nothing ailed the kingbolt, you know, an' when Josh riz up he says, 'Goin' up country for a spell, Mr. Brimblecom?'

[12] A small valley.

"'I be,' says the deacon, lookin' dreadful mortified and cast down.

"'Ain't things turned out well with you an' Sister Wisby?' says Joshuay. 'You had ought to remember that the woman is the weaker vessel.'

"'Hang her, let her carry less sail, then!' the deacon bu'st out, and he stood right up an' shook his fist there by the hen-coop, he was so mad; an' Ezry's hoss was a young creatur' an' started up and set the deacon right over backwards into the chips. We didn't know but he'd broke his neck; but when he see the women folks runnin' out he jumped up quick as a cat, an' clim' into the cart, an' off they went. Ezry said he told him that he couldn't git along with Lizy, she was so fractious° in thundery weather; if there was a rumble in the daytime she must go right to bed an' screech, and if 'twas night she must git right up an' go an' call him out of a sound sleep. But everybody knew he'd never a gone home unless she'd sent him.

"Somehow they made it up ag'in, him an' Lizy, and she had him back. She'd been countin' all along on not havin' to hire nobody to work about the gardin an' so on, an' she said she wa'n't goin' to let him have a whole winter's board for nothin'. So the old hens was moved back, and they was married right off fair an' square, an' I don't know but they got along well as most folks. He brought his youngest girl down to live with 'em after a while, an' she was a real treasure to Lizy; everybody spoke well o' Phoebe Brimble-com. The deacon got over his pious fit, and there was consider'ble work in him if you kept right after him. He was an amazin' cider-drinker, and he airnt the name you know him by in his latter days. Lizy never trusted him with nothin', but she kep' him well. She left everything she owned to Phoebe, when she died, 'cept somethin' to satisfy the law. There, they're all gone now; seems to me some-times, when I get thinkin', as if I'd lived a thousand years!"

I laughed, but I found Mrs. Goodsoe's thoughts had taken a serious turn.

"There, I come by some old graves down here in the lower edge of the pasture," she said as we rose to go. "I couldn't help thinking how I should like to be laid right out in the pasture ground, when my time comes; it looked sort o' comfortable, and I have ranged these slopes so many summers. Seems as if I could see right up through the turf and tell when the weather was pleasant, and get the goodness o' the sweet fern. Now, dear, just hand me my apernful o' mulleins out o' the shade. I hope you won't come to need none this winter, but I'll dry some special for you."

"I'm going by the road," said I, "or else by the path across the meadows, so I will walk as far as the house with you. Aren't you pleased with my company?" for she demurred at my going the least bit out of the way.

So we strolled toward the little gray house, with our plunder of mullein leaves slung on a stick which we carried between us. Of course I went in to make a call, as if I had not seen my hostess before; she is the last maker of muster-gingerbread, and before I came away I was kindly measured for a pair of mittens.

"You'll be sure to come an' see them two peach-trees after I get 'em well growin'?" Mrs. Goodsoe called after me when I had said good-by, and was almost out of hearing down the road.

Do especially Questions 12, 15, 20, 52, 73, 75, 77-81, 83, 103, 105, 107, 108, and 147. Consult the Model Short Story in Volume One.

SARAH ORNE JEWETT *1849-1909*

The scenes of Miss Jewett's birthplace, Maine ports and farmlands, greatly influenced her work and stimulated in her a determination to portray her state's local color. Accompanying her doctor father on sick calls, she observed village types, and developed sympathy for the suffering and admiration for the strength of those less fortunate than herself. She began her writing career early; when she was nineteen the *Atlantic Monthly* accepted one of her stories. Her novels and short stories concentrated on the deterioration of the state from the old days of glory, the deserted harbors and the dying farms of Maine. Among her best works are *A Country Doctor*, *A White Heron*, and *The Country of the Pointed Firs*, which has been called the best piece of regional fiction to appear during the nineteenth century. Her "precise, charmingly subdued vignettes" have secured her place among the regionalists, and have had a marked effect on later writers. Willa Cather, by her own admission, is testament to the influence of Sarah Jewett's accuracy of observation, depth of insight, and poetry of description.

PROBLEM QUESTIONS

1. Compare the following characters: Ethan Brand (Volume One), Captain Ahab (Volume One), Stumpy, Tim Haskins, and old Mrs. Goodsoe.

(a) Compare them according to their appearance, social status, and personal habits.

(b) Compare the characteristics of their thoughts, speech, and actions.

(c) Compare their convictions and beliefs about man, the world, and human destiny.

(d) Compare your empathy towards each of them as personalities.

(e) Compare their concepts of what the "Good Life" is with your own concept.

2. "It is a settled conviction with me," said Hamlin Garland, "that each locality must produce its own literary record, each special phase of life utter its own voice." Discuss the effectiveness of Bret Harte, Hamlin Garland, and Sarah Orne Jewett in recording their particular localities and voicing their views of a special phase of life in their individual regions.

3. Because Western writers wrote mainly for Eastern readers their stories were often filled with the unusual and the picturesque in both the landscape and the characters. Show how this statement is true of "The Luck of Roaring Camp." What aspects of the story are realistic? What aspects are sentimental? Are the characters mere stereotypes or do they have individual personalities?

4. It has been said of Sarah Orne Jewett that she "learned the great trick of true realism: to combine depth of sympathetic involvement with artistic detachment, reaching unity through the establishment of a point of view." What is Miss Jewett's point of view in "The Courting of Sister Wisby"? How does she reveal her sympathetic involvement with her characters while maintaining also a detached viewpoint? In the telling of Mrs. Goodsoe's story, how does Miss Jewett show her appreciation of comedy without a hint of ridicule?

THE NATURALISTIC VOGUE

Writers of the naturalistic school wanted a literature that sought the factual, the honest, the authentic in human life. The positive sciences were examining data with a confidence born of better precision instruments, journalism was becoming less a creative art than a science of accurate fact-finding, and the developing art of photography caught a certain truth about the human face that, it seemed, no flattering portrait painter could improve upon. Naturalistic literature professed to apply these same techniques to life. To some of the naturalistic writers a "scientific" representation of man tended to mean a dissection of man into the biological, economic, and subconscious drives that made him tick. Stephen Crane and Jack London represent this point of view. Others, notably Henry James and William Dean Howells, tended to follow the latter's suggestion that authors exclude everything from the picture of man but "the cleanly respectabilities" and the "smiling aspect" of life. Significantly, however, the best works of all of these authors transcended these differences and produced an image of man struggling against his own nature and the world about him—but at the same time, a free agent, capable of something heroic and redeemable.

The naturalistic preoccupation with the helplessness of man before the indifference and violence of nature or the irony and whimsy of civilized existence can be adequately examined in the fiction of a few writers of that school. O. Henry, whose real name was William S. Porter, a prolific writer of stories with twists and surprise endings, was acutely aware of the irony of life. His stories, each of which is a miniature portrait of life's vagaries and human fallibility, were extremely popular in America and abroad.

The most outspoken naturalist of this period was Jack London. He pictured the world as peopled by animals and supermen, "pursuing and being pursued, hunting and being hunted . . . in blindness and confusion, with violence and disorder, a chaos of gluttony and slaughter, ruled over by chance, merciless, planless, endless." This is the same hopeless, "multiverse" world symbolized by Henry Adams' Dynamo. In "The Open Boat," Stephen Crane describes a struggle between man and nature that is as harsh and instinctive as the gunfight in London's "All Gold Canyon." There is a moment when the wind is quiet at sea, and the four survivors of a shipwreck study a tower on the distant shore: "This tower was a giant, standing with its back to the plight of the ants. It represented in a degree, to the correspondent, the serenity of nature amid the struggles of the individual — nature in the wind, and nature in the vision of men. She did not seem cruel to him then, nor beneficent, nor treacherous, nor wise. But she was indifferent, flatly indifferent."

There is little room for freedom and heroic deeds in this sort of universe pictured by Crane. Collins in "A Mystery of Heroism" was "not a hero," says Crane. "Heroes had no shame in their lives, and as for him [Collins], he remembered borrowing fifteen dollars from a friend and promising to pay it back the next day, and then avoiding that friend for ten months. . . . He saw that, in this matter of the well, the canteens, the shells, he was an intruder in the land of fine deeds."

There may be some advantage in reviewing the various meanings nature has had in early American thought. The concept of "Nature" to Puritan Man had meant corrupt, depraved human nature and a universe that had become disordered after man's Original Sin. To men like Franklin and Jefferson in the Age of Enlightenment it had meant the firm core of reason and common sense in human nature which could be perfected by education and civilization, and which brought order into man's relationship with God and the universe. In the Romantic Period of Emerson and Thoreau "Nature" was a mysterious dynamic force in man himself, in God, and in the surface beauties of the universe; it was the bond of communion between man and God; it reached beyond the limits of common sense into the heights and the depths of man. Finally, to the Naturalists, "Nature" was the dark blind force that ran through all reality, the Darwinist instinctive drive in man for biological survival, the Marxist economic determinism that ruled his social and political life, and the unknown subconscious forces that struggled within man, and were soon to be charted by Sigmund Freud.

The Cop and the Anthem

O. HENRY

On his bench in Madison Square, Soapy moved uneasily. When wild geese honk high of nights, and when women without sealskin coats grow kind to their husbands, and when Soapy moves uneasily on his bench in the park, you may know that winter is near at hand.

A dead leaf fell in Soapy's lap. That was Jack Frost's card. Jack is kind to the regular denizens° of Madison Square and gives fair warning of his annual call. At the corners of four streets he hands his pasteboards to the North Wind, footman of the mansion of All Outdoors, so that the inhabitants thereof may make ready.

Soapy's mind became cognizant° of the fact that the time had come for him to resolve himself into a singular Committee of Ways and Means to provide against the coming rigor. And therefore he moved uneasily on his bench.

The hibernatorial° ambitions of Soapy were not of the

"The Cop and the Anthem" from *The Four Million* by O. Henry. Reprinted by permission of Doubleday & Co. Inc.

highest. In them there were no considerations of Mediterranean cruises, of soporific° Southern skies, or drifting in the Vesuvian Bay. Three months on the Island[1] was what his soul craved. Three months of assured board and bed and congenial company, safe from Boreas[2] and blue-coats, seemed to Soapy the essence of things desirable.

For years the hospitable Blackwell's had been his winter quarters. Just as his more fortunate fellow New Yorkers had bought their tickets to Palm Beach and the Riviera each winter, so Soapy had made his humble arrangements for his annual hegira° to the Island. And now the time was come. On the previous night three Sabbath newspapers, distributed beneath his coat, about his ankles, and over his lap, had failed to repulse the cold as he slept on his bench near the spurting fountain in the ancient square. So the Island loomed big and timely in Soapy's mind. He scorned the provisions made in the name of charity for the city's dependents. In Soapy's opinion the Law was more benign than Philanthropy.° There was an endless round of institutions, municipal and eleemosynary,° on which he might set out and receive lodging and food accordant with the simple life. But to one of Soapy's proud spirit the gifts of charity are encumbered. If not in coin you must pay in humiliation of spirit for every benefit received at the hands of philanthropy. As Caesar had his Brutus, every bed of charity must have its toll of a bath, every loaf of bread its compensation of a private and personal inquisition.° Wherefore it is better to be a guest of the law which, though conducted by rules, does not meddle unduly with a gentleman's private affairs.

Soapy, having decided to go to the Island, at once set about accomplishing his desire. There were many easy ways of doing this. The pleasantest was to dine luxuriously at some expensive restaurant; and then, after declaring insolvency,° be handed over quietly and without uproar to a policeman. An accommodating magistrate would do the rest.

[1]Blackwell's Island lying in the East River, the site of the city workhouse.
[2]The god of the North Wind.

Soapy left his bench and strolled out of the square and across the level sea of asphalt, where Broadway and Fifth Avenue flow together. Up Broadway he turned, and halted at a glittering café, where are gathered together nightly the choicest products of the grape, the silkworm, and the protoplasm.°

Soapy had confidence in himself from the lowest button of his vest upward. He was shaven, and his coat was decent and his neat, black, ready-tied four-in-hand had been presented to him by a lady missionary on Thanksgiving Day. If he could reach a table in the restaurant unsuspected, success would be his. The portion of him that would show above the table would raise no doubt in the waiter's mind. A roasted mallard duck, thought Soapy, would be about the thing—with a bottle of Chablis, and then Camembert, a demi-tasse, and a cigar. One dollar for the cigar would be enough. The total would not be so high as to call forth any supreme manifestation of revenge from the café management; and yet the meat would leave him filled and happy for the journey to his winter refuge.

But as Soapy set foot inside the restaurant door the head waiter's eye fell upon his frayed trousers and decadent° shoes. Strong and ready hands turned him about and conveyed him in silence and haste to the sidewalk and averted the ignoble fate of the menaced mallard.

Soapy turned off Broadway. It seemed that his route to the coveted island was not to be an epicurean° one. Some other way of entering limbo must be thought of.

At a corner of Sixth Avenue electric lights and cunningly displayed wares behind plate glass made a shop window conspicuous. Soapy took a cobblestone and dashed it through the glass. People came running around the corner, a policeman in the lead. Soapy stood still, with his hands in his pockets, and smiled at the sight of brass buttons.

"Where's the man that done that?" inquired the officer excitedly.

"Don't you figure out that I might have had something to do with it?" said Soapy, not without sarcasm, but friendly, as one greets good fortune.

The policeman's mind refused to accept Soapy even as a clue. Men who smash windows do not remain to parley with the law's minions. They take to their heels. The policeman saw a man halfway down the block running to catch a car. With drawn club he joined in the pursuit. Soapy, with disgust in his heart, loafed along, twice unsuccessful.

On the opposite side of the street was a restaurant of no great pretensions. It catered° to large appetites and modest purses. Its crockery and atmosphere were thick; its soup and napery thin. Into this place Soapy took his accusive shoes and telltale trousers without challenge. At a table he sat and consumed beefsteak, flapjacks, doughnuts, and pie. And then to the waiter he betrayed the fact that the minutest coin and himself were strangers.

"Now, get busy and call a cop," said Soapy. "And don't keep a gentleman waiting."

"No cop for youse," said the waiter, with a voice like butter cakes and an eye like the cherry in a Manhattan cocktail. "Hey, Con!"

Neatly upon his left ear on the callous° pavement two waiters pitched Soapy. He arose, joint by joint, as a carpenter's rule opens, and beat the dust from his clothes. Arrest seemed but a rosy dream. The Island seemed very far away. A policeman who stood before a drug store two doors away laughed and walked down the street.

Five blocks Soapy traveled before his courage permitted him to woo capture again. This time the opportunity presented what he fatuously° termed to himself a "cinch." A young woman of a modest and pleasing guise° was standing before a show window gazing with sprightly interest at its display of shaving mugs and inkstands, and two yards from the window a large policeman of severe demeanor° leaned against a water plug.

It was Soapy's design to assume the role of the despicable and execrated° "masher." The refined and elegant appearance of his victim and the contiguity° of the conscientious cop encouraged him to believe that he would soon feel the pleasant official clutch upon his arm that would insure his winter quarters on the right little, tight little isle.

Soapy straightened the lady missionary's ready-made tie, dragged his shrinking cuffs into the open, set his hat at a killing cant, and sidled toward the young woman. He made eyes at her, was taken with sudden coughs and "hems," smiled, smirked, and went brazenly through the impudent and contemptible litany of the "masher." With half an eye Soapy saw that the policeman was watching him fixedly. The young woman moved away a few steps, and again bestowed her absorbed attention upon the shaving mugs. Soapy followed, boldly stepping to her side, raised his hat and said:

"Ah there, Bedelia! Don't you want to come and play in my yard?"

The policeman was still looking. The persecuted young woman had but to beckon a finger and Soapy would be practically en route for his insular haven.° Already he imagined he could feel the cozy warmth of the station house. The young woman faced him and, stretching out a hand, caught Soapy's coat sleeve.

"Sure, Mike," she said joyfully, "if you'll blow me to a pail of suds. I'd have spoke to you sooner, but the cop was watching."

With the young woman playing the clinging ivy to his oak, Soapy walked past the policeman overcome with gloom. He seemed doomed to liberty.

At the next corner he shook off his companion and ran. He halted in the district where by night are found the lightest streets, hearts, vows, and librettos.° Women in furs and men in greatcoats moved gaily in the wintry air. A sudden fear seized Soapy that some dreadful enchantment had rendered him immune to arrest. The thought brought a little of panic upon it, and when he came upon another policeman lounging grandly in front of a transplendent° theater he caught at the immediate straw of "disorderly conduct."

On the sidewalk Soapy began to yell drunken gibberish

at the top of his harsh voice. He danced, howled, raved, and otherwise disturbed the welkin.°

The policeman twirled his club, turned his back to Soapy, and remarked to a citizen:

"'Tis one of them Yale lads celebratin' the goose egg they give to the Hartford College. Noisy; but no harm. We've instructions to lave them be."

Disconsolate, Soapy ceased his unavailing racket. Would never a policeman lay hands on him? In his fancy the Island seemed an unattainable Arcadia.° He buttoned his thin coat against the chilling wind.

In a cigar store he saw a well-dressed man lighting a cigar at a swinging light. His silk umbrella he had set by the door on entering. Soapy stepped inside, secured the umbrella, and sauntered off with it slowly. The man at the cigar light followed hastily.

"My umbrella," he said, sternly.

"Oh, is it?" sneered Soapy, adding insult to petit° larceny. "Well, why don't you call a policeman? I took it. Your umbrella! Why don't you call a cop? There stands one on the corner."

The umbrella owner slowed his steps. Soapy did likewise, with a presentiment° that luck would again run against him. The policeman looked at the two curiously.

"Of course," said the umbrella man — "that is — well, you know how these mistakes occur — I — if it's your umbrella I hope you'll excuse me — I picked it up this morning in a restaurant — if you recognize it as yours, why — I hope you'll — "

"Of course it's mine," said Soapy, viciously.

The ex-umbrella man retreated. The policeman hurried to assist a tall blonde in an opera cloak across the street in front of a streetcar that was approaching two blocks away.

Soapy walked eastward through a street damaged by improvements. He hurled the umbrella wrathfully into an excavation. He muttered against the men who wear helmets and carry clubs. Because he wanted to fall into their clutches, they seemed to regard him as a king who could do no wrong.

At length Soapy reached one of the avenues to the east where the glitter and turmoil was but faint. He set his face down this toward Madison Square, for the homing instinct survives even when the home is a park bench.

But on an unusually quiet corner Soapy came to a standstill. Here was an old church, quaint and rambling and gabled.° Through one violet-stained window a soft light glowed, where, no doubt, the organist loitered over the keys, making sure of his mastery of the coming Sabbath anthem. For there drifted out to Soapy's ears sweet music that caught and held him transfixed° against the convolutions° of the iron fence.

The moon was above, lustrous and serene; vehicles and pedestrians were few; sparrows twittered sleepily in the eaves—for a little while the scene might have been a country churchyard. And the anthem that the organist played cemented Soapy to the iron fence, for he had known it well in the days when his life contained such things as mothers and roses and ambitions and friends and immaculate thoughts and collars.

The conjunction of Soapy's receptive state of mind and the influences about the old church wrought a sudden and wonderful change in his soul. He viewed with swift horror the pit into which he had tumbled, the degraded days, unworthy desires, dead hopes, wrecked faculties, and base motives that made up his existence.

And also in a moment his heart responded thrillingly to this novel mood. An instantaneous and strong impulse moved him to battle with his desperate fate. He would pull himself out of the mire; he would make a man of himself again; he would conquer the evil that had taken possession of him. There was time; he was comparatively young yet; he would resurrect his old eager ambitions and pursue them without faltering. Those solemn but sweet organ notes had set up a revolution in him. Tomorrow he would go into the roaring downtown district and find work. A fur importer had once offered him a place as driver. He would find him tomorrow and ask for the position. He would be somebody in the world. He would—

Soapy felt a hand laid on his arm. He looked quickly around into the broad face of a policeman.

"What are you doin' here?" asked the officer.

"Nothin'," said Soapy.

"Then come along," said the policeman.

"Three months on the Island," said the Magistrate in the Police Court the next morning.

Do especially Questions 48, 73, 77, 82, 83, 84, 86, 94, 95, 106, and 111. Consult the Model Short Story in Volume One.

O. HENRY (WILLIAM SYDNEY PORTER) *1862-1910*

After a diversified early career in Texas as cowboy, banker, editor, and finally embezzler sentenced to five years imprisonment, O. Henry settled down in the East to a contract with the New York *World* for a short story a week. His work represents the concise, tricky, syndicated story characteristic of modern journalism, and the local-color of large-city street and tenement life.

A Mystery of Heroism

STEPHEN CRANE

The dark uniforms of the men were so coated with dust from the incessant° wrestling of the two armies that the regiment almost seemed a part of the clay bank which shielded them from the shells. On the top of the hill a battery was arguing in tremendous roars with some other guns, and to the eye of the infantry the artillerymen, the guns, the caissons,° the horses, were distinctly outlined upon the blue sky. When a piece was fired, a red streak as round as a log flashed low in the heavens, like a monstrous bolt of lightning. The men of the battery wore white duck trousers, which somehow emphasized their legs; and when they ran and crowded in little groups at the bidding of the

"A Mystery of Heroism" and "The Open Boat," from *Stephen Crane: An Omnibus*, edited by Robert Wooster Stallman. By permission of Alfred A. Knopf, Inc.

shouting officers, it was more impressive than usual to the infantry.

Fred Collins, of A Company, was saying: "Thunder! I wisht I had a drink. Ain't there any water round here?" Then somebody yelled: "There goes th' bugler!"

As the eyes of half the regiment swept in one machine-like movement, there was an instant's picture of a horse in a great convulsive° leap of a death wound and a rider leaning back with a crooked arm and spread fingers before his face. On the ground was the crimson terror of an exploding shell, with fibers of flame that seemed like lances. A glittering bugle swung clear of the rider's back as fell headlong the horse and the man. In the air was an odor as from a conflagration.°

Sometimes they of the infantry looked down at a fair little meadow which spread at their feet. Its long green grass was rippling gently in a breeze. Beyond it was the gray form of a house half torn to pieces by shells and by the busy axes of soldiers who had pursued firewood. The line of an old fence was now dimly marked by long weeds and by an occasional post. A shell had blown the well-house to fragments. Little lines of gray smoke ribboning upward from some embers indicated the place where had stood the barn.

From beyond a curtain of green woods there came the sound of some stupendous scuffle, as if two animals of the size of islands were fighting. At a distance there were occasional appearances of swift-moving men, horses, batteries, flags, and with the crashing of infantry volleys° were heard, often, wild and frenzied cheers. In the midst of it all Smith and Ferguson, two privates of A Company, were engaged in a heated discussion which involved the greatest questions of the national existence.

The battery on the hill presently engaged in a frightful duel. The white legs of the gunners scampered this way and that, and the officers redoubled their shouts. The guns, with their demeanors° of stolidity° and courage, were typical of something infinitely self-possessed in this clamor of death that swirled around the hill.

One of a "swing" team was suddenly smitten° quivering to the ground, and his maddened brethren dragged his torn body in their struggle to escape from this turmoil and danger. A young soldier astride one of the leaders swore and fumed in his saddle and furiously jerked at the bridle. An officer screamed out an order so violently that his voice broke and ended the sentence in a falsetto° shriek.

The leading company of the infantry regiment was somewhat exposed, and the colonel ordered it moved more fully under the shelter of the hill. There was the clank of steel against steel.

A lieutenant of the battery rode down and passed them, holding his right arm carefully in his left hand. And it was as if this arm was not at all a part of him, but belonged to another man. His sober and reflective charger went slowly. The officer's face was grimy and perspiring, and his uniform was tousled as if he had been in direct grapple with an enemy. He smiled grimly when the men stared at him. He turned his horse toward the meadow.

Collins, of A Company, said: "I wisht I had a drink. I bet there's water in that there ol' well yonder!"

"Yes; but how you goin' to git it?"

For the little meadow which intervened was now suffering a terrible onslaught of shells. Its green and beautiful calm had vanished utterly. Brown earth was being flung in monstrous handfuls. And there was a massacre of the young blades of grass. They were being torn, burned, obliterated. Some curious fortune of the battle had made this gentle little meadow the object of the red hate of the shells, and each one as it exploded seemed like an imprecation° in the face of a maiden.

The wounded officer who was riding across this expanse said to himself: "Why, they couldn't shoot any harder if the whole army was massed here!"

A shell struck the gray ruins of the house, and as, after the roar, the shattered wall fell in fragments, there was a noise which resembled the flapping of shutters during a wild gale of winter. Indeed, the infantry paused in the shelter of the bank appeared as men standing upon a shore contemplating a madness of the sea. The angel of calamity had under its glance the battery upon the hill. Fewer white-legged men labored about the guns. A shell had smitten one of the pieces, and after the flare, the smoke, the dust, the wrath of this blow were gone, it was possible to see white legs stretched horizontally upon the ground. And at that interval to the rear where it is the business of battery horses to stand with their noses to the fight, await-ing the command to drag their guns out of the destruction, or into it, or wheresoever these incomprehensible humans demanded with whip and spur—in this line of passive and dumb spectators, whose fluttering hearts yet would not let them forget the iron laws of man's control of them—in this rank of brute-soldiers there had been relentless and hideous carnage. From the ruck° of bleeding and pros-trate° horses, the men of the infantry could see one animal raising its stricken body with its forelegs and turning its nose with mystic and profound eloquence toward the sky.

Some comrades joked Collins about his thirst. "Well, if yeh want a drink so bad, why don't yeh go git it?"

"Well, I will in a minnet, if yeh don't shut up!"

A lieutenant of artillery floundered his horse straight down the hill with as little concern as if it were level ground. As he galloped past the colonel of the infantry, he threw up his hand in swift salute. "We've got to get out of that," he roared angrily. He was a black-bearded officer, and his eyes, which resembled beads, sparkled like those of an insane man. His jumping horse sped along the column of infantry.

The fat major, standing carelessly with his sword held horizontally behind him and with his legs far apart, looked after the receding horseman and laughed. "He wants to get back with orders pretty quick, or there'll be no batt'ry left," he observed.

The wise young captain of the second company hazarded to the lieutenant colonel that the enemy's infantry would probably soon attack the hill, and the lieutenant colonel snubbed him.

A private in one of the rear companies looked out over the meadow, and then turned to a companion and said, "Look there, Jim!" It was the wounded officer from the battery, who some time before had started to ride across the meadow, supporting his right arm carefully with his left hand. This man had encountered a shell, apparently, at a time when no one perceived him, and he could now be seen lying face downward with a stirruped foot stretched across the body of his dead horse. A leg of the charger extended slantingly upward, precisely as stiff as a stake. Around this motionless pair the shells still howled.

There was a quarrel in A Company. Collins was shaking his fist in the faces of some laughing comrades. "Dern yeh! I ain't afraid t' go. If yeh say much, I will go!"

"Of course, yeh will! You'll run through that there medder, won't yeh?"

Collins said, in a terrible voice: "You see now!"

At this ominous threat his comrades broke into renewed jeers.

Collins gave them a dark scowl, and went to find his captain. The latter was conversing with the colonel of the regiment.

"Captain," said Collins, saluting and standing at attention—in those days all trousers bagged at the knees—"Captain, I want t' get permission to go git some water from that there well over yonder!"

The colonel and the captain swung about simultaneously and stared across the meadow. The captain laughed. "You must be pretty thirsty, Collins?"

"Yes, sir, I am."

"Well—ah," said the captain. After a moment, he asked, "Can't you wait?"

"No, sir."

The colonel was watching Collins' face. "Look here, my lad," he said in a pious sort of voice—"Look here, my lad"—Collins was not a lad—"don't you think that's taking pretty big risks for a little drink of water?"

"I dunno," said Collins uncomfortably. Some of the resentment toward his companions, which perhaps had forced him into this affair, was beginning to fade. "I dunno w'ether 'tis."

The colonel and the captain contemplated him for a time.

"Well," said the captain finally.

"Well," said the colonel, "if you want to go, why, go."

Collins saluted. "Much obliged t' yeh."

As he moved away the colonel called after him. "Take some of the other boys' canteens with you, an' hurry back."

"Yes, sir, I will."

The colonel and the captain looked at each other then, for it had suddenly occurred that they could not for the life of them tell whether Collins wanted to go or whether he did not.

They turned to regard Collins, and as they perceived him surrounded by gesticulating comrades, the colonel said: "Well, by thunder! I guess he's going."

Collins appeared as a man dreaming. In the midst of the questions, the advice, the warnings, all the excited talk of his company mates, he maintained a curious silence.

They were busy preparing him for his ordeal. When they inspected him carefully, it was somewhat like the examination that grooms give a horse before a race; and they were amazed, staggered, by the whole affair. Their astonishment found vent in strange repetitions.

"Are yeh sure a-goin'?" they demanded again and again.

"Certainly I am," cried Collins at last, furiously.

He strode sullenly° away from them. He was swinging five or six canteens by their cords. It seemed that his cap would not remain firmly on his head, and often he reached and pulled it down over his brow.

There was a general movement in the compact column. The long animal-like thing moved slightly. Its four hundred eyes were turned upon the figure of Collins.

"Well, sir, if that ain't th' derndest thing! I never thought Fred Collins had the blood in him for that kind of business."

"What's he goin' to do, anyhow?"

"He's goin' to that well after water."

"We ain't dyin' of thirst, are we? That's foolishness."

"Well, somebody put him up to it, an' he's doin' it."

"Say, he must be a desperate cuss."

When Collins faced the meadow and walked away from the regiment, he was vaguely conscious that a chasm, the deep valley of all prides, was suddenly between him and his comrades. It was provisional,° but the provision was that he return as a victor. He had blindly been led by quaint emotions, and laid himself under an obligation to walk squarely up to the face of death.

But he was not sure he wished to make a retraction,° even if he could do so without shame. As a matter of truth, he was sure of very little. He was mainly surprised.

It seemed to him supernaturally strange that he had allowed his mind to maneuver his body into such a situation. He understood that it might be called dramatically great.

However, he had no full appreciation of anything, excepting that he was actually conscious of being dazed. He could feel his dulled mind groping after the form and color of this incident. He wondered why he did not feel some keen agony of fear cutting his sense like a knife. He wondered at this, because human expressions had said loudly for centuries that men should feel afraid of certain things, and that all men who did not feel this fear were phenomena—heroes.

He was, then, a hero. He suffered that disappointment which we would all have if we discovered that we were ourselves capable of those deeds which we most admire in history and legend. This, then, was a hero. After all, heroes were not much.

No, it could not be true. He was not a hero. Heroes had no shames in their lives, and, as for him, he remembered borrowing fifteen dollars from a friend and promising to pay it back the next day, and then avoiding that friend for ten months. When, at home, his mother had aroused him for the early labor of his life on the farm, it had often been his fashion to be irritable, childish, diabolical; and his mother had died since he had come to the war.

He saw that, in this matter of the well, the canteens, the shells, he was an intruder in the land of fine deeds.

He was now about thirty paces from his comrades. The regiment had just turned its many faces toward him.

From the forest of terrific noises there suddenly emerged a little uneven line of men. They fired fiercely and rapidly at distant foliage on which appeared little puffs of white smoke. The spatter of skirmish° firing was added to the thunder of the guns on the hill. The little line of men ran forward. A color sergeant fell flat with his flag as if he had slipped on ice. There was hoarse cheering from this distant field.

Collins suddenly felt that two demon fingers were pressed into his ears. He could see nothing but flying arrows, flaming red. He lurched from the shock of this explosion, but he made a mad rush for the house, which he viewed as a man submerged to the neck in a boiling surf might view the shore. In the air little pieces of shell howled, and the earthquake explosions drove him insane with the menace of their roar. As he ran, the canteens knocked together with a rhythmical tinkling.

As he neared the house, each detail of the scene became vivid to him. He was aware of some bricks of the vanished chimney lying on the sod. There was a door which hung by one hinge.

Rifle bullets called forth by the insistent skirmishers came from the far-off bank of foliage. They mingled with the shells and the pieces of shells until the air was torn in all directions by hootings, yells, howls. The sky was full of fiends who directed all their wild rage at his head.

When he came to the well, he flung himself face downward and peered into its darkness. There were furtive silver glintings some feet from the surface. He grabbed one of the canteens, and, unfastening its cap, swung it down by the cord. The water flowed slowly in with an indolent° gurgle.

And now, as he lay with his face turned away, he was suddenly smitten with terror. It came upon his heart like the grasp of claws. All the power faded from his muscles. For an instant he was no more than a dead man.

The canteen filled with a maddening slowness, in the manner of all bottles. Presently he recovered his strength and addressed a screaming oath to it. He leaned over until it seemed as if he intended to try to push water into it with his hands. His eyes as he gazed down into the well shone like two pieces of metal, and in their expression was a great appeal and a great curse. The stupid water derided him.

There was the blaring thunder of a shell. Crimson light shone through the swift-boiling smoke and made a pink reflection on part of the wall of the well. Collins jerked out his arm and canteen with the same motion that a man would use in withdrawing his head from a furnace.

He scrambled erect and glared and hesitated. On the ground near him lay the old well bucket, with a length of rusty chain. He lowered it swiftly into the well. The bucket struck the water and then, turning lazily over, sank. When, with hand reaching tremblingly over hand, he hauled it out, it knocked often against the walls of the well and spilled some of its contents.

In running with a filled bucket, a man can adopt but one kind of gait. So, through this terrible field over which screamed practical angels of death, Collins ran in the manner of a farmer chased out of a dairy by a bull.

His face went staring white with anticipation—anticipation of a blow that would whirl him around and down. He would fall as he had seen other men fall, the life knocked out of them so suddenly that their knees were no more quick to touch the ground than their heads. He saw the long blue line of the regiment, but his comrades were standing looking at him from the edge of an impossible star. He was aware of some deep wheel-ruts and hoof-prints in the sod beneath his feet.

The artillery officer who had fallen in this meadow had been making groans in the teeth of the tempest of sound. These futile cries, wrenched from him by his agony, were heard only by shells, bullets. When wild-eyed Collins came running, this officer raised himself. His face contorted and blanched° from pain, he was about to utter some great beseeching cry. But suddenly his face straightened, and he called: "Say, young man, give me a drink of water, will you?"

Collins had no room amid his emotions for surprise. He was mad from the threats of destruction.

"I can't!" he screamed, and in his reply was a full description of his quaking apprehension. His cap was gone and his hair was riotous. His clothes made it appear that he had been dragged over the ground by the heels. He ran on.

The officer's head sank down, and one elbow crooked. His foot in its brass-bound stirrup still stretched over the body of his horse, and the other leg was under the steed.

But Collins turned. He came dashing back. His face had now turned gray, and in his eyes was all terror. "Here it is! here it is!"

The officer was as a man gone in drink. His arm bent like a twig. His head drooped as if his neck were of willow. He was sinking to the ground, to lie face downward.

Collins grabbed him by the shoulder. "Here it is. Here's your drink. Turn over. Turn over, man!"

With Collins hauling at his shoulder, the officer twisted his body and fell with his face turned toward that region where lived the unspeakable noises of the swirling missiles. There was the faintest shadow of a smile on his lips as he looked at Collins. He gave a sigh, a little primitive breath like that from a child.

Collins tried to hold the bucket steadily, but his shaking hands caused the water to splash all over the face of the dying man. Then he jerked it away and ran on.

The regiment gave him a welcoming roar. The grimed faces were wrinkled in laughter.

His captain waved the bucket away. "Give it to the men!"

The two genial, skylarking young lieutenants were the first to gain possession of it. They played over it in their fashion.

When one tried to drink, the other teasingly knocked his elbow. "Don't, Billie! You'll make me spill it," said the one. The other laughed.

Suddenly there was an oath, the thud of wood on the ground, and a swift murmur of astonishment among the ranks. The two lieutenants glared at each other. The bucket lay on the ground, empty.

Do especially Questions 32, 41, 58, 61, 82, 89, 90, 94, 98, 103, and 146. Consult the Model Short Story in Volume One.

The Open Boat

STEPHEN CRANE

A Tale Intended to Be After the Fact: Being the Experience of Four Men from the Sunk Steamer *Commodore*.

None of them knew the color of the sky. Their eyes glanced level, and were fastened upon the waves that swept toward them. These waves were of the hue of slate, save for the tops, which were of foaming white, and all of the men knew the colors of the sea. The horizon narrowed and widened, and dipped and rose, and at all times its edge was jagged with waves that seemed thrust up in points like rocks. Many a man ought to have a bathtub larger than the boat which here rode upon the sea. These waves were most wrongfully and barbarously abrupt and tall, and each froth-top was a problem in small-boat navigation.

The cook squatted in the bottom and looked with both eyes at the six inches of gunwale° which separated him from the ocean. His sleeves were rolled over his fat forearms, and the two flaps of his unbuttoned vest dangled as he bent to bail out the boat. Often he said: "Gawd! That was a narrow clip." As he remarked it he invariably gazed eastward over the broken sea.

The oiler, steering with one of the two oars in the boat, sometimes raised himself suddenly to keep clear of water that swirled in over the stern. It was a thin little oar and it seemed often ready to snap.

The correspondent, pulling at the other oar, watched the waves and wondered why he was there.

The injured captain, lying in the bow, was at this time buried in that profound dejection and indifference which comes, temporarily at least, to even the bravest and most enduring when, willy-nilly, the firm fails, the army loses, the ship goes down. The mind of the master of a vessel is rooted deep in the timbers of her, though he command for a day or a decade, and this captain had on him the stern impression of a scene in the grays of dawn of seven turned faces, and later a stump of a top-mast with a white ball on it that slashed to and fro at the waves, went low and lower, and down. Thereafter there was something strange in his voice. Although steady, it was deep with mourning, and of a quality beyond oration or tears.

"Keep 'er a little more south, Billie," said he.

"A little more south, sir," said the oiler in the stern.

A seat in this boat was not unlike a seat upon a bucking broncho, and by the same token, a broncho is not much smaller. The craft pranced and reared, and plunged like an animal. As each wave came, and she rose for it, she seemed like a horse making at a fence outrageously high. The manner of her scramble over these walls of water is a mystic thing, and, moreover, at the top of them were ordinarily these problems in white water, the foam racing down from the summit of each wave, requiring a new leap, and a leap from the air. Then, after scornfully bumping a crest, she would slide, and race, and splash down a long incline, and arrive bobbing and nodding in front of the next menace.

A singular disadvantage of the sea lies in the fact that after successfully surmounting one wave you discover that there is another behind it just as important and just as nervously anxious to do something effective in the way of swamping boats. In a ten-foot dinghy° one can get an idea of the resources of the sea in the line of waves that is not probable to the average experience which is never at sea in a dinghy. As each slaty wall of water approached, it shut all else from the view of the men in the boat, and it was not difficult to imagine that this particular wave was the final outburst of the ocean, the last effort of the grim water. There was a terrible grace in the move of the waves, and they came in silence, save for the snarling of the crests.

In the wan light, the faces of the men must have been gray. Their eyes must have glinted in strange ways as they gazed steadily astern. Viewed from a balcony, the whole thing would doubtless have been weirdly picturesque. But the men in the boat had no time to see it, and if they had had leisure there were other things to occupy their minds. The sun swung steadily up the sky, and they knew it was broad day because the color of the sea changed from slate to emerald-green, streaked with amber lights, and the foam was like tumbling snow. The process of the breaking day was unknown to them. They were aware only of this effect upon the color of the waves that rolled toward them.

In disjointed sentences the cook and the correspondent argued as to the difference between a life-saving station and a house of refuge. The cook had said: "There's a house of refuge just north of the Mosquito Inlet Light,[1] and as soon as they see us, they'll come off in their boat and pick us up."

"As soon as who see us?" said the correspondent.

"The crew," said the cook.

"Houses of refuge don't have crews," said the correspondent. "As I understand them, they are only places where clothes and grub are stored for the benefit of ship-wrecked people. They don't carry crews."

"Oh, yes, they do," said the cook.

"No, they don't," said the correspondent.

"Well, we're not there yet, anyhow," said the oiler, in the stern.

"Well," said the cook, "perhaps it's not a house of refuge that I'm thinking of as being near Mosquito Inlet Light. Perhaps it's a life-saving station."

"We're not there yet," said the oiler, in the stern.

2

As the boat bounced from the top of each wave, the wind tore through the hair of the hatless men, and as the craft plopped her stern down again the spray splashed past them. The crest of each of these waves was a hill, from

[1]All the places mentioned here and later are on the east coast of Florida.

the top of which the men surveyed, for a moment, a broad tumultuous expanse, shining and wind-riven. It was probably splendid. It was probably glorious, this play of the free sea, wild with lights of emerald and white and amber.

"Bully good thing it's an on-shore wind," said the cook. "If not, where would we be? Wouldn't have a show."

"That's right," said the correspondent.

The busy oiler nodded his assent.

Then the captain, in the bow, chuckled in a way that expressed humor, contempt, tragedy, all in one. "Do you think we've got much of a show now, boys?" said he.

Whereupon the three were silent, save for a trifle of hemming and hawing. To express any particular optimism at this time they felt to be childish and stupid, but they all doubtless possessed this sense of the situation in their mind. A young man thinks doggedly at such times. On the other hand, the ethics of their condition was decidedly against any open suggestion of hopelessness. So they were silent.

"Oh, well," said the captain, soothing his children, "we'll get ashore all right."

But there was that in his tone which made them think, so the oiler quoth: "Yes! If this wind holds!"

The cook was bailing: "Yes! If we don't catch hell in the surf."

Canton-flannel gulls flew near and far. Sometimes they sat down on the sea, near patches of brown seaweed that rolled over the waves with a movement like carpets on a line in a gale. The birds sat comfortably in groups, and they were envied by some in the dinghy, for the wrath of the sea was no more to them than it was to a covey° of prairie chickens a thousand miles inland. Often they came very close and stared at the men with black bead-like eyes. At these times they were uncanny and sinister in their unblinking scrutiny, and the men hooted angrily at them, telling them to be gone. One came, and evidently decided to light on the top of the captain's head. The bird flew parallel to the boat and did not circle, but made short sidelong jumps in the air in chicken fashion. His black eyes were wistfully fixed upon the captain's head. "Ugly brute," said the oiler to the bird. "You look as if you were made with a jack-knife." The cook and the correspondent swore darkly at the creature. The captain naturally wished to knock it away with the end of the heavy painter;[2] but he did not dare do it, because anything resembling an emphatic gesture would have capsized this freighted boat, and so with his open hand, the captain gently and carefully waved the gull away. After it had been discouraged from the pursuit the captain breathed easier on account of his hair, and others breathed easier because the bird struck their minds at this time as being somehow gruesome and ominous.°

In the meantime the oiler and the correspondent rowed. And also they rowed.

They sat together in the same seat, and each rowed an oar. Then the oiler took both oars; then the correspondent took both oars; then the oiler; then the correspondent. They rowed and they rowed. The very ticklish part of the business was when the time came for the reclining one in the stern to take his turn at the oars. By the very last star of truth, it is easier to steal eggs from under a hen than it was to change seats in the dinghy. First the man in the stern slid his hand along the thwart[3] and moved with care, as if he were of Sèvres.[4] Then the man in the rowing seat slid his hand along the other thwart. It was all done with the most extraordinary care. As the two sidled° past each other, the whole party kept watchful eyes on the coming wave, and the captain cried: "Look out now! Steady there!"

The brown mats of seaweed that appeared from time to time were like islands, bits of earth. They were traveling, apparently, neither one way nor the other. They were, to all intents, stationary. They informed the men in the boat that it was making progress slowly toward the land.

[2]Rope.
[3]A seat across a boat.
[4]Breakable porcelain.

The captain, rearing cautiously in the bow, after the dinghy soared on a great swell, said that he had seen the lighthouse at Mosquito Inlet. Presently the cook remarked that he had seen it. The correspondent was at the oars then, and for some reason he too wished to look at the lighthouse, but his back was toward the far shore and the waves were important, and for some time he could not seize an opportunity to turn his head. But at last there came a wave more gentle than the others, and when at the crest of it he swiftly scoured the western horizon.

"See it?" said the captain.

"No," said the correspondent slowly, "I didn't see anything."

"Look again," said the captain. He pointed. "It's exactly in that direction."

At the top of another wave, the correspondent did as he was bid, and this time his eyes chanced on a small thing on the edge of the swaying horizon. It was precisely like the point of a pin. It took an anxious eye to find a lighthouse so tiny.

"Think we'll make it, captain?"

"If this wind holds and the boat don't swamp, we can't do much else," said the captain.

The little boat, lifted by each towering sea, and splashed viciously by the crests, made progress that in the absence of seaweed was not apparent to those in her. She seemed just a wee thing wallowing, miraculously top-up, at the mercy of five oceans. Occasionally a great spread of water, like white flames, swarmed into her.

"Bail her, cook," said the captain serenely.

"All right, captain," said the cheerful cook.

3

It would be difficult to describe the subtle brotherhood of men that was here established on the seas. No one said that it was so. No one mentioned it. But it dwelt in the boat, and each man felt it warm him. They were a captain, an oiler, a cook, and a correspondent, and they were friends, friends in a more curiously iron-bound degree than may be common. The hurt captain, lying against the water-jar in the bow, spoke always in a low voice and calmly, but he could never command a more ready and swiftly obedient crew than the motley° three of the dinghy. It was more than a mere recognition of what was best for the common safety. There was surely in it a quality that was personal and heartfelt. And after this devotion to the commander of the boat there was this comradeship that the correspondent, for instance, who had been taught to be cynical of men, knew even at the time was the best experience of his life. But no one said that it was so. No one mentioned it.

"I wish we had a sail," remarked the captain. "We might try my overcoat on the end of an oar and give you two boys a chance to rest." So the cook and the correspondent held the mast and spread wide the overcoat. The oiler steered, and the little boat made good way with her new rig.° Sometimes the oiler had to scull sharply to keep a sea from breaking into the boat, but otherwise sailing was a success.

Meanwhile the lighthouse had been growing slowly larger. It had now almost assumed color, and appeared like a little gray shadow on the sky. The man at the oars could not be prevented from turning his head rather often to try for a glimpse of this little gray shadow.

At last, from the top of each wave the men in the tossing boat could see land. Even as the lighthouse was an upright shadow on the sky, this land seemed but a long black shadow on the sea. It certainly was thinner than paper. "We must be about opposite New Smyrna," said the cook, who had coasted this shore often in schooners. "Captain, by the way, I believe they abandoned that life-saving station there about a year ago."

"Did they?" said the captain.

The wind slowly died away. The cook and the correspondent were not now obliged to slave in order to hold high the oar. But the waves continued their old impetuous swooping at the dinghy, and the little craft, no longer under

way, struggled woundily⁵ over them. The oiler or the
correspondent took the oars again.

Shipwrecks are *à propos°* of nothing. If men could only
train for them and have them occur when the men had
reached pink condition, there would be less drowning
at sea. Of the four in the dinghy none had slept any time
worth mentioning for two days and two nights previous
to embarking in the dinghy, and in the excitement of
clambering about the deck of a foundering° ship they had
also forgotten to eat heartily.

For these reasons, and for others, neither the oiler nor
the correspondent was fond of rowing at this time. The
correspondent wondered ingenuously how in the name
of all that was sane could there be people who thought it
amusing to row a boat. It was not an amusement; it was a
diabolical punishment, and even a genius of mental
aberrations° could never conclude that it was anything
but a horror to the muscles and a crime against the back.
He mentioned to the boat in general how the amusement
of rowing struck him, and the weary-faced oiler smiled in
full sympathy. Previously to the foundering, by the way,
the oiler had worked double-watch in the engine-room of
the ship.

"Take her easy, now, boys," said the captain. "Don't
spend yourselves. If we have to run a surf you'll need all
your strength, because we'll sure have to swim for it.
Take your time."

Slowly the land arose from the sea. From a black line it
became a line of black and a line of white, trees and sand.
Finally, the captain said that he could make out a house
on the shore. "That's the house of refuge, sure," said the
cook. "They'll see us before long, and come out after us."

The distant lighthouse reared high. "The keeper ought
to be able to make us out now, if he's looking through a
glass," said the captain. "He'll notify the life-saving
people."

⁵Twistedly.

"None of those other boats could have got ashore to give word of the wreck," said the oiler, in a low voice. "Else the lifeboat would be out hunting us."

Slowly and beautifully the land loomed out of the sea. The wind came again. It had veered from the northeast to the southeast. Finally, a new sound struck the ears of the men in the boat. It was the low thunder of the surf on the shore. "We'll never be able to make the lighthouse now," said the captain. "Swing her head a little more north, Billie," said he.

"A little more north, sir," said the oiler.

Whereupon the little boat turned her nose once more down the wind, and all but the oarsman watched the shore grow. Under the influence of this expansion doubt and direful° apprehension was leaving the minds of the men. The management of the boat was still most absorbing, but it could not prevent a quiet cheerfulness. In an hour, perhaps, they would be ashore.

Their backbones had become thoroughly used to balancing in the boat, and they now rode this wild colt of a dinghy like circus men. The correspondent thought that he had been drenched to the skin, but happening to feel in the top pocket of his coat, he found therein eight cigars. Four of them were soaked with seawater; four were perfectly scatheless. After a search, somebody produced three dry matches, and thereupon the four waifs° rode impudently in their little boat, and with an assurance of an impending rescue shining in their eyes, puffed at the big cigars and judged well and ill of all men. Everybody took a drink of water.

4

"Cook," remarked the captain, "there don't seem to be any signs of life about your house of refuge."

"No," replied the cook. "Funny they don't see us!"

A broad stretch of lowly coast lay before the eyes of the men. It was of low dunes topped with dark vegetation. The roar of the surf was plain, and sometimes they could see the white lip of a wave as it spun up the beach. A tiny house was blocked out black upon the sky. Southward, the slim lighthouse lifted its little gray length.

Tide, wind, and waves were swinging the dinghy northward. "Funny they don't see us," said the men.

The surf's roar was here dulled, but its tone was, nevertheless, thunderous and mighty. As the boat swam over the great rollers, the men sat listening to this roar. "We'll swamp sure," said everybody.

It is fair to say here that there was not a life-saving station within twenty miles in either direction, but the men did not know this fact, and in consequence they made dark and opprobrious° remarks concerning the eyesight of the nation's life-savers. Four scowling men sat in the dinghy and surpassed records in the invention of epithets.°

"Funny they don't see us."

The light-heartedness of a former time had completely faded. To their sharpened minds it was easy to conjure pictures of all kinds of incompetency and blindness and, indeed, cowardice. There was the shore of the populous land, and it was bitter and bitter to them that from it came no sign.

"Well," said the captain, ultimately, "I suppose we'll have to make a try for ourselves. If we stay out here too long, we'll none of us have strength left to swim after the boat swamps."

And so the oiler, who was at the oars, turned the boat straight for the shore. There was a sudden tightening of muscles. There was some thinking.

"If we don't all get ashore—" said the captain. "If we don't all get ashore, I suppose you fellows know where to send news of my finish?"

They then briefly exchanged some addresses and admonitions.° As for the reflections of the men, there was a great deal of rage in them. Perchance they might be formulated thus: "If I am going to be drowned—if I am going to be drowned—if I am going to be drowned, why, in the name of the seven mad gods who rule the sea, was I allowed to come thus far and contemplate sand and trees? Was I brought here merely to have my nose dragged away as

I was about to nibble the sacred cheese of life? It is preposterous. If this old ninny-woman, Fate, cannot do better than this, she should be deprived of the management of men's fortunes. She is an old hen who knows not her intention. If she has decided to drown me, why did she not do it in the beginning and save me all this trouble? The whole affair is absurd.... But no, she cannot mean to drown me. She dare not drown me. She cannot drown me. Not after all this work." Afterward the man might have had an impulse to shake his fist at the clouds: "Just you drown me, now, and then hear what I call you!"

The billows that came at this time were more formidable. They seemed always just about to break and roll over the little boat in a turmoil of foam. There was a preparatory and long growl in the speech of them. No mind unused to the sea would have concluded that the dinghy could ascend these sheer heights in time. The shore was still afar. The oiler was a wily surfman. "Boys," he said swiftly, "she won't live three minutes more, and we're too far out to swim. Shall I take her to sea again, captain?"

"Yes! Go ahead!" said the captain.

This oiler, by a series of quick miracles, and fast and steady oarsmanship, turned the boat in the middle of the surf and took her safely to sea again.

There was a considerable silence as the boat bumped over the furrowed sea to deeper water. Then somebody in the gloom spoke. "Well, anyhow, they must have seen us from the shore by now."

The gulls went in slanting flight up the wind toward the gray desolate east. A squall, marked by dingy clouds, and clouds brick-red, like smoke from a burning building, appeared from the southeast.

"What do you think of those life-saving people? Ain't they peaches?"

"Funny they haven't seen us."

"Maybe they think we're out here for sport! Maybe they think we're fishin'. Maybe they think we're damned fools."

It was a long afternoon. A changed tide tried to force

them southward, but the wind and wave said northward. Far ahead, where coastline, sea, and sky formed their mighty angle, there were little dots which seemed to indicate a city on the shore.

"St. Augustine?"

The captain shook his head: "Too near Mosquito Inlet."

And the oiler rowed, and then the correspondent rowed. Then the oiler rowed. It was a weary business. The human back can become the seat of more aches and pains than are registered in books for the composite anatomy of a regiment. It is a limited area, but it can become the theatre of innumerable muscular conflicts, tangles, wrenches, knots, and other comforts.

"Did you ever like to row, Billie?" asked the correspondent.

"No," said the oiler. "Hang it!"

When one exchanged the rowing-seat for a place in the bottom of the boat, he suffered a bodily depression that caused him to be careless of everything save an obligation to wiggle one finger. There was cold sea-water swashing to and fro in the boat, and he lay in it. His head, pillowed on a thwart, was within an inch of the swirl of a wave crest, and sometimes a particularly obstreperous° sea came inboard and drenched him once more. But these matters did not annoy him. It is almost certain that if the boat had capsized he would have tumbled comfortably out upon the ocean as if he felt sure that it was a great soft mattress.

"Look! There's a man on the shore!"

"Where?"

"There! See 'im? See 'im?"

"Yes, sure! He's walking along."

"Now he's stopped. Look! He's facing us!"

"He's waving at us!"

"So he is! By thunder!"

"Ah, now we're all right! Now we're all right! There'll be a boat out here for us in half-an-hour."

"He's going on. He's running. He's going up to that house there."

The remote beach seemed lower than the sea, and it

required a searching glance to discern the little black figure. The captain saw a floating stick and they rowed to it. A bath-towel was by some weird chance in the boat, and, tying this on the stick, the captain waved it. The oarsman did not dare turn his head, so he was obliged to ask questions.

"What's he doing now?"

"He's standing still again. He's looking, I think.... There he goes again. Toward the house.... Now he's stopped again."

"Is he waving at us?"

"No, not now! He was, though."

"Look! There comes another man!"

"He's running."

"Look at him go, would you."

"Why, he's on a bicycle. Now he's met the other man. They're both waving at us. Look!"

"There comes something up the beach."

"What the devil is that thing?"

"Why it looks like a boat."

"Why, certainly it's a boat."

"No, it's on wheels."

"Yes, so it is. Well, that must be the life-boat. They drag them along shore on a wagon."

"That's the life-boat, sure."

"No, by—, it's—it's an omnibus."°

"I tell you it's a life-boat."

"It is not! It's an omnibus. I can see it plain. See? One of these big hotel omnibuses."

"By thunder, you're right. It's an omnibus, sure as fate. What do you suppose they are doing with an omnibus? Maybe they are going around collecting the life-crew, hey?"

"That's it, likely. Look! There's a fellow waving a little black flag. He's standing on the steps of the omnibus. There come those other two fellows. Now they're all talking together. Look at the fellow with the flag. Maybe he ain't waving it."

"That ain't a flag, is it? That's his coat. Why, certainly, that's his coat."

"So it is. It's his coat. He's taken it off and is waving it around his head. But would you look at him swing it."

"Oh, say, there isn't any life-saving station there. That's just a winter resort hotel omnibus that has brought over some of the boarders to see us drown."

"What's that idiot with the coat mean? What's he signaling, anyhow?"

"It looks as if he were trying to tell us to go north. There must be a life-saving station up there."

"No! He thinks we're fishing. Just giving us a merry hand. See? Ah, there, Willie!"

"Well, I wish I could make something out of those signals. What do you suppose he means?"

"He don't mean anything. He's just playing."

"Well, if he'd just signal us to try the surf again, or to go to sea and wait, or go north, or go south, or go to hell— there would be some reason in it. But look at him. He just stands there and keeps his coat revolving like a wheel. The fool!"

"There come more people."

"Now there's quite a mob. Look! Isn't that a boat?"

"Where? Oh, I see where you mean. No, that's no boat."

"That fellow is still waving his coat."

"He must think we like to see him do that. Why don't he quit it? It don't mean anything."

"I don't know. I think he is trying to make us go north. It must be that there's a life-saving station there somewhere."

"Say, he ain't tired yet. Look at 'im wave."

"Wonder how long he can keep that up. He's been revolving his coat ever since he caught sight of us. He's an idiot. Why aren't they getting men to bring a boat out? A fishing boat—one of those big yawls°—could come out here all right. Why don't he do something?"

"Oh, it's all right, now."

"They'll have a boat out here for us in less than no time, now that they've seen us."

A faint yellow tone came into the sky over the low land. The shadows on the sea slowly deepened. The wind bore coldness with it, and the men began to shiver.

"Holy smoke!" said one, allowing his voice to express his impious mood, "if we keep on monkeying out here! If we've got to flounder out here all night!"

"Oh, we'll never have to stay here all night! Don't you worry. They've seen us now, and it won't be long before they'll come chasing out after us."

The shore grew dusky. The man waving a coat blended gradually into this gloom, and it swallowed in the same manner the omnibus and the group of people. The spray, when it dashed uproariously over the side, made the voyagers shrink and swear like men who were being branded.

"I'd like to catch the chump who waved the coat. I feel like soaking him one, just for luck."

"Why? What did he do?"

"Oh, nothing, but then he seemed so damned cheerful."

In the meantime the oiler rowed, and then the correspondent rowed, and then the oiler rowed. Gray-faced and bowed forward, they mechanically, turn by turn, plied the leaden oars. The form of the lighthouse had vanished from the southern horizon, but finally a pale star appeared, just lifting from the sea. The streaked saffron° in the west passed before the all-merging darkness, and the sea to the east was black. The land had vanished, and was expressed only by the low and drear thunder of the surf.

"If I am going to be drowned — if I am going to be drowned — if I am going to be drowned, why, in the name of the seven mad gods who rule the sea, was I allowed to come thus far and contemplate sand and trees? Was I brought here merely to have my nose dragged away as I was about to nibble the sacred cheese of life?"

The patient captain, drooped over the water-jar, was sometimes obliged to speak to the oarsman.

"Keep her head up! Keep her head up!"

"Keep her head up, sir." The voices were weary and low.

This was surely a quiet evening. All save the oarsman lay heavily and listlessly in the boat's bottom. As for him, his eyes were just capable of noting the tall black waves that swept forward in a most sinister silence, save for an occasional subdued growl of a crest.

The cook's head was on a thwart, and he looked without interest at the water under his nose. He was deep in other scenes. Finally he spoke. "Billie," he murmured, dreamfully, "what kind of pie do you like best?"

5

"Pie," said the oiler and the correspondent, agitatedly. "Don't talk about those things, blast you!"

"Well," said the cook, "I was just thinking about ham sandwiches, and—"

A night on the sea in an open boat is a long night. As darkness settled finally, the shine of the light, lifting from the sea in the south, changed to full gold. On the northern horizon a new light appeared, a small bluish gleam on the edge of the waters. These two lights were the furniture of the world. Otherwise there was nothing but waves.

Two men huddled in the stern, and distances were so magnificent in the dinghy that the rower was enabled to keep his feet partly warmed by thrusting them under his companions. Their legs indeed extended far under the rowing-seat until they touched the feet of the captain forward. Sometimes, despite the efforts of the tired oarsman, a wave came piling into the boat, an icy wave of the night, and the chilling water soaked them anew. They would twist their bodies for a moment and groan, and sleep the dead sleep once more, while the water in the boat gurgled about them as the craft rocked.

The plan of the oiler and the correspondent was for one to row until he lost the ability, and then arouse the other from his sea-water couch in the bottom of the boat.

The oiler plied° the oars until his head drooped forward, and the overpowering sleep blinded him. And he rowed yet afterward. Then he touched a man in the bottom of the boat, and called his name. "Will you spell me for a little while?" he said, meekly.

"Sure, Billie," said the correspondent, awakening and

dragging himself to a sitting position. They exchanged places carefully, and the oiler, cuddling down in the sea-water at the cook's side, seemed to go to sleep instantly.

The particular violence of the sea had ceased. The waves came without snarling. The obligation of the man at the oars was to keep the boat headed so that the tilt of the rollers would not capsize her, and to preserve her from filling when the crests rushed past. The black waves were silent and hard to be seen in the darkness. Often one was almost upon the boat before the oarsman was aware.

In a low voice the correspondent addressed the captain. He was not sure that the captain was awake, although this iron man seemed to be always awake. "Captain, shall I keep her making for that light north, sir?"

The same steady voice answered him. "Yes. Keep it about two points off the port bow."

The cook had tied a life-belt around himself in order to get even the warmth which this clumsy cork contrivance could donate, and he seemed almost stove-like when a rower, whose teeth invariably chattered wildly as soon as he ceased his labor, dropped down to sleep.

The correspondent, as he rowed, looked down at the two men sleeping underfoot. The cook's arm was around the oiler's shoulders, and, with their fragmentary clothing and haggard faces, they were the babes of the sea, a grotesque rendering of the old babes in the wood.

Later he must have grown stupid at his work, for suddenly there was a growling of water, and a crest came with a roar and a swash into the boat, and it was a wonder that it did not set the cook afloat in his life-belt. The cook continued to sleep, but the oiler sat up, blinking his eyes and shaking with the new cold.

"Oh, I'm awful sorry, Billie," said the correspondent contritely.

"That's all right, old boy," said the oiler, and lay down again and was asleep.

Presently it seemed that even the captain dozed, and the correspondent thought that he was the one man afloat on all the oceans. The wind had a voice as it came over the waves, and it was sadder than the end.

There was a long, loud swishing astern of the boat, and a gleaming trail of phosphorescence, like blue flame, was furrowed on the black waters. It might have been made by a monstrous knife.

Then there came a stillness, while the correspondent breathed with the open mouth and looked at the sea.

Suddenly there was another swish and another long flash of bluish light, and this time it was alongside the boat, and might almost have been reached with an oar. The correspondent saw an enormous fin speed like a shadow through the water, hurling the crystalline spray and leaving the long glowing trail.

The correspondent looked over his shoulder at the captain. His face was hidden, and he seemed to be asleep. He looked at the babes of the sea. They certainly were asleep. So, being bereft of sympathy, he leaned a little way to one side and swore softly into the sea.

But the thing did not then leave the vicinity of the boat. Ahead or astern, on one side or the other, at intervals long or short, fled the long sparkling streak, and there was to be heard the whirroo of the dark fin. The speed and power of the thing was greatly to be admired. It cut the water like a gigantic and keen projectile.

The presence of this biding thing did not affect the man with the same horror that it would if he had been a picnicker. He simply looked at the sea and swore in an undertone.

Nevertheless, it is true that he did not wish to be alone. He wished one of his companions to awaken by chance and keep him company with it. But the captain hung motionless over the water-jar, and the oiler and the cook in the bottom of the boat were plunged in slumber.

6

"If I am going to be drowned — if I am going to be drowned — if I am going to be drowned, why, in the name of the seven mad gods who rule the sea, was I allowed to come thus far and contemplate sand and trees?"

During this dismal night, it may be remarked that a man would conclude that it was really the intention of the seven mad gods to drown him, despite the abominable injustice of it. For it was certainly an abominable injustice to drown a man who had worked so hard, so hard. The man felt it would be a crime most unnatural. Other people had drowned at sea since galleys swarmed with painted sails, but still—

When it occurs to a man that nature does not regard him as important, and that she feels she would not maim the universe by disposing of him, he at first wishes to throw bricks at the temple, and he hates deeply the fact that there are no brick and no temples. Any visible expression of nature would surely be pelleted with his jeers.

Then, if there be no tangible thing to hoot he feels, perhaps, the desire to confront a personification and indulge in pleas, bowed to one knee, and with hands supplicant, saying: "Yes, but I love myself."

A high cold star on a winter's night is the word he feels that she says to him. Thereafter he knows the pathos of his situation.

The men in the dinghy had not discussed these matters, but each had, no doubt, reflected upon them in silence and according to his mind. There was seldom any expression upon their faces save the general one of complete weariness. Speech was devoted to the business of the boat.

To chime the notes of his emotion, a verse mysteriously entered the correspondent's head. He had even forgotten that he had forgotten this verse, but it suddenly was in his mind.

A soldier of the Legion lay dying in Algiers,
There was a lack of woman's nursing, there was dearth of woman's tears;
But a comrade stood beside him, and he took that comrade's hand,
And he said: "I shall never see my own, my native land."

In his childhood, the correspondent had been made acquainted with the fact that a soldier of the Legion lay dying in Algiers, but he had never regarded the fact as important. Myriads of his school-fellows had informed him of the soldier's plight, but the dinning° had naturally ended by making him perfectly indifferent. He had never considered it his affair that a soldier of the Legion lay dying in Algiers, nor had it appeared to him as a matter for sorrow. It was less to him than the breaking of a pencil's point.

Now, however, it quaintly came to him as a human, living thing. It was no longer merely a picture of a few throes in the breast of a poet, meanwhile drinking tea and warming his feet at the grate; it was an actuality — stern, mournful, and fine.

The correspondent plainly saw the soldier. He lay on the sand with his feet out straight and still. While his pale left hand was upon his chest in an attempt to thwart the going of his life, the blood came between his fingers. In the far Algerian distance, a city of low square forms was set against a sky that was faint with the last sunset hues. The correspondent, plying the oars and dreaming of the slow and slower movements of the lips of the soldier, was moved by a profound and perfectly impersonal comprehension. He was sorry for the soldier of the Legion who lay dying in Algiers.

The thing which had followed the boat and waited had evidently grown bored at the delay. There was no longer to be heard the slash of the cut-water, and there was no longer the flame of the long trail. The light in the north still glimmered, but it was apparently no nearer to the boat. Sometimes the boom of the surf rang in the correspondent's ears, and he turned the craft seaward then and rowed harder. Southward, someone had evidently built a watch-fire on the beach. It was too low and too far to be seen, but it made a shimmering, roseate° reflection upon the bluff back of it, and this could be discerned from the boat. The wind came stronger, and sometimes a wave suddenly raged out like a mountain-cat, and there was to be seen the sheen and sparkle of a broken crest.

The captain, in the bow, moved on his water-jar and sat

erect. "Pretty long night," he observed to the correspondent. He looked at the shore. "Those life-saving people take their time."

"Did you see that shark playing around?"

"Yes, I saw him. He was a big fellow, all right."

"Wish I had known you were awake."

Later the correspondent spoke into the bottom of the boat.

"Billie!" There was a slow and gradual disentanglement. "Billie, will you spell me?"

"Sure," said the oiler.

As soon as the correspondent touched the cold comfortable sea-water in the bottom of the boat, and had huddled close to the cook's life-belt. he was deep in sleep, despite the fact that his teeth played all the popular airs. This sleep was so good to him that it was but a moment before he heard a voice call his name in a tone that demonstrated the last stages of exhaustion. "Will you spell me?"

"Sure, Billie."

The light in the north had mysteriously vanished, but the correspondent took his course from the wide-awake captain.

Later in the night they took the boat farther out to sea, and the captain directed the cook to take one oar at the stern and keep the boat facing the seas. He was to call out if he should hear the thunder of the surf. This plan enabled the oiler and the correspondent to get respite° together. "We'll give those boys a chance to get into shape again," said the captain. They curled down and, after a few preliminary chatterings and trembles, slept once more the dead sleep. Neither knew they had bequeathed to the cook the company of another shark, or perhaps the same shark.

As the boat caroused° on the waves, spray occasionally bumped over the side and gave them a fresh soaking, but this had no power to break their repose. The ominous slash of the wind and the water affected them as it would have affected mummies.

"Boys," said the cook, with the notes of every reluctance in his voice, "she's drifted in pretty close, I guess one of you had better take her to sea again." The correspondent, aroused, heard the crash of the toppled crests.

As he was rowing, the captain gave him some whiskey-and-water, and this steadied the chills out of him. "If I ever get ashore and anybody shows me even a photo-graph of an oar—"

At last there was a short conversation.

"Billie .... Billie, will you spell me?"

"Sure," said the oiler.

7

When the correspondent again opened his eyes, the sea and the sky were each of the gray hue of the dawning. Later, carmine and gold was painted upon the waters. The morning appeared finally, in its splendor, with a sky of pure blue, and the sunlight flamed on the tips of the waves.

On the distant dunes were set many little black cottages, and a tall white windmill reared above them. No man, nor dog, nor bicycle appeared on the beach. The cottages might have formed a deserted village.

The voyagers scanned the shore. A conference was held in the boat. "Well," said the captain, "if no help is coming we might better try a run through the surf right away. If we stay out here much longer we will be too weak to do anything for ourselves at all." The others silently acquiesced in this reasoning. The boat was headed for the beach. The correspondent wondered if none ever ascended the tall wind-tower, and if then they never looked seaward. This tower was a giant, standing with its back to the plight of the ants. It represented in a degree, to the correspondent, the serenity of nature amid the strug-gles of the individual—nature in the wind, and nature in the vision of men. She did not seem cruel to him then, nor beneficent, nor treacherous, nor wise. But she was indifferent, flatly indifferent. It is, perhaps, plausible that a man in this situation, impressed with the unconcern of the universe, should see the innumerable flaws of his life, and have them taste wickedly in his mind and wish for another chance. A distinction between right and wrong seems absurdly clear to him, then, in this new ignorance of the grave-edge, and he understands that if he were given another opportunity he would mend his conduct and his words, and be better and brighter during an introduction or at a tea.

"Now, boys," said the captain, "she is going to swamp, sure. All we can do is to work her in as far as possible, and then when she swamps, pile out and scramble for the beach. Keep cool now, and don't jump until she swamps sure."

The oiler took the oars. Over his shoulders he scanned the surf. "Captain," he said, "I think I'd better bring her about, and keep her head-on to the seas and back her in."

"All right, Billie," said the captain. "Back her in." The oiler swung the boat then and, seated in the stern, the cook and the correspondent were obliged to look over their shoulders to contemplate the lonely and indifferent shore.

The monstrous in-shore rollers heaved the boat high until the men were again enabled to see the white sheets of water scudding up the slanted beach. "We won't get in very close," said the captain. Each time a man could wrest his attention from the rollers, he turned his glance toward the shore, and in the expression of the eyes during this contemplation there was a singular quality. The correspondent, observing the others, knew that they were not afraid, but the full meaning of their glances was shrouded.

As for himself, he was too tired to grapple fundamentally with the fact. He tried to coerce his mind into thinking of it, but the mind was dominated at this time by the muscles, and the muscles said they did not care. It merely occurred to him that if he should drown it would be a shame.

There were no hurried words, no pallor, no plain agitation. The men simply looked at the shore. "Now, remember to get well clear of the boat when you jump," said the captain.

Seaward the crest of a roller suddenly fell with a thunderous crash, and the long white comber came roaring down upon the boat.

"Steady now," said the captain. The men were silent. They turned their eyes from the shore to the comber and waited. The boat slid up the incline, leaped at the furious top, bounced over it, and swung down the long back of the wave. Some water had been shipped and the cook bailed it out.

But the next crest crashed also. The tumbling, boiling flood of white water caught the boat and whirled it almost perpendicular. Water swarmed in from all sides. The correspondent had his hands on the gunwale at this time, and when the water entered at that place he swiftly withdrew his fingers, as if he objected to wetting them.

The little boat, drunken with this weight of water, reeled and snuggled deeper into the sea.

"Bail her out, cook! Bail her out," said the captain.

"All right, captain," said the cook.

"Now, boys, the next one will do for us, sure," said the oiler. "Mind to jump clear of the boat."

The third wave moved forward, huge, furious, implacable.° It fairly swallowed the dinghy, and almost simultaneously the men tumbled into the sea. A piece of lifebelt had lain in the bottom of the boat, and as the correspondent went overboard he held this to his chest with his left hand.

The January water was icy, and he reflected immediately that it was colder than he had expected to find it off the coast of Florida. This appeared to his dazed mind as a fact important enough to be noted at the time. The coldness of the water was sad; it was tragic. This fact was somehow so mixed and confused with his opinion of his own situation that it seemed almost a proper reason for tears. The water was cold.

When he came to the surface he was conscious of little but the noisy water. Afterward he saw his companions in the sea. The oiler was ahead in the race. He was swimming strongly and rapidly. Off to the correspondent's left, the cook's great white and corked back bulged out of the water, and in the rear the captain was hanging with his one good hand to the keel of the overturned dinghy.

There is a certain immovable quality to a shore, and the correspondent wondered at it amid the confusion of the sea.

It seemed also very attractive, but the correspondent knew that it was a long journey, and he paddled leisurely. The piece of life-preserver lay under him, and sometimes he whirled down the incline of a wave as if he were on a hand-sled.

But finally he arrived at a place in the sea where travel was beset with difficulty. He did not pause swimming to inquire what manner of current had caught him, but there his progress ceased. The shore was set before him like a bit of scenery on a stage, and he looked at it and understood with his eyes each detail of it.

As the cook passed, much farther to the left, the captain was calling to him. "Turn over on your back, cook! Turn over on your back and use the oar."

"All right, sir," The cook turned on his back, and paddling with an oar, went ahead as if he were a canoe.

Presently the boat passed to the left of the correspondent with the captain clinging with one hand to the keel. He would have appeared like a man raising himself to look over a board fence, if it were not for the extraordinary gymnastics of the boat. The correspondent marvelled that the captain could still hold to it.

They passed on, nearer to the shore—the oiler, the cook, the captain—and following them went the water-jar, bouncing gaily over the seas.

The correspondent remained in the grip of this strange new enemy—a current. The shore, with its white slope of sand and its green bluff, topped with little silent cottages, was spread like a picture before him. It was very near to him then, but he was impressed as one who in a gallery looks at a scene from Brittany or Algiers.

He thought: "I am going to drown? Can it be possible? Can it be possible? Can it be possible?" Perhaps an individual must consider his own death to be the final phenomenon of nature.

But later a wave perhaps whirled him out of this small, deadly current, for he found suddenly that he could again make progress toward the shore. Later still, he was aware that the captain, clinging with one hand to the keel of the dinghy, had his face turned away from the shore and toward him, and was calling his name. "Come to the boat! Come to the boat!"

In his struggle to reach the captain and the boat, he reflected that when one gets properly wearied, drowning must really be a comfortable arrangement, a cessation of hostilities accompanied by a large degree of relief, and he was glad of it, for the main thing in his mind for some moments had been horror of the temporary agony. He did not wish to be hurt.

Presently he saw a man running along the shore. He was undressing with most remarkable speed. Coat, trousers, shirt, everything flew magically off him.

"Come to the boat," called the captain.

"All right, captain." As the correspondent paddled, he saw the captain let himself down to bottom and leave the boat. Then the correspondent performed his one little marvel of the voyage. A large wave caught him and flung him with ease and supreme speed completely over the boat and far beyond it. It struck him even then as an event in gymnastics, and a true miracle of the sea. An overturned boat in the surf is not a plaything to a swimming man.

The correspondent arrived in water that reached only to his waist, but his condition did not enable him to stand for more than a moment. Each wave knocked him into a heap, and the undertow pulled at him.

Then he saw the man who had been running and undressing, and undressing and running, come bounding into the water. He dragged ashore the cook, and then waded toward the captain, but the captain waved him away, and sent him to the correspondent. He was naked, naked as a tree in winter, but a halo was about his head, and he shone like a saint. He gave a strong pull, and a long drag, and a bully heave at the correspondent's hand. The correspondent, schooled in the minor formulae, said: "Thanks, old man." But suddenly the man cried: "What's that?" He pointed a swift finger. The correspondent said: "Go."

In the shallows, face downward, lay the oiler. His forehead touched sand that was periodically, between each wave, clear of the sea.

The correspondent did not know all that transpired afterward. When he achieved safe ground he fell, striking the sand with each particular part of his body. It was as if he had dropped from a roof, but the thud was grateful to him.

It seems that instantly the beach was populated with men with blankets, clothes, and flasks, and women with coffee-pots and all the remedies sacred to their minds. The welcome of the land to the men from the sea was warm and generous, but a still and dripping shape was carried slowly up the beach, and the land's welcome for it could only be the different and sinister hospitality of the grave.

When it came night, the white waves paced to and fro in the moonlight, and the wind brought the sound of the great sea's voice to the men on shore, and they felt that they could then be interpreters.

Do especially Questions 15-20, 33, 35, 45, 58, 61, 64, 82, 91, 96, 107, 108, 113, 116, 117, 133, 149, and 157. Consult the Model Short Story in Volume One.

STEPHEN CRANE   *1871-1900*

Into his twenty-nine years, Stephen Crane pressed an intense, frenzied career that rapidly burned itself out. Born in New Jersey of two deeply religious parents, he shocked the world by producing at the age of twenty the tough and sordid short novel *Maggie: A Girl of the Streets,* which anticipated a whole stream of present-day naturalist novels on sex and slum-life. His greatest work followed in 1895—*The Red Badge of Courage,* a psychological study of fear and disillusionment in the ordinary soldier, pieced together not from any actual experience on the battlefield but from photographs and memoirs that Crane found in books and newspapers. He modeled many of his battle scenes on those in Stendhal's *La Chartreuse de Parme,* and even excelled Stendhal in his ability to create scenes and sensations from the point of view of an actual participant. Crane spent the last years of his life recklessly exposing himself as war-correspondent in the Greco-Turkish War, the insurrection in Cuba, and the Spanish-American War. "The Open Boat" (1898), which Howells called "the finest short story in English," resulted from an actual experience during Crane's assignment to Cuba. He and three other men struggled for two days in a heavy sea after the sinking of the steamer *Commodore.* Dead of tuberculosis at the dawn of the twentieth century, Crane left behind him twelve volumes, including two widely acclaimed volumes of lucid, bitter poetry.

All Gold Canyon

JACK LONDON

It was the green heart of the canyon, where the walls swerved back from the rigid plan and relieved their harshness of line by making a little sheltered nook and filling it to the brim with sweetness and roundness and softness. Here all things rested. Even the narrow stream ceased its turbulent down-rush long enough to form a quiet pool. Knee-deep in the water, with drooping head and half-shut eyes, drowsed a red-coated, many-antlered buck.

On one side, beginning at the very lip of the pool, was a tiny meadow, a cool, resilient° surface of green that extended to the base of the frowning wall. Beyond the pool a gentle slope of earth ran up and up to meet the opposing wall. Fine grass covered the slope — grass that was spangled with flowers, with here and there patches of color — orange and purple and golden. Below, the canyon was shut in. There was no view. The walls leaned together abruptly, and the canyon ended in a chaos of rocks, moss-covered and hidden by a green screen of vines and creepers and boughs of trees. Up the canyon rose far hills and peaks, the big foot-hills, pine-covered and remote. And far beyond, like clouds upon the border of the sky, towered minarets° of white, where the Sierra's eternal snows flashed austerely the blazes of the sun.

There was no dust in the canyon. The leaves and flowers were clean and virginal. The grass was young velvet. Over the pool three cottonwoods sent their snowy fluffs fluttering down the quiet air. On the slope the blossoms of the wine-wooded manzanita[1] filled the air with springtime odors, while the leaves, wise with experience, were already be-ginning their vertical twist against the coming aridity of summer. In the open spaces on the slope, beyond the farthest shadow reach of the manzanita, poised the mari-posa[2] lilies like so many flights of jeweled moths suddenly arrested and on the verge of trembling into flight again. Here and there that woods harlequin,° the madrone, per-mitting itself to be caught in the act of changing its pea-green trunk to madder red, breathed its fragrance into the air from great clusters of waxen bells. Creamy white were these bells, shaped like lilies of the valley, with the sweet-ness of perfume that is of the springtime.

There was not a sigh of wind. The air was drowsy with its weight of perfume. It was a sweetness that would have been cloying had the air been heavy and humid. But the air was sharp and thin. It was as starlight transmuted° into atmosphere, shot through and warmed by sunshine, and flower-drenched with sweetness.

An occasional butterfly drifted in and out through the patches of light and shade. And from all about rose the low and sleepy hum of mountain bees—feasting sybarites° that jostled one another good-naturedly at the board, nor found time for rough discourtesy. So quietly did the little stream drip and ripple its way through the canyon that it spoke only in faint and occasional gurgles. The voice of

[1]A shrub or small tree.
[2]The Spanish name for "butterfly"—a brilliant, tulip-like flower.

the stream was as a drowsy whisper, ever interrupted by dozings and silences, ever lifted again in the awakenings.

The motion of all things was a drifting in the heart of the canyon. Sunshine and butterflies drifted in and out among the trees. The hum of the bees and the whisper of the stream were a drifting of sound. And the drifting sound and drifting color seemed to weave together in the making of a delicate and intangible° fabric which was the spirit of the place. It was a spirit of peace that was not of death, but of smooth-pulsing life, of quietude that was not silence, of movement that was not action, of repose that was quick with existence without being violent with struggle and travail. The spirit of the place was the spirit of the peace of the living, somnolent° with the easement and content of prosperity, and undisturbed by rumors of far wars.

The red-coated, many-antlered buck acknowledged the lordship of the spirit of the place and dozed knee-deep in the cool, shaded pool. There seemed no flies to vex him, and he was languid with rest. Sometimes his ears moved when the stream awoke and whispered; but they moved lazily, with foreknowledge that it was merely the stream grown garrulous° at discovery that it had slept.

But there came a time when the buck's ears lifted and tensed with swift eagerness for sound. His head was turned down the canyon. His sensitive, quivering nostrils scented the air. His eyes could not pierce the green screen through which the stream rippled away, but to his ears came the voice of a man. It was a steady, monotonous, singsong voice. Once the buck heard the harsh clash of metal upon rock. At the sound he snorted with a sudden start that jerked him through the air from water to meadow, and his feet sank into the young velvet, while he pricked his ears and again scented the air. Then he stole across the tiny meadow, pausing once and again to listen, and faded away out of the canyon like a wraith,° soft-footed and without sound.

The clash of steel-shod soles against the rocks began to be heard, and the man's voice grew louder. It was raised in a sort of chant and became distinct with nearness, so that the words could be heard:

> Tu'n around an' tu'n yo' face
> Untoe them sweet hills of grace
>   (D' pow'rs of sin yo' am scornin'!).
> Look about an' look aroun',
> Fling yo' sin-pack on d' groun'
>   (Yo' will meet wid d'Lord in d'mornin'!).

A sound of scrambling accompanied the song, and the spirit of the place fled away on the heels of the red-coated buck. The green screen was burst asunder, and a man peered out at the meadow and the pool and the sloping sidehill. He was a deliberate sort of man. He took in the scene with one embracing glance, then ran his eyes over the details to verify the general impression. Then, and not until then, did he open his mouth in vivid and solemn approval: "Smoke of life an' snakes of purgatory! Will you just look at that! Wood an' water an' grass an' a side-hill! A pocket[3] hunter's delight an' a cayuse's[4] paradise! Cool green for tired eyes! Pink pills for pale people ain't in it. A secret pasture for prospectors and a resting place for tired burros, by damn!"

He was a sandy-complexioned man in whose face geniality and humor seemed the salient characteristics. It was a mobile face, quick-changing to inward mood and thought. Thinking was in him a visible process. Ideas chased across his face like wind flaws across the surface of a lake. His hair, sparse and unkempt of growth, was as indeterminate and colorless as his complexion. It would seem that all the color of his frame had gone into his eyes, for they were startlingly blue. Also, they were laughing and merry eyes, within them much of the naïveté° and wonder of the child; and yet, in an unassertive way, they contained much of calm self-reliance and strength of purpose founded upon self-experience and experience of the world.

From out the screen of vines and creepers he flung ahead

---

[3]A cavity of gold.
[4]An Indian pony.

of him a miner's pick and shovel and gold pan. Then he crawled out himself into the open. He was clad in faded overalls and black cotton shirt, with hobnailed brogans on his feet, and on his head a hat whose shapelessness and stains advertised the rough usage of wind and rain and sun and camp smoke. He stood erect, seeing wide-eyed the secrecy of the scene and sensuously inhaling the warm, sweet breath of the canyon garden through nostrils that dilated and quivered with delight. His eyes narrowed to laughing slits of blue, his face wreathed itself in joy, and his mouth curled in a smile as he cried aloud: "Jumping dandelions and happy hollyhocks, but that smells good to me! Talk about your attar° o' roses an' cologne factories! They ain't in it!"

He had the habit of soliloquy.° His quick-changing facial expressions might tell every thought and mood, but the tongue, perforce, ran hard after, repeating, like a second Boswell.[5]

The man lay down on the lip of the pool and drank long and deep of its water. "Tastes good to me," he murmured, lifting his head and gazing across the pool at the sidehill, while he wiped his mouth with the back of his hand. The sidehill attracted his attention. Still lying on his stomach, he studied the hill formation long and carefully. It was a practiced eye that traveled up the slope to the crumbling canyon wall and back and down again to the edge of the pool. He scrambled to his feet and favored the sidehill with a second survey.

"Looks good to me," he concluded, picking up his pick and shovel and gold pan. He crossed the stream below the pool, stepping agilely from stone to stone. Where the sidehill touched the water he dug up a shovelful of dirt and put it into the gold pan. He squatted down, holding the pan in his two hands and partly immersing it in the stream. Then he imparted to the pan a deft circular motion that sent the water sluicing in and out through the dirt and gravel. The larger and the lighter particles worked to the surface, and these, by a skillful dipping movement of the

[5]James Boswell (1740-1795) recorded conversations like a dictaphone in perhaps the greatest biography of all time, *The Life of Samuel Johnson.*

pan, he spilled out and over the edge. Occasionally, to ex-
pedite° matters, he rested the pan and with his fingers
raked out the large pebbles and pieces of rock.

The contents of the pan diminished rapidly until only
fine dirt and the smallest bits of gravel remained. At this
stage he began to work very deliberately and carefully. It
was fine washing, and he washed fine and finer, with a keen
scrutiny° and delicate and fastidious° touch. At last the
pan seemed empty of everything but water; but with a
quick semicircular flirt° that sent the water flying over the
shallow rim into the stream, he disclosed a layer of black
sand on the bottom of the pan. So thin was this layer that
it was like a streak of paint. He examined it closely. In
the midst of it was a tiny golden speck. He dribbled a
little water in over the depressed edge of the pan. With
a quick flirt he sent the water sluicing° across the bottom,
turning the grains of black sand over and over. A second
tiny golden speck rewarded his effort.

The washing had now become very fine — fine beyond
all need of ordinary placer mining. He worked the black
sand, a small portion at a time, up the shallow rim of the
pan. Each small portion he examined sharply, so that his
eyes saw every grain of it before he allowed it to slide over
the edge and away. Jealously, bit by bit, he let the black
sand slip away. A golden speck, no larger than a pin point,
appeared on the rim, and by his manipulation of the water
it returned to the bottom of the pan. And in such fashion
another speck was disclosed, and another. Great was his
care of them. Like a shepherd he herded his flock of golden
specks so that not one should be lost. At last, of the pan of
dirt nothing remained but his golden herd. He counted it,
and then, after all his labor, sent it flying out of the pan
with one final swirl of water.

But his blue eyes were shining with desire as he rose to
his feet. "Seven," he muttered aloud, asserting the sum of
the specks for which he had toiled so hard and which he
had so wantonly° thrown away. "Seven," he repeated with
the emphasis of one trying to impress a number on his
memory.

He stood still a long while, surveying the hillside. In

his eyes was a curiosity, new aroused and burning. There was an exultance about his bearing and a keenness like that of a hunting animal catching the fresh scent of game.

He moved down the stream a few steps and took a second panful of dirt.

Again came the careful washing, the jealous herding of the golden specks, and the wantonness with which he sent them flying into the stream when he had counted their number.

"Five," he muttered, and repeated, "five."

He could not forbear another survey of the hill before filling the pan farther down the stream. His golden herds diminished. "Four, three, two, two, one," were his memory tabulations as he moved down the stream. When but one speck of gold rewarded his washing, he stopped and built a fire of dry twigs. Into this he thrust the gold pan and burned it till it was blue-black. He held up the pan and examined it critically. Then he nodded approbation. Against such a color background he could defy the tiniest yellow speck to elude him.

Still moving down the stream, he panned again. A single speck was his reward. A third pan contained no gold at all. Not satisfied with this, he panned three times again, taking his shovels of dirt within a foot of one another. Each pan proved empty of gold, and the fact, instead of discouraging him, seemed to give him satisfaction. His elation increased with each barren washing, until he arose, exclaiming jubilantly, "If it ain't the real thing, may God knock off my head with sour apples!"

Returning to where he had started operations, he began to pan up the stream. At first his golden herds increased— increased prodigiously.° "Fourteen, eighteen, twenty-one, twenty-six," ran his memory tabulations. Just above the pool he struck his richest pan—thirty-five colors.

"Almost enough to save," he remarked regretfully, as he allowed the water to sweep them away.

The sun climbed to the top of the sky. The man worked on. Pan by pan he went up the stream, the tally of results steadily decreasing.

"It's just booful, the way it peters out," he exulted when

a shovelful of dirt contained no more than a single speck of gold.

And when no specks at all were found in several pans, he straightened up and favored the hillside with a confident glance.

"Ah, ha! Mr. Pocket!" he cried out, as though to an auditor hidden somewhere above him beneath the surface of the slope. "Ah, ha! Mr. Pocket! I'm a-comin', I'm a-comin', and I'm shorely gwine to get yer! You heah me, Mr. Pocket? I'm gwine to get yer as shore as punkins ain't cauliflowers!"

He turned and flung a measuring glance at the sun poised above him in the azure° of the cloudless sky. Then he went down the canyon, following the line of shovel holes he had made in filling the pans. He crossed the stream below the pool and disappeared through the green screen. There was little opportunity for the spirit of the place to return with its quietude and repose, for the man's voice, raised in ragtime song, still dominated the canyon with possession.

After a time, with a greater clashing of steel-shod feet on rock, he returned. The green screen was tremendously agitated. It surged back and forth in the throes of a struggle. There was a loud grating and clanging of metal. The man's voice leaped to a higher pitch and was sharp with imperativeness. A large body plunged and panted. There was a snapping and ripping and rending, and amid a shower of falling leaves a horse burst through the screen. On its back was a pack, and from this trailed broken vines and torn creepers. The animal gazed with astonished eyes at the scene into which it had been precipitated,° then dropped its head to the grass and began contentedly to graze. A second horse scrambled into view, slipping once on the mossy rocks and regaining equilibrium when its hoofs sank into the yielding surface of the meadow. It was riderless, though on its back was a high-horned Mexican saddle, scarred and discolored by long usage.

The man brought up the rear. He threw off pack and saddle, with an eye to camp location, and gave the animals their freedom to graze. He unpacked his food and got out frying pan and coffeepot. He gathered an armful of dry wood, and with a few stones made a place for his fire.

"My!" he said, "but I've got an appetite. I could scoff iron filings an' horseshoe nails an' thank you kindly, ma'am, for a second helpin'."

He straightened up, and while he reached for matches in the pocket of his overalls his eyes traveled across the pool to the sidehill. His fingers had clutched the matchbox, but they relaxed their hold and the hand came out empty. The man wavered perceptibly. He looked at his preparations for cooking and he looked at the hill.

"Guess I'll take another whack at her," he concluded, starting to cross the stream.

"They ain't no sense in it, I know," he mumbled apologetically. "But keepin' grub back an hour ain't goin' to hurt none, I reckon."

A few feet back from his first line of test pans he started a second line. The sun dropped down the western sky, the shadows lengthened, but the man worked on. He began a third line of test pans. He was crosscutting the hillside, line by line, as he ascended. The center of each line produced the richest pans, while the ends came where no colors showed in the pan. And as he ascended the hillside the lines grew perceptibly shorter. The regularity with which their length diminished served to indicate that somewhere up the slope the last line would be so short as to have scarcely length at all, and that beyond could come only to a point. The design was growing into an inverted V. The converging° sides of this V marked the boundaries of the gold-bearing dirt.

The apex° of the V was evidently the man's goal. Often he ran his eye along the converging sides and on up the hill, trying to divine the apex—the point where the gold-bearing dirt must cease. Here resided "Mr. Pocket," for so the man familiarly addressed the imaginary point above him on the slope, crying out: "Come down out o' that, Mr. Pocket! Be right smart an' agreeable, an' come down!"

"All right," he would add later, in a voice resigned to

determination. "All right, Mr. Pocket. It's plain to me I got to come right up an' snatch you out bald-headed. An' I'll do it! I'll do it!" he would threaten still later.

Each pan he carried down to the water to wash, and as he went higher up the hill the pans grew richer, until he began to save the gold in an empty baking-powder can which he carried carelessly in his hip pocket. So engrossed was he in his toil that he did not notice the long twilight of oncoming night. It was not until he tried vainly to see the gold colors in the bottom of the pan that he realized the passage of time. He straightened up abruptly. An expression of whimsical wonderment and awe overspread his face as he drawled, "Gosh darn my buttons! if I didn't plum forget dinner!"

He stumbled across the stream in the darkness and lighted his long-delayed fire. Flapjacks and bacon and warmed-over beans constituted his supper. Then he smoked a pipe by the smoldering coals, listening to the night noises and watching the moonlight stream through the canyon. After that he unrolled his bed, took off his heavy shoes, and pulled the blankets up to his chin. His face showed white in the moonlight, like the face of a corpse. But it was a corpse that knew its resurrection, for the man rose suddenly on one elbow and gazed across at his hillside.

"Good night, Mr. Pocket," he called sleepily. "Good night."

He slept through the early gray of morning until the direct rays of the sun smote his closed eyelids, when he awoke with a start and looked about him until he had established the continuity of his existence and identified his present self with the days previously lived.

To dress he had merely to buckle on his shoes. He glanced at his fireplace and at his hillside, wavered, but fought down the temptation and started the fire.

"Keep yer shirt on, Bill; keep yer shirt on," he admonished himself. "What's the good of rushin'? No use in gettin' all het up and sweaty. Mr. Pocket'll wait for you. He ain't a-runnin' away before you can get yer breakfast.

Now, what you want, Bill, is something fresh in yer bill o' fare. So it's up to you to go an' get it."

He cut a short pole at the water's edge and drew from one of his pockets a bit of line and a draggled fly that had once been a royal coachman.[6]

"Mebbe they'll bite in the early morning," he muttered as he made his first cast into the pool. And a moment later he was gleefully crying: "What'd I tell you, eh? What'd I tell you?"

He had no reel, nor any inclination to waste time, and by main strength, and swiftly, he drew out of the water a flashing ten-inch trout. Three more, caught in rapid succession, furnished his breakfast. When he came to the stepping-stones on his way to his hillside, he was struck by a sudden thought, and paused.

"I'd just better take a hike downstream a ways," he said. "There's no tellin' what cuss may be snoopin' around."

But he crossed over on the stones, and with a "I really oughter take that hike," the need of the precaution passed out of his mind and he fell to work.

At nightfall he straightened up. The small of his back was stiff from stooping toil, and as he put his hand behind him to soothe the protesting muscles, he said: "Now what d'ye think of that, by damn? I clean forgot my dinner again! If I don't watch out, I'll sure be degeneratin' into a two-meal-a-day crank."

"Pockets is the damnedest things I ever see for makin' a man absent-minded," he communed that night, as he crawled into his blankets. Nor did he forget to call up the hillside, "Good night, Mr. Pocket! Good night!"

Rising with the sun and snatching a hasty breakfast, he was early at work. A fever seemed to be growing in him, nor did the increasing richness of the test pans allay this fever. There was a flush in his cheek other than that made by the heat of the sun, and he was oblivious° to fatigue and the passage of time. When he filled a pan with dirt, he ran down the hill to wash it; nor could he forbear running up

[6]A type of artificial fly.

the hill again, panting and stumbling profanely, to refill the pan.

He was now a hundred yards from the water, and the inverted V was assuming definite proportions. The width of the pay dirt steadily decreased, and the man extended in his mind's eye the sides of the V to their meeting place far up the hill. This was his goal, the apex of the V, and he panned many times to locate it.

"Just about two yards above that manzanita bush an' a yard to the right," he finally concluded.

Then the temptation seized him. "As plain as the nose on your face," he said as he abandoned his laborious cross-cutting and climbed to the indicated apex. He filled a pan and carried it down the hill to wash. It contained no trace of gold. He dug deep, and he dug shallow, filling and washing a dozen pans, and was unrewarded even by the tiniest golden speck. He was enraged at having yielded to the temptation, and cursed himself blasphemously and pridelessly. Then he went down the hill and took up the crosscutting.

"Slow an' certain, Bill; slow an' certain," he crooned. "Short cuts to fortune ain't in your line, and it's about time you know it. Get wise, Bill; get wise. Slow and certain's the only hand you can play; so go to it, an' keep to it, too."

As the crosscuts decreased, showing that the sides of the V were converging, the depth of the V increased. The gold trace was dipping into the hill. It was only at thirty inches beneath the surface that he could get colors in his pan. The dirt he found at twenty-five inches from the surface, and at thirty-five inches, yielded barren pans. At the base of the V, by the water's edge, he had found the gold colors at the grass roots. The higher he went up the hill, the deeper the gold dipped. To dig a hole three feet deep in order to get one test pan was a task of no mean magnitude; while between the man and the apex intervened an untold number of such holes to be dug. "An' there's no tellin' how much deeper it'll pitch," he sighed, in a moment's pause, while his fingers soothed his aching back.

Feverish with desire, with aching back and stiffening muscles, with pick and shovel gouging and mauling° the soft brown earth, the man toiled up the hill. Before him was the smooth slope, spangled with flowers and made sweet with their breath. Behind him was devastation. It looked like some terrible eruption breaking out on the smooth skin of the hill. His slow progress was that of a slug,° befouling beauty with a monstrous trail.

Though the dipping gold trace increased the man's work, he found consolation in the increasing richness of the pans. Twenty cents, thirty cents, fifty cents, sixty cents, were the values of the gold found in the pans, and at nightfall he washed his banner pan which gave him a dollar's worth of gold dust from a shovelful of dirt.

"I'll just bet it's my luck to have some inquisitive cuss come buttin' in here on my pasture," he mumbled sleepily that night as he pulled the blankets up to his chin.

Suddenly he sat upright. "Bill!" he called sharply. "Now, listen to me, Bill; d'ye hear! It's up to you, tomorrow mornin', to mosey round an' see what you can see. Understand? Tomorrow morning, an' don't you forget it!"

He yawned and glanced across at his sidehill. "Good night, Mr. Pocket," he called.

In the morning he stole a march on the sun, for he had finished breakfast when its first rays caught him, and he was climbing the wall of the canyon where it crumbled away and gave footing. From the outlook at the top he found himself in the midst of loneliness. As far as he could see, chain after chain of mountains heaved themselves into his vision. To the east his eyes, leaping the miles between range and range and between many ranges, brought up at last against the white-peaked Sierras—the main crest, where the backbone of the Western world reared itself against the sky. To the north and south he could see more distinctly the cross systems that broke through the main trend of the sea of mountains. To the west the ranges fell away, one behind the other, diminishing and fading into the gentle foothills that, in turn, descended into the great valley which he could not see.

And in all that mighty sweep of earth he saw no sign of man nor the handiwork of man, save only the torn bosom of the hillside at his feet. The man looked long and carefully. Once, far down his own canyon he thought he saw in the air a faint hint of smoke. He looked again and decided that it was the purple haze of the hills made dark by a convolution° of the canyon wall at its back.

"Hey, you, Mr. Pocket!" he called down into the canyon. "Stand out from under! I'm a-comin', Mr. Pocket! I'm a-comin'!"

The heavy brogans° on the man's feet made him appear clumsy-footed, but he swung down from the giddy° height as lightly and airily as a mountain goat. A rock, turning under his foot on the edge of the precipice, did not disconcert him. He seemed to know the precise time required for the turn to culminate in disaster, and in the meantime he utilized the false footing itself for the momentary earth contact necessary to carry him on into safety. Where the earth sloped so steeply that it was impossible to stand for a second upright, the man did not hesitate. His foot pressed the impossible surface for but a fraction of the fatal second and gave him the bound that carried him onward. Again, where even the fraction of a second's footing was out of the question, he would swing his body past by a moment's handgrip on a jutting knob of rock, a crevice, or a precariously rooted shrub. At last, with a wild leap and yell, he exchanged the face of the wall for an earth slide and finished the descent in the midst of several tons of sliding earth and gravel.

His first pan of the morning washed out over two dollars in coarse gold. It was from the center of the V. To either side the diminution in the values of the pans was swift. His lines of crosscutting holes were growing very short. The converging sides of the inverted V were only a few yards apart. Their meeting point was only a few yards above him. But the pay streak was dipping deeper and deeper into the earth. By early afternoon he was sinking the test holes five feet before the pans could show the gold trace.

For that matter, the gold trace had become something more than a trace; it was a placer mine in itself, and the man resolved to come back, after he had found the pocket, and work over the ground. But the increasing richness of the pans began to worry him. By later afternoon the worth of the pans had grown to three and four dollars. The man scratched his head perplexedly and looked a few feet up the hill at the manzanita bush that marked approximately the apex of the V. He nodded his head and said oracularly: "It's one o' two things, Bill; one o' two things. Either Mr. Pocket's spilled himself all out an' down the hill, or else Mr. Pocket's that damned rich you maybe won't be able to carry him all away with you. And that'd be terrible, wouldn't it, now?" He chuckled at contemplation of so pleasant a dilemma.

Nightfall found him by the edge of the stream, his eyes wrestling with the gathering darkness over the washing of a five-dollar pan.

"Wisht I had an electric light to go on working," he said.

He found sleep difficult that night. Many times he composed himself and closed his eyes for slumber to overtake him; but his blood pounded with too strong desire, and as many times his eyes opened and he murmured wearily, "Wisht it was sun-up."

Sleep came to him in the end, but his eyes were open with the first paling of the stars, and the gray of dawn caught him with breakfast finished and climbing the hillside in the direction of the secret abiding place of Mr. Pocket.

The first crosscut the man made, there was space for only three holes, so narrow had become the pay streak and so close was he to the fountain head of the golden stream he had been following for four days.

"Be ca'm, Bill; be ca'm," he admonished himself as he broke ground for the final hole where the sides of the V had at last come together in a point.

"I've got the almighty cinch on you, Mr. Pocket, an' you can't lose me," he said many times as he sank the hole deeper and deeper.

Four feet, five feet, six feet, he dug his way down into the earth. The digging grew harder. His pick grated on broken rock. He examined the rock. "Rotten quartz" was his conclusion as, with the shovel, he cleared the bottom of the hole of loose dirt. He attacked the crumbling quartz with the pick, bursting the disintegrating rock asunder with every stroke.

He thrust his shovel into the loose mass. His eye caught a gleam of yellow. He dropped the shovel and squatted suddenly on his heels. As a farmer rubs the clinging earth from fresh-dug potatoes, so the man, a piece of rotten quartz held in both hands, rubbed the dirt away.

"Sufferin' Sardanapolis!" he cried. "Lumps an' chunks of it! Lumps an' chunks of it!"

It was only half rock he held in his hand. The other half was virgin gold. He dropped it into his pan and examined another piece. Little yellow was to be seen, but with his strong fingers he crumbled the rotten quartz away till both hands were filled with glowing yellow. He rubbed the dirt away from fragment after fragment, tossing them into the gold pan. It was a treasure hole. So much had the quartz rotted away that there was less of it than there was of gold. Now and again he found a piece to which no rock clung—a piece that was all gold. A chunk where the pick had laid open the heart of the gold glittered like a handful of yellow jewels, and he cocked his head at it and slowly turned it around and over to observe the rich play of the light upon it.

"Talk about yer Too Much Gold[7] diggin's!" the man snorted contemptuously. "Why, this diggin' 'd make it look like thirty cents. This diggin' is All Gold. An' right here an' now, I name this yere canyon 'All Gold Canyon,' b'gosh!"

Still squatting on his heels, he continued examining the fragments and tossing them into the pan. Suddenly there came to him a premonition° of danger. It seemed a shadow had fallen upon him. But there was no shadow. His heart had given a great jump up into his throat and was choking

[7]The name of a famous gold strike.

him. Then his blood slowly chilled and he felt the sweat of his shirt cold against his flesh.

He did not spring up nor look around. He did not move. He was considering the nature of the premonition he had received, trying to locate the source of the mysterious force that had warned him, striving to sense the imperative presence of the unseen thing that threatened him. There is an aura° of things hostile, made manifest by messengers too refined for the senses to know; and this aura he felt, but knew not how he felt it. His was the feeling as when a cloud passes over the sun. It seemed that between him and life had passed something dark and smothering and menacing, a gloom, as it were, that swallowed up life and made for death—his death.

Every force of his being impelled him to spring up and confront the unseen danger, but his soul dominated the panic, and he remained squatting on his heels, in his hands a chunk of gold. He did not dare to look around, but he knew by now that there was something behind him and above him. He made believe to be interested in the gold in his hand. He examined it critically, turned it over and over, and rubbed the dirt from it. And all the time he knew that something behind him was looking at the gold over his shoulder.

Still feigning interest in the chunk of gold in his hand, he listened intently, and he heard the breathing of the thing behind him. His eyes searched the ground in front of him for a weapon, but they saw only the uprooted gold, worthless to him now in his extremity. There was his pick, a handy weapon on occasion; but this was not such an occasion. The man realized his predicament. He was in a narrow hole that was seven feet deep. His head did not come to the surface of the ground. He was in a trap.

He remained squatting on his heels. He was quite cool and collected; but his mind, considering every factor, showed him only his helplessness. He continued rubbing the dirt from the quartz fragments and throwing the gold into the pan. There was nothing else for him to do. Yet he knew that he would have to rise up, sooner or later, and face the danger that breathed at his back. The minutes passed and with the passage of each minute he knew that by so much he was nearer the time when he must stand up, or else—and his wet shirt went cold against his flesh again at the thought—or else he might receive death as he stooped there over his treasure.

Still he squatted on his heels, rubbing dirt from gold and debating in just what manner he should rise up. He might rise up with a rush and claw his way out of the hole to meet whatever threatened on the even footing above ground; or he might rise up slowly and carelessly, and feign casually to discover the thing that breathed at his back. His instinct and every fighting fiber of his body favored the mad, clawing rush to the surface. His intellect, and the craft thereof, favored the slow and cautious meeting with the thing that menaced and that he could not see. And while he debated, a loud, crashing noise burst on his ear. At the same instant he received a stunning blow on the left side of the back, and from the point of impact felt a rush of flame through his flesh. He sprang up in the air, but halfway to his feet collapsed. His body crumpled in like a leaf withered in sudden heat, and he came down, his chest across his pan of gold, his face in the dirt and rock, his legs tangled and twisted because of the restricted space at the bottom of the hole. His legs twitched convulsively several times. His body was shaken as with a mighty ague.° There was a slow expansion of the lungs, accompanied by a deep sigh. Then the air was slowly, very slowly, exhaled, and his body as slowly flattened itself down into inertness.

Above, revolver in hand, a man was peering down over the edge of the hole. He peered for a long time at the prone and motionless body beneath him. After a while the stranger sat down on the edge of the hole so that he could see into it, and rested the revolver on his knee. Reaching his hand into a pocket, he drew out a wisp of brown paper. Into this he dropped a few crumbs of tobacco. The combination became a cigarette, brown and squat, with the ends turned in. Not once did he take his eyes from the body at the bottom of the hole. He lighted the cigarette and drew its smoke into his lungs with a caressing intake of the breath. He smoked slowly. Once the cigarette went out and he relighted it. And all the while he studied the body beneath him.

In the end he tossed the cigarette stub away and rose to his feet. He moved to the edge of the hole. Spanning it, a hand resting on each edge, and with the revolver still in the right hand, he muscled his body down into the hole. While his feet were yet a yard from the bottom he released his hands and dropped down.

At the instant his feet struck bottom he saw the pocket miner's arm leap out, and his own legs knew a swift, jerking grip that overthrew him. In the nature of the jump his revolver hand was above his head. Swiftly as the grip had flashed about his legs, just as swiftly he brought the revolver down. He was still in the air, his fall in process of completion, when he pulled the trigger. The explosion was deafening in the confined space. The smoke filled the hole so that he could see nothing. He struck the bottom on his back, and like a cat's the pocket miner's body was on top of him. Even as the miner's body passed on top the stranger crooked in his right arm to fire; and even in that instant the miner, with a quick thrust of elbow, struck his wrist. The muzzle was thrown up, and the bullet thudded into the dirt of the side of the hole.

The next instant the stranger felt the miner's hand grip his wrist. The struggle was now for the revolver. Each man strove to turn it against the other's body. The smoke in the hole was clearing. The stranger, lying on his back, was beginning to see dimly. But suddenly he was blinded by a handful of dirt deliberately flung into his eyes by his antagonist. In that moment of shock his grip on the revolver was broken. In the next moment he felt a smashing darkness descend upon his brain, and in the midst of the darkness even the darkness ceased.

But the pocket miner fired again and again, until the revolver was empty. Then he tossed it from him and, breathing heavily, sat down on the dead man's legs.

The miner was sobbing and struggling for breath.

"Measly skunk!" he panted; "a-campin' on my trail an' lettin' me do the work, an' then shootin' me in the back!"

He was half crying from anger and exhaustion. He peered at the face of the dead man. It was sprinkled with loose dirt and gravel, and it was difficult to distinguish the features.

"Never laid eyes on him before," the miner concluded his scrutiny. "Just a common an' ordinary thief, damn him! An' he shot me in the back! He shot me in the back!"

He opened his shirt and felt himself front and back on his left side.

"Went clean through, and no harm done!" he cried jubilantly. "I'll bet he aimed all right, all right; but he drew the gun over when he pulled the trigger—the cuss! But I fixed 'm! Oh, I fixed 'm!"

His fingers were investigating the bullet hole in his side, and a shade of regret passed over his face. "It's goin' to be stiff," he said. "An' it's up to me to get mended an' get out o' here."

He crawled out of the hole and went down the hill to his camp. Half an hour later he returned, leading his pack horse. His open shirt disclosed the rude bandages with which he had dressed his wounds. He was slow and awkward with his left-hand movements, but that did not prevent his using the arm.

The bight[8] of the pack rope under the dead man's shoulders enabled him to heave the body out of the hole. Then he set to work gathering up his gold. He worked steadily for several hours, pausing often to rest his stiffening shoulder and to exclaim: "He shot me in the back, the measly skunk! He shot me in the back!"

When his treasure was quite cleaned up and wrapped securely into a number of blanket-covered parcels, he made an estimate of its value.

"Four hundred pounds, or I'm a Hottentot," he concluded. "Say two hundred in quartz an' dirt; that leaves two hundred pounds of gold. Bill! Wake up. Two hundred

[8]Loop.

pounds of gold! Forty thousand dollars! An' it's yourn—
all yourn!"

He scratched his head delightedly and his fingers
blundered into an unfamiliar groove. They quested along it
for several inches. It was a crease through his scalp where
the second bullet had plowed.

He walked angrily over to the dead man.

"You would, would you?" he bullied. "You would, eh?
Well, I fixed you good an' plenty, and I'll give you decent
burial, too. That's more 'n you'd have done for me."

He dragged the body to the edge of the hole and toppled
it in. It struck the bottom with a dull crash, on its side,
the face twisted up to the light. The miner peered down
at it.

"An' you shot me in the back!" he said accusingly.

With pick and shovel he filled the hole. Then he loaded
the gold on his horse. It was too great a load for the animal,
and when he had gained his camp he transferred part of
it to his saddle horse. Even so, he was compelled to abandon a portion of his outfit—pick and shovel and gold pan,
extra food and cooking utensils, and divers odds and ends.

The sun was at the zenith when the man forced the horses
at the screen of vines and creepers. To climb the huge
boulders the animals were compelled to uprear and struggle blindly through the tangled mass of vegetation. Once
the saddle horse fell heavily, and the man removed the
pack to get the animal on his feet. After it started on its
way again the man thrust his head out from among the
leaves and peered up at the sidehill.

"The measly skunk!" he said, and disappeared.

There was a ripping and tearing of vines and boughs.
The trees surged back and forth, marking the passage of
the animals through the midst of them. There was a clashing of steel-shod hoofs on stone, and now and again an
oath or a sharp cry of command. Then the voice of the man
was raised in song:

> Tu'n around an' tu'n yo' face
> Untoe them sweet hills of grace
>   (D' pow'rs of sin yo' am scornin'!)

> Look about an' look aroun',
> Fling yo' sin-pack on d' groun'
> (Yo' will meet wid d'Lord in d'mornin'!).

The song grew faint and fainter, and through the silence crept back the spirit of the place. The stream once more drowsed and whispered; the hum of the mountain bees rose sleepily. Down through the perfume-weighted air fluttered the snowy fluffs of the cottonwoods. The butterflies drifted in and out among the trees, and over all blazed the quiet sunshine. Only remained the hoof marks in the meadow and the torn hillside to mark the boisterous trail of the life that had broken the peace of the place and passed on.

Do especially Questions 11, 73, 75-83, 89-93, and 103. Consult the Model Short Story in Volume One.

JACK LONDON   *1876-1916*

A tramp on the waterfront in San Francisco, a sailor, and a socialist agitator, London headed for the Klondike in 1897 when gold was discovered there. After a period as war-correspondent in Japan, London settled down to produce about fifty books, which earned him over a million dollars. "All Gold Canyon" (1905) catches his preoccupation with nature and the crude instinctive struggle between men which dominates *The Call of the Wild* and so many of his other stories about animals.

PROBLEM QUESTIONS

1. Detailed descriptions of setting are often a major part of naturalistic stories. Compare the mood evoked by the descriptions of setting in "All Gold Canyon," and "The Open Boat"; what does the mood of each suggest about the philosophies of Stephen Crane and Jack London with regard to man's place in the natural world?

2. The main characters in "A Mystery of Heroism," "All Gold Canyon," and "The Open Boat" are all depicted in times of crisis. Compare their reactions to their respective crises. What constitutes the "heroism" in each story?

3. Compare the reasons for and kinds of isolation of Bill in "All Gold Canyon" and Soapy in "The Cop and the Anthem." Is either character lonely, or just alone? Explain. How do you think Soapy would have reacted in Bill's situation and vice versa?

Unit Five

THE AMERICAN DESIGN

The intellectual and external forces that influenced short-story writing in pre-World War I America have already been described. It is therefore important to discover what of significance influenced the rise of the American novel. The novel in America was slow to emerge and for very good reasons. The inhabitants of this new land were so deeply involved in subduing their environment, protecting themselves from natural and social enemies, and carving out the foundations of the first truly democratic government that they had no time for entertainments that required sustained leisure and cultural exposure. Even had the leisure been available, the appearance of the novel would have been curtailed by other obstacles: America was so large and so diverse that language spoken in one section of it could hardly be understood in another. The dialects brought by immigrants from England, Scotland, and the Continent underwent a metamorphosis that made them even more disparate than they had been originally. Roads and means of communication were, of course, rudimentary; news and ideas traveled so slowly that it was not easy for persons in Massachusetts to think of themselves as related to those in Virginia. The interests, laws, problems, and economies of these colonies were so dissimilar that had a novelist appeared, full-blown, as it were, he could not feel himself "American," let alone write to please "Americans." No real American existed. More important, the colonists who had come from the British Isles felt no dearth of literary heritage, for, as William Cullen Bryant said: "We were contented with considering ourselves as participating in the literary fame of that nation, of which we were a part, and of which many of us were native, and aspired to no separate distinction."

All of these factors then, to which can be added the absence of widespread education and the dearth of publishers, served to prohibit the emergence of literature *per se* and novels in particular.

The American novel, therefore, did not make its appearance until the late eighteenth century. But it must be recalled that the English novel itself was unknown before 1719. Novels are inevitably among the latest literary forms to appear in any culture. *The Power of Sympathy* (1789) by William Hill Brown is accepted generally as the first American novel. Susanna Rowson's *Charlotte Temple,* however, received in 1794 more attention than Brown's book not only because it was superior but because *The Power of Sympathy,* in spite of its moral admonitions, was suppressed as libelous.

Following these two early novelists were several whose achievements were uneven and whose popularity was dramatic if short. The one characteristic common to most eighteenth-century American novels was a necessary subjugation of artistic interests to didacticism. The books were replete with strong arguments designed to insure good behavior, proper conduct, and clean, if not clear, thinking. Unfortunately, the novelist, then as now, chose to dissuade his public from evil by describing it, and the warnings and lessons were sometimes lost in the lurid and exciting details of the effects of sin and unleashed passion. These novels are of a class known as the sentimental novel.

Nevertheless, as early as 1792, when Hugh H. Brackenridge published the first two volumes of *Modern Chivalry,* American fiction began to reflect adult interests from an adult point of view. Brackenridge proposed, as did William Hill Brown and Susanna Rowson, to examine problems of human existence, but he did not feel, as they did, that these problems were limited to the outcomes of love affairs, the avoidance of incest, and the details of suicide, or that the solutions to them were all available in the prose of every child's primer. *Modern Chivalry* is the first American novel of satire.

Other kinds of novels which made their appearance during this early period were novels of historical romance and Gothic romance. It is within this first category that we find James Fenimore Cooper, certainly the most noteworthy of the writers of early American romance. Along with Washington Irving, Cooper, the creator of Natty Bumppo and the Leatherstocking series, put the American novel on a par with the English novel of that kind. More important, Cooper's novels were clearly American. The *Last of the Mohicans, The Spy, The Deerslayer, The Pathfinder* — these are some of the perennial favorites.

There were many writers who followed closely in the wake of Cooper — James Kirke Paulding (1778-1860) and William Gilmore Simms (1806-1870) to name two — but in his own area no one surpassed him. It was some thirty years later that the real giants of American literature began to produce novels of national, international, and unequivocal stature.

In 1850 Nathaniel Hawthorne published *The Scarlet Letter.* Before 1837 when *Twice-Told Tales* appeared, Hawthorne had received only grudging and faint praise. Suggestions as to why Hawthorne's appeal was not general are offered by a literary historian: "Uninterested in Indian legend, inexperienced on the sea, meager in powers of invention, not gifted in characterization, possessed of no ready fund of tearful sentiment, seldom moved by the comic, inclined toward careful finish rather than intensity, interested in line more than color or mass, he produced faint ethereal etchings which were tossed aside by the multitude who stood agape before the larger, more lurid canvases of Cooper and Simms and the charming Dutch realism of Irving. He steadily practiced a genre in which mingled realism and fantasy contended for empire with a heavier strain of philosophizing than most readers of fiction welcomed."

Another of the early giants of American literature, whose work in many ways parallels Hawthorne's, is Herman Melville. Achieving fame with his first novels *Typee* (1846) and

Omoo (1847), Melville was, like Hawthorne, not content with a literary examination of the more superficial aspects of American life, nor were either of them mollified by the easy aphorisms of the sentimental novelists, or enchanted with the static adventures of historical romanticists. The trials and inevitable successes of rough but noble country boys in their efforts to win from sophisticated, somehow sinister, noblemen, the hand of the virtuous maiden, was the typical theme of American novels in 1850. Hawthorne and Melville were unimpressed. They preferred rather to focus their attention on the nature of the universe and the soul of man. When Melville went to Pittsfield, where he wrote *Moby Dick,* he and Hawthorne began one of the most mutually rewarding of literary and personal friendships. Melville's dedication of *Moby Dick* to Nathaniel Hawthorne is testament to the warmth and sincerity of that liaison. Ironically, *Moby Dick,* now ranked among the finest novels in any language, was as poorly received as its author's early works were well received. His later years were like Hawthorne's early years—nothing he wrote seemed to please. He wrote, therefore, what his own integrity demanded. "Benito Cereno" is a good example of his work during this period.

It had become increasingly obvious by mid-nineteenth century that America was more than its thirty-one states. Although the holocaust of 1861-1865 proved how great still was the disparity between agrarian America and industrial America, between employed laborers and owned laborers, between state supremacy and federal supremacy, in literature the outlines of an American could be detected. In order to discover what this American was or seemed to be becoming, we must know what aspects of his life interested the major writers of the day, for what these writers chose to illuminate is a good index to what was significant about Americans.

The themes chosen by the novelists who reached their peak between 1865 and 1914 are not themselves unique— nor could they be and remain art. The universality of art precludes the possibility of aboriginal themes. It is only in the exploration of the themes—the treatment, comprehension, and expression of them—that literature is national. American writers toward the end of the nineteenth century, like their Russian contemporaries Chekhov and Tolstoy, like their French contemporaries Zola and Anatole France, like their British contemporaries Thomas Hardy and George Eliot, were concerned about man in conflict with nature, man in conflict with society, and man in conflict with evil. The questions put were the same; the difference lay in the answers suggested.

Mark Twain (like Melville, like Tolstoy, like Thomas Hardy) studied the behavior of man in a natural and civilized environment. He, too, considered the soothing effects of nature at her most benevolent, the terror of nature at her most violent, the problems of social class in a fluid society, the pitfalls of urbanity and ultrasophistication. In his nonfiction, where the European dandy is met with stubborn contempt and raucous humor, and in his novels such as *The Adventures of Huckleberry Finn, Pudd'nhead Wilson,* and *The Adventures of Tom Sawyer,* where the effects of civilization and Sunday-school morality are made the subject of charming good humor, he is suggesting a point of view about humans, and the point of view is American: beneath the bantering good humor lies a seriousness, shrewdness, and facility that were more and more to become generally accepted characteristics of an American. Victor Hugo, in *Les Misérables,* had portrayed a man plagued all of his life by the cruel and exacting Arm of Law for the theft of a loaf of bread; Twain, in *Tom Sawyer,* makes a delightful but realistic distinction between stealing and borrowing, and the Law in America, far from being absolute, was a matter of taste, region, and personality.

For a more comprehensive view of the national quality of Twain's art, there is no better example than *The Adventures of Huckleberry Finn.* Published in 1884, this novel marks a peak of achievement in American letters. Huck and Jim, a runaway slave, band together against the whole of nineteenth-century, near-west America in one of the most noble and enviable friendships recounted in literature. Huck, a homeless juvenile with scant education and no family to speak of (his wastrel father is one of the villains of the story), lives by his wits, holding civilization at bay, and creates out of his innocence, ignorance, native intelligence, and cunning a moral fabric no less "just" or demanding than that of Jonathan Edwards. He is a truly American hero. The evil and hostile forces that alternately threaten and protect Huck and Jim are Americana: riverboat gamblers, well-meaning but short-sighted Sunday-school teachers, traveling show people, confidence men — and through the entire novel, perhaps the real hero, the Mississippi River. Like the Pacific Ocean in *Moby Dick* with almost as many faces as tides, sometimes life-giving, sometimes fatal, the Mississippi River is the guiding force of the book. While it provides Huck and Jim with food, shelter, means of escape, it also foists on them cut-throats, thieves, malingerers, and imminent death. Huck and Jim are able to cope with the natural world — the world of the Mississippi, but they are misfits when they encounter civilized America. The river gives them the strength they need to combat the restrictions, injustices, indifference, and villainy of the pseudo-civilized American West.

It is impossible, of course, to represent here the magnitude of *The Adventures of Huckleberry Finn*, but perhaps the following chapters can illustrate in part the language, the humor, the cunning, and the morality which make Twain's work so very much Americana, and so very much Art.

From Chapters X and XI

Next morning I said it was getting slow and dull, and I wanted to get a stirring-up some way. I said I reckoned I would slip over the river[1] and find out what was going on. Jim liked that notion; but he said I must go in the dark and look sharp. Then he studied it over and said, couldn't I put on some of them old things and dress up

[1] That is, to the town Huck and Jim had run away from.

From Chapters X and XI *The Adventures of Huckleberry Finn* by Mark Twain. Reprinted by permission of Harper & Row, Publishers.

like a girl? That was a good notion, too. So we shortened up one of the calico gowns,[2] and I turned up my
trouser-legs to my knees and got into it. Jim hitched it
behind with the hooks, and it was a fair fit. I put on the
sun-bonnet and tied it under my chin, and then for a
body to look in and see my face was like looking down a
joint of stovepipe. Jim said nobody would know me,
even in the daytime, hardly. I practiced around all day
to get the hang of the things, and by and by I could do
pretty well in them, only Jim said I didn't walk like a
girl; and he said I must quit pulling up my gown to get
at my britches-pocket. I took notice, and done better.

I started up the Illinois shore in the canoe just after
dark.

I started across to the town from a little below the
ferry-landing; and the drift of the current fetched me in
at the bottom of the town. I tied up and started along
the bank. There was a light burning in a little shanty
that hadn't been lived in for a long time, and I wondered who had took up quarters there. I slipped up and
peeped in at the window. There was a woman about
forty year old in there knitting by a candle that was on a
pine table. I didn't know her face; she was a stranger,
for you couldn't start a face in that town that I didn't
know. Now this was lucky, because I was weakening; I
was getting afraid I had come; people might know my
voice and find me out. But if this woman had been in
such a little town two days she could tell me all I
wanted to know; so I knocked at the door, and made up
my mind I wouldn't forget I was a girl.

"Come in," says the woman, and I did. She says:
"Take a cheer."

I done it. She looked me all over with her little shiny
eyes, and says:

"What might your name be?"

"Sarah Williams."

"Where 'bouts do you live? In this neighborhood?"

[2]These had been found in a house that came floating down the Mississippi
at flood stage.

"No'm. In Hookerville, seven mile below. I've walked all the way and I'm all tired out."

"Hungry, too, I reckon. I'll find you something."

"No'm, I ain't hungry. I was so hungry I had to stop two miles below here at a farm; so I ain't hungry no more. It's what makes me so late. My mother's down sick, and out of money and everything, and I come to tell my uncle Abner Moore. He lives at the upper end of the town, she says. I hain't ever been here before. Do you know him?"

"No; but I don't know everybody yet. I haven't lived here quite two weeks. It's a considerable ways to the upper end of the town. You better stay here all night. Take off your bonnet."

"No," I says; "I'll rest awhile, I reckon, and go on. I ain't afeard of the dark."

She said she wouldn't let me go by myself, but her husband would be in by and by, maybe in a hour and a half, and she'd send him along with me. Then she got to talking about her husband, and about her relations up the river, and her relations down the river, and about how much better off they used to was, and how they didn't know but they'd made a mistake coming to our town, instead of letting well alone—and so on and so on, till I was afeard *I* had made a mistake coming to her to find out what was going on in the town; but by and by she dropped on to Pap and the murder, and then I was pretty willing to let her chatter right along. She told about me and Tom Sawyer finding the twelve thousand dollars[3] (only she got it twenty) and all about Pap and what a hard lot he was, and what a hard lot I was, and at last she got down to where I was murdered. I says:

"Who done it? We've heard considerable about these goings-on down in Hookerville, but we don't know who 'twas that killed Huck Finn."

"Well, I reckon there's a right smart chance[4] of peo-

[3]In Twain's earlier novel, *The Adventures of Tom Sawyer,* Huck and his friend Tom had discovered a hoard of gold coins.
[4]Quantity or number.

ple *here* that'd like to know who killed him. Some think
old Finn done it himself."

"No—is that so?"

"Most everybody thought it at first. He'll never
know how nigh he come to getting lynched. But before
night they changed around and judged it was done by a
runaway slave named Jim."

"Why *he*—"

I stopped. I reckoned I better keep still. She run on,
and never noticed I had put in at all:

"The slave run off the very night Huck Finn was
killed. So there's a reward out for him—three hundred
dollars. . . . They'll get him pretty soon now, and maybe
they can scare it out of him."

"Why, are they after him yet?"

"Well, you're innocent, ain't you! Does three hundred dollars lay around every day for people to pick up?
Some folks think the slave ain't far from here. I'm one
of them—but I hain't talked it around. A few days ago I
was talking with an old couple that lives next door in
the log shanty, and they happened to say hardly anybody ever goes to that island over yonder that they call
Jackson's Island. Don't anybody live there? says I.
No, nobody, says they. I didn't say any more, but I
done some thinking. I was pretty near certain I'd seen
smoke over there, about the head of the island, a day or
two before that, so I says to myself, like as not that
slave's hiding over there; anyway, says I, it's worth the
trouble to give the place a hunt. I hain't seen any
smoke sence, so I reckon maybe he's gone, it if was
him; but husband's going over to see—him and another
man. He was gone up the river; but he got back today,
and I told him as soon as he got here two hours ago."

I had got so uneasy I couldn't set still. I had to do
something with my hands; so I took up a needle off of
the table and went to threading it. My hands shook,
and I was making a bad job of it. When the woman
stopped talking I looked up, and she was looking at me
pretty curious and smiling a little. I put down the

needle and thread, and let on to be interested—and I was, too—and says:

"Three hundred dollars is a power of money. I wish my mother could get it. Is your husband going over there tonight?"

"Oh, yes. He went up-town with the man I was telling you of, to get a boat and see if they could borrow another gun. They'll go over after midnight."....

The woman kept looking at me pretty curious, and I didn't feel a bit comfortable. Pretty soon she says:

"What did you say your name was, honey?"

"M—Mary Williams."

Somehow it didn't seem to me that I said it was Mary before, so I didn't look up—seemed to be I said it was Sarah; so I felt sort of cornered, and was afeard maybe I was looking it, too. I wished the woman would say something more; the longer she set still the uneasier I was. But now she says:

"Honey, I thought you said it was Sarah when you first come in?"

"Oh, yes'm, I did. Sarah Mary Williams. Sarah's my first name. Some calls me Sarah, some calls me Mary."

"Oh, that's the way of it?"

"Yes'm."

I was feeling better then, but I wished I was out of there, anyway. I couldn't look up yet.

Well, the woman fell to talking about how hard times was, and how poor they had to live, and how the rats was as free as if they owned the place, and so forth and so on, and then I got easy again. She was right about the rats. You'd see one stick his nose out of a hole in the corner every little while. She said she had to have things handy to throw at them when she was alone, or they wouldn't give her no peace. She showed me a bar of lead twisted up into a knot, and said she was a good shot with it generly, but she'd wrenched her arm a day or two ago, and didn't know whether she could throw true now. But she watched for a chance, and directly banged away at a rat; but she missed him wide, and said, "Ouch!" it hurt her arm so. Then she told me to try for the next one. I wanted to be getting away before the old man got back, but of course I didn't let on. I got the thing, and the first rat that showed his nose I let drive, and if he'd 'a' stayed where he was he'd 'a' been a tolerable sick rat. She said that was first-rate, and she reckoned I would hive the next one. She went and got the lump of lead and fetched it back, and brought along a hank of yarn which she wanted me to help her with. I held up my two hands and she put the hank over them, and went on talking about her and her husband's matters. But she broke off to say:

"Keep your eye on the rats. You better have the lead in your lap, handy."

So she dropped the lump into my lap just at that moment, and I clapped my legs together on it and she went on talking. But only about a minute. Then she took off the hank and looked me straight in the face, and very pleasant, and says:

"Come, now, what's your real name?"

"Wh-hat, mum?"

"What's your real name? Is it Bill, or Tom, or Bob?—or what is it?"

I reckon I shook like a leaf, and I didn't know hardly what to do. But I says:

"Please to don't poke fun at a poor girl like me, mum. If I'm in the way here, I'll—"

"No, you won't. Set down and stay where you are. I ain't going to hurt you, and I ain't going to tell on you, nuther. You just tell me your secret, and trust me. I'll keep it; and what's more, I'll help you. So'll my old man if you want him to. You see, you're a runaway 'prentice,[5] that's all. It ain't anything. There ain't no harm in it. You've been treated bad, and you made up your mind to cut. Bless you, child, I wouldn't tell on you. Tell me all about it, now—that's a good boy."

So I said it wouldn't be no use to try to play it any

[5] A boy who has been "bound" legally to work a certain number of years as an apprentice without pay, but has run away from his master.

longer, and I would just make a clean breast and tell her everything, but she mustn't go back on her promise. Then I told her my father and mother was dead, and the law had bound me out to a mean old farmer in the country thirty mile back from the river, and he treated me so bad I couldn't stand it no longer; he went away to be gone a couple of days, and so I took my chance and stole some of his daughter's old clothes and cleared out, and I had been three nights coming the thirty miles. I traveled nights, and hid daytimes and slept, and the bag of bread and meat I carried from home lasted me all the way, and I had a-plenty. I said I believed my uncle Abner Moore would take care of me, and so that was why I struck out for this town of Goshen.

"Goshen, child? This ain't Goshen. This is St. Petersburg. Goshen's ten mile further up the river. Who told you this was Goshen?"

"Why, a man I met at daybreak this morning, just as I was going to turn into the woods for my regular sleep. He told me when the roads forked I must take the right hand, and five mile would fetch me to Goshen."

"He was drunk, I reckon. He told you just exactly wrong."

"Well, he did act like he was drunk, but it ain't no matter now. I got to be moving along. I'll fetch Goshen before daylight."

"Hold on a minute. I'll put you up a snack to eat. You might want it."

So she put me up a snack, and says:

"Say, when a cow's laying down, which end of her gets up first? Answer up prompt now—don't stop to study over it. Which end gets up first?"

"The hind end, mum."

"Well, then, a horse?"

"The for'rard end, mum."

"Which side of a tree does the moss grow on?"

"North side."

"If fifteen cows is browsing on a hillside, how many of them eats with their heads pointed the same direction?"

"The whole fifteen, mum."

"Well, I reckon you *have* lived in the country. I thought maybe you was trying to hocus me again. What's your real name, now?"

"George Peters, mum."

"Well, try to remember it, George. Don't forget and tell me it's Elexander before you go, and then get out by saying it's George Elexander when I catch you. And don't go about women in that old calico. You do a girl tolerable poor, but you might fool men, maybe. Bless you, child, when you set out to thread a needle don't hold the thread still and fetch the needle up to it; hold the needle still and poke the thread at it; that's the way a woman most always does, but a man always does t'other way. And when you throw at a rat or anything, hitch yourself up a-tiptoe and fetch your hand up over your head as awkward as you can, and miss your rat about six or seven foot. Throw stiff-armed from the shoulder, like there was a pivot there for it to turn on, like a girl; not from the wrist and elbow, with your arm out to one side, like a boy. And, mind you, when a girl tries to catch anything in her lap she throws her knees apart; she don't clap them together, the way you did when you catched the lump of lead. Why, I spotted you for a boy when you was threading the needle; and I contrived the other things just to make certain. Now trot along to your uncle, Sarah Mary Williams George Elexander Peters, and if you get into trouble you send word to Mrs. Judith Loftus, which is me, and I'll do what I can to get you out of it. Keep the river road all the way, and next time you tramp take shoes and socks with you. The river road's a rocky one, and your feet'll be in a condition when you get to Goshen, I reckon."

I went up the bank about fifty yards, and then I

doubled on my tracks and slipped back to where my
canoe was, a good piece below the house. I jumped in,
and was off in a hurry....

I landed, and slopped through the timber and up the
ridge and into the cavern. There Jim laid, sound asleep
on the ground. I roused him out and says:

"Git up and hump yourself, Jim! There ain't a minute to lose. They're after us!"...

Then we got out the raft and slipped along down in
the shade, past the foot of the island dead still—never
saying a word.

What Mark Twain did for frontier-town Western society,
other writers did for big-city Eastern society. It is important
to recall that in the three or four decades immediately
preceding World War I the face of America had changed
greatly from the days of Poe and Irving. With expansion,
investments in the products and raw materials of the South
and West, means by which the products could be shipped,
ways by which they could be processed and sold, much
money was made and a leisure class had emerged. This
class had the dilemma of drawing its own lines of financial
and cultural demarcation and remaining at the same time
part of the Democratic System. It was a difficult task. The
transitions from anonymity to sudden wealth, from undis-
tinguished lineage to positions of power and influence, are
problems found in the upper middle classes of any country.
But to maintain one's exclusiveness in a theoretically class-
less society, to have the means to acquire the artifacts of
culture, but not the taste to appreciate them—this was a
particularly knotty problem for Americans. Then, too, how
was the extraordinarily wealthy man to justify his wealth in
terms of Christian heritage, and particularly, his American
Puritan heritage?

William Dean Howells had examined these social and
moral problems in *The Rise of Silas Lapham;* Edith Wharton was to do the same with an eye for deeper meaning and
the less "smiling aspects" of life. In *The Age of Innocence,*
Miss Wharton probes with irony and understanding the

falsity of Victorian mores and New York high society, where form had become formality and tradition had become habit.

The following chapters from *The Age of Innocence* reveal both Miss Wharton's mastery of her medium and the essence of monied New York society at the turn of the century.

Chapter I

On a January evening of the early seventies, Christine Nilsson was singing in *Faust* at the Academy of Music in New York.

Though there was already talk of the erection, in remote metropolitan distances "above the Forties," of a new Opera House which should compete in costliness and splendour with those of the great European capitals, the world of fashion was still content to reassemble every winter in the shabby red and gold boxes of the sociable old Academy. Conservatives cherished it for being small and inconvenient, and thus keeping out the "new people" whom New York was beginning to dread and yet be drawn to; and the sentimental clung to it for its historic associations, and the musical for its excellent acoustics, always so problematic a quality in halls built for the hearing of music.

It was Madame Nilsson's first appearance that winter, and what the daily press had already learned to describe as "an exceptionally brilliant audience" had gathered to hear her, transported through the slippery, snowy streets in private broughams,° in the spacious family landau,° or in the humbler but more convenient "Brown *coupé*." To come to the Opera in a Brown *coupé* was almost as honourable a way of arriving as in one's own carriage; and departure by the same means had the immense advantage of enabling one (with a playful allusion to democratic principles) to scramble into the first Brown conveyance in the line, instead of waiting till the cold-and-gin congested nose of one's own coachman gleamed under the portico of the Academy. It was one of the great livery-stableman's most masterly intuitions to have discovered that Americans want to get away from amusement even more quickly than they want to get to it.

When Newland Archer opened the door at the back of the club box the curtain had just gone up on the garden scene. There was no reason why the young man should not have come earlier, for he had dined at seven, alone with his mother and sister, and had lingered afterward over a cigar in the Gothic library with glazed black-walnut bookcases and finial-topped chairs which was the only room in the house where Mrs. Archer allowed smoking. But, in the first place, New York was a metropolis, and perfectly aware that in metropolises it was "not the thing" to arrive early at the opera; and what was or was not "the thing" played a part as important in Newland Archer's New York as the inscrutable totem° terrors that had ruled the destinies of his forefathers thousands of years ago.

The second reason for his delay was a personal one. He had dawdled over his cigar because he was at heart a dilettante,° and thinking over a pleasure to come often gave him a subtler satisfaction than its realisation. This was especially the case when the pleasure was a delicate one, as his pleasures mostly were; and on this occasion the moment he looked forward to was so rare and exquisite in quality that—well, if he had timed his arrival in accord with the prima donna's stage-manager he could not have entered the Academy at a more significant moment than just as she was singing: "He loves me—he loves me not—*he loves me!*" and sprinkling the falling daisy petals with notes as clear as dew.

She sang, of course, "*M'ama!*" and not "he loves me," since an unalterable and unquestioned law of the musical world required that the German text of French operas sung by Swedish artists should be translated into Italian for the clearer understanding of English-speaking audiences. This seemed as natural to Newland Archer as all the other conventions on which his life was moulded: such as the duty of using two silver-backed brushes with his monogram in blue enamel to part his hair, and of never appearing in society without a flower (preferably a gardenia) in his buttonhole.

"M'ama...non m'ama..." the prima donna sang, and "M'ama!", with a final burst of love triumphant, as she pressed the dishevelled daisy to her lips and lifted her large eyes to the sophisticated countenance of the little brown Faust-Capoul, who was vainly trying, in a tight purple velvet doublet and plumed cap, to look as pure and true as his artless victim.

Newland Archer, leaning against the wall at the back of the club box, turned his eyes from the stage and scanned the opposite side of the house. Directly facing him was the box of old Mrs. Manson Mingott, whose monstrous obesity had long since made it impossible for her to attend the Opera, but who was always represented on fashionable nights by some of the younger members of the family. On this occasion, the front of the box was filled by her daughter-in-law, Mrs. Lovell Mingott, and her daughter, Mrs. Welland; and slightly withdrawn behind these brocaded matrons sat a young girl in white with eyes ecstatically fixed on the stage-lovers. As Madame Nilsson's "M'ama!" thrilled out above the silent house (the boxes always stopped talking during the Daisy Song) a warm pink mounted to the girl's cheek, mantled her brow to the roots of her fair braids, and suffused the young slope of her breast to the line where it met a modest tulle tucker fastened with a single gardenia. She dropped her eyes to the immense bouquet of lilies-of-the-valley on her knee, and Newland Archer saw her white-gloved finger-tips touch the flowers softly. He drew a breath of satisfied vanity and his eyes returned to the stage.

No expense had been spared on the setting, which was acknowledged to be very beautiful even by people who shared his acquaintance with the Opera houses of Paris and Vienna. The foreground, to the footlights, was covered with emerald green cloth. In the middle distance symmetrical mounds of woolly green moss bounded by croquet hoops formed the base of shrubs shaped like orange-trees but studded with large pink and red roses. Gigantic pansies, considerably larger than the roses, and closely resembling the floral pen-wipers made by female parishioners for fashionable clergymen, sprang from the moss beneath the rose-trees; and here and there a daisy grafted on a rose-branch flowered with a luxuriance prophetic of Mr. Luther Burbank's[1] far-off prodigies.

In the centre of this enchanted garden Madame Nilsson, in white cashmere slashed with pale blue satin, a reticule° dangling from a blue girdle, and large yellow braids carefully disposed on each side of her muslin chemisette, listened with downcast eyes to M. Capoul's impassioned wooing, and affected a guileless incomprehension of his designs whenever, by word or glance, he persuasively indicated the ground floor window of the neat brick villa projecting obliquely from the right wing.

"The darling!" thought Newland Archer, his glance flitting back to the young girl with the lilies-of-the-valley. "She doesn't even guess what it's all about." And he contemplated her absorbed young face with a thrill of possessorship in which pride in his own masculine initiation was mingled with a tender reverence for her abysmal purity. "We'll read *Faust* together . . . by the Italian lakes . . ." he thought, somewhat hazily confusing the scene of his projected honey-moon with the masterpieces of literature which it would be his manly privilege to reveal to his bride. It was only that afternoon that May Welland had let him guess that she "cared" (New York's consecrated phrase of maiden avowal), and already his imagination, leaping ahead of the engagement ring, the betrothal kiss, and the march from Lohengrin, pictured her at his side in some scene of old European witchery.

[1]Luther Burbank (1849-1926) experimented with plant breeding and developed many new varieties.

He did not in the least wish the future Mrs. Newland Archer to be a simpleton. He meant her (thanks to his enlightening companionship) to develop a social tact and readiness of wit enabling her to hold her own with the most popular married women of the "younger set," in which it was the recognised custom to attract masculine homage while playfully discouraging it. If he had probed to the bottom of his vanity (as he sometimes nearly did) he would have found there the wish that his wife should be as worldly-wise and as eager to please as the married lady whose charms had held his fancy through two mildly agitated years; without, of course, any hint of the frailty which had so nearly marred that unhappy being's life, and had disarranged his own plans for a whole winter.

How this miracle of fire and ice was to be created, and to sustain itself in a harsh world, he had never taken the time to think out; but he was content to hold his view without analysing it, since he knew it was that of all the carefully-brushed, white-waistcoated, button-hole-flowered gentlemen who succeeded each other in the club box, exchanged friendly greetings with him, and turned their opera-glasses critically on the circle of ladies who were the product of the system. In matters intellectual and artistic Newland Archer felt himself distinctly the superior of these chosen specimens of old New York gentility; he had probably read more, thought more, and even seen a good deal more of the world, than any other man of the number. Singly they betrayed their inferiority; but grouped together they represented "New York," and the habit of masculine solidarity made him accept their doctrine on all the issues called moral. He instinctively felt that in this respect it would be troublesome — and also rather bad form — to strike out for himself.

"Well — upon my soul!" exclaimed Lawrence Lefferts, turning his opera-glass abruptly away from the stage. Lawrence Lefferts was, on the whole, the foremost authority on "form" in New York. He had probably devoted more time than anyone else to the study of this intricate and fascinating question; but study alone could not account for his complete and easy competence. One had only to look at him, from the slant of his bald forehead and the curve of his beautiful fair moustache to the long patent-leather feet at the other end of his lean and elegant person, to feel that the knowledge of "form" must be congenital in any one who knew how to wear such good clothes so carelessly and carry such height with so much lounging grace. As a young admirer had once said of him: "If anybody can tell a fellow just when to wear a black tie with evening clothes and when not to, it's Larry Lefferts." And on the question of pumps versus patent-leather "Oxfords" his authority had never been disputed.

"My God!" he said; and silently handed his glass to old Sillerton Jackson.

Newland Archer, following Lefferts' glance, saw with surprise that his exclamation had been occasioned by the entry of a new figure into old Mrs. Mingott's box. It was that of a slim young woman, a little less tall than May Welland, with brown hair growing in close curls about her temples and held in place by a narrow band of diamonds. The suggestion of this headdress, which gave her what was then called a "Josephine look," was carried out in the cut of the dark blue velvet gown rather theatrically caught up under her bosom by a girdle with a large old-fashioned clasp. The wearer of this unusual dress, who seemed quite unconscious of the attention it was attracting, stood a moment in the centre of the box, discussing with Mrs. Welland the propriety of taking the latter's place in the front right-hand corner; then she yielded with a slight smile, and seated herself in line with Mrs. Welland's sister-in-law, Mrs. Lovell Mingott, who was installed in the opposite corner.

Mr. Sillerton Jackson had returned the opera-glass to Lawrence Lefferts. The whole of the club turned instinctively, waiting to hear what the old man had to say; for old Mr. Jackson was as great an authority on

"family" as Lawrence Lefferts was on "form." He
knew all the ramifications of New York's cousinships;
and could not only elucidate such complicated questions as that of the connection between the Mingotts
(through the Thorleys) with the Dallases of South Caro-
lina, and that of the relationship of the elder branch of
Philadelphia Thorleys to the Albany Chiverses (on no
account to be confused with the Manson Chiverses of
University Place), but could also enumerate the leading characteristics of each family: as, for instance, the
fabulous stinginess of the younger lines of Leffertses
(the Long Island ones); or the fatal tendency of the
Rushworths to make foolish matches; or the insanity
recurring in every second generation of the Albany
Chiverses, with whom their New York cousins had
always refused to intermarry — with the disastrous exception of poor Medora Manson, who, as everybody
knew . . . but then her mother was a Rushworth.

In addition to this forest of family trees, Mr. Sillerton
Jackson carried between his narrow hollow temples,
and under his soft thatch of silver hair, a register of
most of the scandals and mysteries that had smouldered
under the unruffled surface of New York society within
the last fifty years. So far indeed did his information
extend, and so acutely retentive was his memory, that
he was supposed to be the only man who could have
told you who Julius Beaufort, the banker, really was,
and what had become of handsome Bob Spicer, old
Mrs. Manson Mingott's father, who had disappeared so
mysteriously (with a large sum of trust money) less than
a year after his marriage, on the very day that a beautiful Spanish dancer who had been delighting thronged
audiences in the old Opera-house on the Battery had
taken ship for Cuba. But these mysteries, and many
others, were closely locked in Mr. Jackson's breast; for
not only did his keen sense of honour forbid his repeating anything privately imparted, but he was fully aware
that his reputation for discretion increased his opportunities of finding out what he wanted to know.

The club box, therefore, waited in visible suspense while Mr. Sillerton Jackson handed back Lawrence Lefferts' opera-glass. For a moment he silently scrutinised the attentive group out of his filmy blue eyes overhung by old veined lids; then he gave his moustache a thoughtful twist, and said simply: "I didn't think the Mingotts would have tried it on."

Chapter II

Newland Archer, during this brief episode, had been thrown into a strange state of embarrassment.

It was annoying that the box which was thus attracting the undivided attention of masculine New York should be that in which his betrothed was seated between her mother and aunt; and for a moment he could not identify the lady in the Empire dress, nor imagine why her presence created such excitement among the initiated. Then light dawned on him, and with it came a momentary rush of indignation. No, indeed; no one would have thought the Mingotts would have tried it on!

But they had; they undoubtedly had; for the low-toned comments behind him left no doubt in Archer's mind that the young woman was May Welland's cousin, the cousin always referred to in the family as "poor Ellen Olenska." Archer knew that she had suddenly arrived from Europe a day or two previously; he had even heard from Miss Welland (not disapprovingly) that she had been to see poor Ellen, who was staying with old Mrs. Mingott. Archer entirely approved of family solidarity, and one of the qualities he most admired in the Mingotts was their resolute championship of the few black sheep that their blameless stock had produced. There was nothing mean or ungenerous in the young man's heart, and he was glad that his future wife should not be restrained by false prudery from being kind (in private) to her unhappy cousin; but to receive Countess Olenska in the family circle was a different thing from producing her in public, at the Opera of all places, and in the very box with the young girl whose engagement to him, Newland Archer, was to be announced within a few weeks. No, he felt as old Sillerton Jackson felt; he did not think the Mingotts would have tried it on!

He knew, of course, that whatever man dared (within Fifth Avenue's limits) that old Mrs. Manson Mingott, the Matriarch of the line, would dare. He had always admired the high and mighty old lady, who, in spite of having been only Catherine Spicer of Staten Island, with a father mysteriously discredited, and neither money nor position enough to make people forget it, had allied herself with the head of the wealthy Mingott line, married two of her daughters to "foreigners" (an Italian Marquis and an English banker), and put the crowning touch to her audacities by building a large house of pale cream-coloured stone (when brown sandstone seemed as much the only wear as a frock-coat in the afternoon) in an inaccessible wilderness near the Central Park.

Old Mrs. Mingott's foreign daughters had become a legend. They never came back to see their mother, and the latter being, like many persons of active mind and dominating will, sedentary and corpulent in her habit, had philosophically remained at home. But the cream-coloured house (supposed to be modelled on the private hotels of the Parisian aristocracy) was there as a visible proof of her moral courage, and she throned in it, among pre-Revolutionary furniture and souvenirs of the Tuileries of Louis Napoleon (where she had shone in her middle age), as placidly as if there were nothing peculiar in living above Thirty-fourth Street, or in having French windows that opened like doors instead of sashes that pushed up.

Everyone (including Mr. Sillerton Jackson) was agreed that old Catherine had never had beauty — a gift which, in the eyes of New York, justified every success, and excused a certain number of failings. Unkind people said that, like her Imperial namesake, she had won her way to success by strength of will and hardness of heart, and a kind of haughty effrontery that was somehow justified by the extreme decency and dignity of her private life. Mr. Manson Mingott had died when she was only twenty-eight, and had "tied up" the money with an additional caution born of the general distrust of the Spicers; but his bold young widow went her way fearlessly, mingled freely in foreign society, married her daughters in heaven knew what corrupt and fashionable circles, hobnobbed with Dukes and Ambassadors, associated familiarly with Papists, entertained Opera singers, and was the intimate friend of Mme. Taglioni; and all the while (as Sillerton Jackson was the first to proclaim) there had never been a breath on her reputation; the only respect, he always added, in which she differed from the earlier Catherine.

Mrs. Manson Mingott had long since succeeded in untying her husband's fortune, and had lived in affluence for half a century; but memories of her early straits had made her excessively thrifty, and though, when she bought a dress or a piece of furniture, she took care that it should be of the best, she could not bring herself to spend much on the transient pleasures of the table. Therefore, for totally different reasons, her food was as poor as Mrs. Archer's, and her wines did nothing to redeem it. Her relatives considered that the penury of her, table discredited the Mingott name, which had always been associated with good living; but people continued to come to her in spite of the "made dishes" and flat champagne, and in reply to the remonstrances of her son Lovell (who tried to retrieve the family credit by having the best *chef* in New York) she used to say laughingly: "What's the use of two good cooks in one family, now that I've married the girls and can't eat sauces?"

Newland Archer, as he mused on these things, had once more turned his eyes toward the Mingott box. He saw that Mrs. Welland and her sister-in-law were facing their semi-circle of critics with the Mingottian *aplomb*° which old Catherine had inculcated in all her tribe, and that only May Welland betrayed, by a heightened colour (perhaps due to the knowledge that he was watching her) a sense of the gravity of the situation. As for the cause of the commotion, she sat gracefully in her corner of the box, her eyes fixed on the stage, and revealing, as she leaned forward, a little more shoulder and bosom than New York was accustomed to seeing, at least in ladies who had reasons for wishing to pass unnoticed.

Few things seemed to Newland Archer more awful than an offence against "Taste," that far-off divinity of whom "Form" was the mere visible representative and vicegerent.° Madame Olenska's pale and serious face appealed to his fancy as suited to the occasion and to her unhappy situation; but the way her dress (which had no tucker) sloped away from her thin shoulders shocked and troubled him. He hated to think of May Welland's being exposed to the influence of a young woman so careless of the dictates of Taste.

"After all," he heard one of the younger men begin behind him (everybody talked through the Mephisto-pheles-and-Martha scenes), "after all, just *what* happened?"

"Well—she left him; nobody attempts to deny that."

"He's an awful brute, isn't he?" continued the young enquirer, a candid Thorley, who was evidently preparing to enter the lists as the lady's champion.

"The very worst; I knew him at Nice," said Lawrence Lefferts with authority. "A half-paralysed white sneering fellow—rather handsome head, but eyes with a lot of lashes. Well, I'll tell you the sort: when he wasn't with women he was collecting china. Paying any price for both, I understand."

There was a general laugh, and the young champion said: "Well, then—?"

"Well, then; she bolted with his secretary."

"Oh, I see." The champion's face fell.

"It didn't last long, though: I heard of her a few months later living alone in Venice. I believe Lovell Mingott went out to get her. He said she was desperately unhappy. That's all right—but this parading her at the Opera's another thing."

"Perhaps," young Thorley hazarded, "she's too unhappy to be left at home."

This was greeted with an irreverent laugh, and the youth blushed deeply, and tried to look as if he had meant to insinuate what knowing people called a *"double entendre."*°

"Well—it's queer to have brought Miss Welland, anyhow," someone said in a low tone, with a sideglance at Archer.

"Oh, that's part of the campaign: Granny's orders, no doubt," Lefferts laughed. "When the old lady does a thing she does it thoroughly."

The act was ending, and there was a general stir in the box. Suddenly Newland Archer felt himself impelled to decisive action. The desire to be the first man to enter Mrs. Mingott's box, to proclaim to the waiting world his engagement to May Welland, and to see her through whatever difficulties her cousin's anomalous° situation might involve her in; this impulse had abruptly overruled all scruples and hesitations, and sent him hurrying through the red corridors to the farther side of the house.

As he entered the box his eyes met Miss Welland's, and he saw that she had instantly understood his motive, though the family dignity which both considered so high a virtue would not permit her to tell him so. The persons of their world lived in an atmosphere of faint implications and pale delicacies, and the fact that he and she understood each other without a word seemed to the young man to bring them nearer than any explanation would have done. Her eyes said: "You see why Mamma brought me," and his answered: "I would not for the world have had you stay away."

"You know my niece Countess Olenska?" Mrs. Welland enquired as she shook hands with her future son-in-law. Archer bowed without extending his hand, as was the custom on being introduced to a lady; and Ellen Olenska bent her head slightly, keeping her own pale-gloved hands clasped on her huge fan of eagle feathers. Having greeted Mrs. Lovell Mingott, a large blonde lady in creaking satin, he sat down beside his betrothed, and said in a low tone: "I hope you've told Madame Olenska that we're engaged? I want every-body to know—I want you to let me announce it this evening at the ball."

Miss Welland's face grew rosy as the dawn, and she looked at him with radiant eyes. "If you can persuade Mamma," she said; "but why should we change what is already settled?" He made no answer but that which his eyes returned, and she added, still more confidently smiling: "Tell my cousin yourself: I give you leave. She says she used to play with you when you were children."

She made way for him by pushing back her chair, and promptly, and a little ostentatiously, with the desire that the whole house should see what he was doing, Archer seated himself at the Countess Olenska's side.

"We *did* use to play together, didn't we?" she asked, turning her grave eyes to his. "You were a horrid boy, and kissed me once behind a door; but it was your cousin Vandie Newland, who never looked at me, that I was in love with." Her glance swept the horse-shoe curve of boxes. "Ah, how this brings it all back to me—I see everybody here in knickerbockers and panta-lettes," she said, with her trailing slightly foreign ac-cent, her eyes returning to his face.

Agreeable as their expression was, the young man was shocked that they should reflect so unseemly a picture of the august tribunal before which, at that very moment, her case was being tried. Nothing could be in worse taste than misplaced flippancy; and he answered somewhat stiffly: "Yes, you have been away a very long time."

"Oh, centuries and centuries; so long," she said, "that

I'm sure I'm dead and buried, and this dear old place is heaven"; which, for reasons he could not define, struck Newland Archer as an even more disrespectful way of describing New York society.

It was Henry James, however, who did most to transform the purpose of the novel from being a remarkably good story to a serious art form. Even Hawthorne and Melville had addressed themselves initially to the telling of a good story. Emphasis on the structure of the novel was a new idea begun in Europe and applied in fine by Henry James. Although he rejected America as being incompatible with the life of an artist, he did not cut off all ties with his homeland. As a matter of fact he understood far more about a certain class of Americans than did his more patriotic contemporaries, and centered most of his best works around American characters.

Whether or not Americans were the central figures of his works, James viewed American life differently from his predecessors. The themes he generally chose to illuminate can be called examinations of the moral intellect. This concern for tenets of morality in the wholly independent intellect, the truly free spirit, was rare in American letters. Perhaps this is why Jamesian fiction is usually "traced" to certain characteristics in Hawthorne, who was also interested in the moral concepts of the unencumbered, rebellious intellect, although his point of departure was deeply religious. James's villains were those persons whose values were reluctantly accepted by high society in England and America—social climbing, social solidarity, greed— values frowned upon as in "bad taste." The behavior, tastes, and ambitions of his heroes and heroines were founded not on religious instruction or social commandments, but on a complex cerebral requirement. They exercised, so to speak, the "will to be good."

In *Washington Square* the plain, dull Catherine Sloper emerges as a woman of subdued but invulnerable moral fiber. In *The Portrait of a Lady*, the drama consists of Isabel

Archer's struggle to maintain integrity in a situation of delicate sensibilities. Hyacinth Robinson, in *The Princess Casamassima,* when faced with the dilemma of breaking a pledge of faith and violating his own sense of honor, resolves it in the one manner he could without giving up pledge or honor.

A less weighty, but certainly most fascinating study of this theme of integrity versus evil can be seen in *The Turn of the Screw,* which comprises this unit.

It is from the modes of these writers, then — romanticism, sentimentality, satire and allegory, regionalism and nationalism — that modern American fiction writers received their literary heritage. What they did with this heritage is yet another book.

The Turn of the Screw

HENRY JAMES

The story had held us, round the fire, sufficiently breathless, but except the obvious remark that it was gruesome, as, on Christmas eve in an old house, a strange tale should essentially be, I remember no comment uttered till somebody happened to say that it was the only case he had met in which such a visitation had fallen on a child. The case, I may mention, was that of an apparition in just such an old house as had gathered us for the occasion — an appearance, of a dreadful kind, to a little boy sleeping in the room with his mother and waking her up in the terror of it; waking her not to dissipate° his dread and soothe him to sleep again, but to encounter also, herself, before she had succeeded in doing so, the same sight that had shaken him. It was this observation that drew from Douglas — not immediately, but later in the evening — a reply that had the interesting consequence to which I call attention. Someone else told a story not particularly effective, which I saw he was not following. This I took for a sign that he had himself something to produce and that we should only have to wait. We waited in fact till two nights later; but that same evening, before we scattered, he brought out what was in his mind.

"I quite agree — in regard to Griffin's ghost, or whatever it was — that its appearing first to the little boy, at so tender an age, adds a particular touch. But it's not the first occurrence of its charming kind that I know to have involved a child. If the child gives the effect another turn of the screw, what do you say to *two* children — ?"

"We say, of course," somebody exclaimed, "that they give two turns! Also that we want to hear about them."

I can see Douglas there before the fire, to which he had got up to present his back, looking down at his interlocutor° with his hands in his pockets. "Nobody but me, till now, has ever heard. It's quite too horrible." This, naturally, was declared by several voices to give the thing the utmost price, and our friend, with quiet art, prepared his triumph by turning his eyes over the rest of us and going on: "It's beyond everything. Nothing at all that I know touches it."

"For sheer terror?" I remember asking.

He seemed to say it was not so simple as that; to be really at a loss how to qualify it. He passed his hand over his eyes, made a little wincing grimace. "For dreadful—dreadfulness!"

"Oh, how delicious!" cried one of the women.

He took no notice of her; he looked at me, but as if, instead of me, he saw what he spoke of. "For general uncanny ugliness and horror and pain."

"Well then," I said, "just sit right down and begin."

He turned round to the fire, gave a kick to a log, watched it an instant. Then as he faced us again: "I can't begin. I shall have to send to town." There was a unanimous groan at this, and much reproach; after which, in his preoccupied way, he explained. "The story's written. It's in a locked drawer—it has not been out for years. I could write to my man and enclose the key; he could send down the packet as he finds it." It was to me in particular that he appeared to propound this—appeared almost to appeal for aid not to hesitate. He had broken a thickness of ice, the formation of many a winter; had had his reasons for a long silence. The others resented postponement, but it was just his scruples that charmed me. I adjured him to write by the first post and to agree with us for an early hearing; then I asked him if the experience in question had been his own. To this his answer was prompt. "Oh, thank God, no!"

"And is the record yours? You took the thing down?"

"Nothing but the impression. I took that *here*"—he tapped his heart. "I've never lost it."

"Then your manuscript—?"

"Is in old, faded ink, and in the most beautiful hand." He hung fire again. "A woman's. She has been dead these twenty years. She sent me the pages in question before she died." They were all listening now, and of course there was somebody to be arch, or at any rate to draw the inference. But if he put the inference by without a smile it was also without irritation. "She was a most charming person, but

she was ten years older than I. She was my sister's governess," he quietly said. "She was the most agreeable woman
I've ever known in her position; she would have been
worthy of any whatever. It was long ago, and this episode
was long before. I was at Trinity, and I found her at home
on my coming down the second summer. I was much there
that year — it was a beautiful one; and we had, in her off-
hours some strolls and talks in the garden — talks in which
she struck me as awfully clever and nice. Oh yes; don't
grin: I liked her extremely and am glad to this day to think
she liked me too. If she hadn't she wouldn't have told me.
She had never told anyone. It wasn't simply that she said
so, but that I knew she hadn't. I was sure; I could see.
You'll easily judge why when you hear."

"Because the thing had been such a scare?"

He continued to fix me. "You'll easily judge," he repeated: "*you* will."

I fixed him too. "I see. She was in love."

He laughed for the first time. "You *are* acute. Yes, she
was in love. That is, she had been. That came out — she
couldn't tell her story without its coming out. I saw it, and
she saw I saw it; but neither of us spoke of it. I remember
the time and the place — the corner of the lawn, the shade of
the great beeches and the long, hot summer afternoon. It
wasn't a scene for a shudder; but oh — !" He quitted the fire
and dropped back into his chair.

"You'll receive the packet Thursday morning?" I inquired.

"Probably not till the second post."

"Well then; after dinner — "

"You'll all meet me here?" He looked us round again.
"Isn't anybody going?" It was almost the tone of hope.

"Everybody will stay!"

"*I* will — and *I* will!" cried the ladies whose departure
had been fixed. Mrs. Griffin, however, expressed the need
for a little more light. "Who was it she was in love with?"

"The story will tell," I took upon myself to reply.

"Oh, I can't wait for the story!"

"The story *won't* tell," said Douglas; "not in any literal,
vulgar way."

"More's the pity, then. That's the only way I ever understand."

"Won't *you* tell, Douglas?" somebody else inquired.

He sprang to his feet again. "Yes—tomorrow. Now I must go to bed. Good-night." And quickly catching up a candlestick, he left us slightly bewildered. From our end of the great brown hall we heard his step on the stair; whereupon Mrs. Griffin spoke. "Well, if I don't know who she was in love with, I know who *he* was."

"She was ten years older," said her husband.

"*Raison de plus*[1]—at that age! But it's rather nice, his long reticence."

"Forty years!" Griffin put in.

"With this outbreak at last."

"The outbreak," I returned, "will make a tremendous occasion of Thursday night"; and everyone so agreed with me that, in the light of it, we lost all attention for everything else. The last story, however incomplete and like the mere opening of a serial, had been told; we handshook and "candlestuck," as somebody said, and went to bed.

I knew the next day that a letter containing the key had, by the first post, gone off to his London apartments; but in spite of—or perhaps just on account of—the eventual diffusion of this knowledge we quite let him alone till after dinner, till such an hour of the evening, in fact, as might best accord with the kind of emotion on which our hopes were fixed. Then he became as communicative as we could desire and indeed gave us his best reason for being so. We had it from him again before the fire in the hall, as we had had our mild wonders of the previous night. It appeared that the narrative he had promised to read us really required for a proper intelligence a few words of prologue. Let me say here distinctly, to have done with it, that this narrative, from an exact transcript of my own made much later, is what I shall presently give. Poor Douglas, before his death—when it was in sight—committed to me the manuscript that reached him on the third of these days and that, on the same spot, with immense effect, he began to

[1] Reason enough.

read to our hushed little circle on the night of the fourth. The departing ladies who had said they would stay didn't, of course, thank heaven, stay: they departed, in consequence of arrangements made, in a rage of curiosity, as they professed, produced by the touches with which he had already worked us up. But that only made his little final auditory more compact and select, kept it, round the hearth, subject to a common thrill.

The first of these touches conveyed that the written statement took up the tale at a point after it had, in a manner, begun. The fact to be in possession of was therefore that his old friend, the youngest of several daughters of a poor country parson, had, at the age of twenty, on taking service for the first time in the schoolroom, come up to London, in trepidation, to answer in person an advertisement that had already placed her in brief correspondence with the advertiser. This person proved, on her presenting herself, for judgment, at a house in Harley Street, that impressed her as vast and imposing—this prospective patron proved a gentleman, a bachelor in the prime of life, such a figure as had never risen, save in a dream or an old novel, before a fluttered, anxious girl out of a Hampshire vicarage. One could easily fix his type; it never, happily, dies out. He was handsome and bold and pleasant, off-hand and gay and kind. He struck her, inevitably, as gallant and splendid, but what took her most of all and gave her the courage she afterwards showed was that he put the whole thing to her as a kind of favour, an obligation he should gratefully incur. She conceived him as rich, but as fearfully extravagant—saw him all in a glow of high fashion, of good looks, of expensive habits, of charming ways with women. He had for his own town residence a big house filled with the spoils of travel and the trophies of the chase; but it was to his country home, an old family place in Essex, that he wished her immediately to proceed.

He had been left, by the death of their parents in India, guardian to a small nephew and a small niece, children of a younger, a military brother, whom he had lost two years before. These children were, by the strangest of chances for a man in his position—a lone man without the right sort of experience or a grain of patience—very heavily on his hands. It had all been a great worry and, on his own part doubtless, a series of blunders, but he immensely pitied the poor chicks and had done all he could: had in particular sent them down to his other house, the proper place for them being of course the country, and kept them there, from the first, with the best people he could find to look after them, parting even with his own servants to wait on them and going down himself, whenever he might, to see how they were doing. The awkward thing was that they had practically no other relations and that his own affairs took up all his time. He had put them in possession of Bly, which was healthy and secure, and had placed at the head of their little establishment—but below stairs only—an excellent woman, Mrs. Grose, whom he was sure his visitor would like and who had formerly been maid to his mother. She was now housekeeper and was also acting for the time as superintendent to the little girl, of whom, without children of her own, she was, by good luck, extremely fond. There were plenty of people to help, but of course the young lady who should go down as governess would be in supreme authority. She would also have, in holidays, to look after the small boy, who had been for a term at school— young as he was to be sent, but what else could be done?— and who, as the holidays were about to begin, would be back from one day to the other. There had been for the two children at first a young lady whom they had had the misfortune to lose. She had done for them quite beautifully —she was a most respectable person—till her death, the great awkwardness of which had, precisely, left no alternative but the school for little Miles. Mrs. Grose, since then, in the way of manners and things, had done as she could for Flora; and there were, further, a cook, a housemaid, a dairywoman, an old pony, an old groom, and an old gardener, all likewise thoroughly respectable.

So far had Douglas presented his picture when someone put a question. "And what did the former governess die of? —of so much respectability?"

Our friend's answer was prompt. "That will come out. I don't anticipate."

"Excuse me—I thought that was just what you *are* doing."

"In her successor's place," I suggested, "I should have wished to learn if the office brought with it—"

"Necessary danger to life?" Douglas completed my thought. "She did wish to learn, and she did learn. You shall hear tomorrow what she learnt. Meanwhile, of course, the prospect struck her as slightly grim. She was young, untried, nervous: it was a vision of serious duties and little company, of really great loneliness. She hesitated—took a couple of days to consult and consider. But the salary offered much exceeded her modest measure, and on a second interview she faced the music, she engaged." And Douglas, with this, made a pause that, for the benefit of the company, moved me to throw in—

"The moral of which was of course the seduction exercised by the splendid young man. She succumbed to it."

He got up and, as he had done the night before, went to the fire, gave a stir to a log with his foot, then stood a moment with his back to us. "She saw him only twice."

"Yes, but that's just the beauty of her passion."

A little to my surprise, on this, Douglas turned round to me. "It *was* the beauty of it. There were others," he went on, "who hadn't succumbed. He told her frankly all his difficulty—that for several applicants the conditions had been prohibitive. They were, somehow, simply afraid. It sounded dull—it sounded strange; and all the more so because of his main condition."

"Which was—?"

"That she should never trouble him—but never, never: neither appeal nor complain nor write about anything; only meet all questions herself, receive all moneys from his solicitor,° take the whole thing over and let him alone. She promised to do this, and she mentioned to me that when, for a moment, disburdened, delighted, he held her hand, thanking her for the sacrifice, she already felt rewarded."

"But was that all her reward?" one of the ladies asked.

"She never saw him again."

"Oh!" said the lady; which, as our friend immediately left us again, was the only other word of importance contributed to the subject till, the next night, by the corner of the hearth, in the best chair, he opened the faded red cover of a thin old-fashioned gilt-edged album. The whole thing took indeed more nights than one, but on the first occasion the same lady put another question. "What is your title?"

"I haven't one."

"Oh, *I* have!" I said. But Douglas, without heeding me, had begun to read with a fine clearness that was like a rendering to the ear of the beauty of his author's hand.

I

I remember the whole beginning as a succession of flights and drops, a little see-saw of the right throbs and the wrong. After rising, in town, to meet his appeal, I had at all events a couple of very bad days — found myself doubtful again, felt indeed sure I had made a mistake. In this state of mind I spent the long hours of bumping, swinging coach that carried me to the stopping-place at which I was to be met by a vehicle from the house. This convenience, I was told, had been ordered, and I found, toward the close of the June afternoon, a commodious fly° in waiting for me. Driving at that hour, on a lovely day, through a country to which the summer sweetness seemed to offer me a friendly welcome, my fortitude mounted afresh and, as we turned into the avenue, encountered a reprieve that was probably but a proof of the point to which it had sunk. I suppose I had expected, or had dreaded, something so melancholy that what greeted me was a good surprise. I remember as a most pleasant impression the broad, clear front, its open windows and fresh curtains and the pair of maids looking out; I remember the lawn and the bright flowers and the crunch of my wheels on the gravel and the clustered treetops over which the rooks° circled and cawed in the golden sky. The scene had a greatness that made it a different affair from my own scant home, and there immediately appeared at the door, with a little girl in her hand, a civil person who dropped me as decent a curtsey as if I had been the mistress or a distinguished visitor. I had received in Harley Street a narrower notion of the place, and that, as I recalled it, made me think the proprietor still more of a gentleman, suggested that what I was to enjoy might be something beyond his promise.

I had no drop again till the next day, for I was carried triumphantly through the following hours by my introduction to the younger of my pupils. The little girl who accompanied Mrs. Grose appeared to me on the spot a creature so charming as to make it a great fortune to have to do with her. She was the most beautiful child I had ever seen, and I afterwards wondered that my employer had not told me more of her. I slept little that night—I was too much excited; and this astonished me too, I recollect, remained with me, adding to my sense of the liberality with which I was treated. The large, impressive room, one of the best in the house, the great state bed, as I almost felt it, the full, figured draperies, the long glasses in which, for the first time, I could see myself from head to foot, all struck me—like the extraordinary charm of my small charge—as so many things thrown in. It was thrown in as well, from the first moment, that I should get on with Mrs. Grose in a relation over which, on my way, in the coach, I fear I had rather brooded. The only thing indeed that in this early outlook might have made me shrink again was the clear circumstance of her being so glad to see me. I perceived within half an hour that she was so glad—stout, simple, plain, clean, wholesome woman—as to be positively on her guard against showing it too much. I wondered even then a little why she should wish not to show it, and that, with reflection, with suspicion, might of course have made me uneasy.

But it was a comfort that there could be no uneasiness in a connection with anything so beatific° as the radiant image of my little girl, the vision of whose angelic beauty had probably more than anything else to do with the restlessness that, before morning, made me several times rise and wander about my room to take in the whole picture and prospect; to watch, from my open window, the faint summer dawn, to look at such portions of the rest of the house as I could catch, and to listen, while, in the fading dusk, the first birds began to twitter, for the possible recurrence of a sound or two, less natural and not without, but within, that I had fancied I heard. There had been a moment when I believed I recognised, faint and far, the cry of a child; there had been another when I found myself just consciously starting as at the passage, before my door, of a light footstep. But these fancies were not marked enough not to be thrown off, and it is only in the light, or the gloom, I should rather say, of other and subsequent matters that they now come back to me. To watch, teach, "form" little Flora would too evidently be the making of a happy and useful life. It had been agreed between us downstairs that after this first occasion I should have her as a matter of course at night, her small white bed being already arranged, to that end, in my room. What I had undertaken was the whole care of her, and she had remained, just this last time, with Mrs. Grose only as an effect of our consideration for my inevitable strangeness and her natural timidity. In spite of this timidity—which the child herself, in the oddest way in the world, had been perfectly frank and brave about, allowing it, without a sign of uncomfortable consciousness, with the deep, sweet serenity indeed of one of Raphael's holy infants, to be discussed, to be imputed° to her and to determine us—I felt quite sure she would presently like me. It was part of what I already liked Mrs. Grose herself for, the pleasure I could see her feel in my admiration and wonder as I sat at supper with four tall candles and with my pupil, in a high chair and a bib, brightly facing me, between them, over bread and milk. There were naturally things that in Flora's presence could pass between us only as prodigious and gratified looks, obscure and round-about allusions.

"And the little boy—does he look like her? Is he too so very remarkable?"

One wouldn't flatter a child. "Oh, Miss, *most* remarkable. If you think well of this one!"—and she stood there with a plate in her hand, beaming at our companion, who looked from one of us to the other with placid heavenly eyes that contained nothing to check us.

"Yes; if I do—?"

"You *will* be carried away by the little gentleman!"

"Well, that, I think, is what I came for—to be carried away. I'm afraid, however," I remember feeling the impulse to add, "I'm rather easily carried away. I was carried away in London!"

I can still see Mrs. Grose's broad face as she took this in. "In Harley Street?"

"In Harley Street."

"Well, Miss, you're not the first—and you won't be the last."

"Oh, I've no pretension," I could laugh, "to being the only one. My other pupil, at any rate, as I understand, comes back tomorrow?"

"Not tomorrow—Friday, Miss. He arrives, as you did, by the coach, under care of the guard, and is to be met by the same carriage."

I forthwith expressed that the proper as well as the pleasant and friendly thing would be therefore that on the arrival of the public conveyance I should be in waiting for him with his little sister; an idea in which Mrs. Grose concurred so heartily that I somehow took her manner as a kind of comforting pledge—never falsified, thank heaven!—that we should on every question be quite at one. Oh, she was glad I was there!

What I felt the next day was, I suppose, nothing that could be fairly called a reaction from the cheer of my arrival; it was probably at the most only a slight oppression produced by a fuller measure of the scale, as I walked round them, gazed up at them, took them in, of my new circumstances. They had, as it were, an extent and mass for which I had not been prepared and in the presence of which I found myself, freshly, a little scared as well as a little proud. Lessons, in this agitation, certainly suffered some delay; I reflected that my first duty was, by the gentlest arts I could contrive, to win the child into the sense of knowing me. I spent the day with her out of doors; I arranged with her, to her great satisfaction, that it should be she, she only, who might show me the place. She showed it step by step and room by room and secret by secret, with droll, delightful, childish talk about it and with the result, in half an hour, of our becoming immense friends. Young as she was, I was struck, throughout our little tour, with her confidence and courage with the way, in empty chambers and dull corridors, on crooked staircases that made me pause and even on the summit of an old machicolated° square tower that made me dizzy, her morning music, her disposition to tell me so many more things than she asked, rang out and led me on. I have not seen Bly since the day I left it, and I dare say that to my older and more informed eyes it would now appear sufficiently contracted. But as my little conductress, with her hair of gold and her frock of blue, danced before me round corners and pattered down passages, I had the view of a castle of romance inhabited by a rosy sprite, such a place as would somehow, for diversion of the young idea, take all colour out of storybooks and fairy-tales. Wasn't it just a storybook over which I had fallen a-doze and a-dream? No; it was a big, ugly, antique, but convenient house, embodying a few features of a building still older, half replaced and half utilised, in which I had the fancy of our being almost as lost as a handful of passengers in a great drifting ship. Well, I was, strangely, at the helm!

II

This came home to me when, two days later, I drove over with Flora to meet, as Mrs. Grose said, the little gentleman; and all the more for an incident that, presenting itself the second evening, had deeply disconcerted° me. The first day had been, on the whole, as I have expressed, reassuring; but I was to see it wind up in keen apprehension. The postbag, that evening—it came late—contained a letter for me, which, however, in the hand of my employer, I found to be composed but of a few words enclosing another, addressed to himself, with a seal still unbroken. "This, I recognise, is from the head-master, and the head-master's an awful bore. Read him, please; deal with him; but mind you don't report. Not a word. I'm off!" I broke the seal with a great effort—so great a one that I was a long time coming to it; took the unopened missive at last up to my room and only attacked it just before going to bed. I had better have let it wait till morning, for it gave me a second sleepless night. With no counsel to take, the next day, I was full of distress; and it finally got so the better of me that I determined to open myself at least to Mrs. Grose.

"What does it mean? The child's dismissed his school."

She gave me a look that I remarked at the moment; then, visibly, with a quick blankness, seemed to try to take it back. "But aren't they all—?"

"Sent home—yes. But only for the holidays. Miles may never go back at all."

Consciously, under my attention, she reddened. "They won't take him?"

"They absolutely decline."

At this she raised her eyes, which she had turned from me; I saw them fill with good tears. "What has he done?"

I hesitated; then I judged best simply to hand her my letter—which, however, had the effect of making her, without taking it, simply put her hands behind her. She shook her head sadly. "Such things are not for me, Miss."

My counsellor couldn't read! I winced at my mistake, which I attenuated° as I could, and opened my letter again to repeat it to her; then, faltering in the act and folding it up once more, I put it back in my pocket. "Is he really *bad?*"

The tears were still in her eyes. "Do the gentlemen say so?"

"They go into no particulars. They simply express their regret that it should be impossible to keep him. That can have only one meaning." Mrs. Grose listened with dumb emotion; she forebore to ask me what this meaning might be; so that, presently, to put the thing with some coherence and with the mere aid of her presence to my own mind, I went on: "That he's an injury to the others."

At this, with one of the quick turns of simple folk, she suddenly flamed up. "Master Miles! *him* an injury?"

There was such a flood of good faith in it that, though I had not yet seen the child, my very fears made me jump to the absurdity of the idea. I found myself, to meet my friend the better, offering it, on the spot, sarcastically. "To his poor little innocent mates!"

"It's too dreadful," cried Mrs. Grose, "to say such cruel things! Why, he's scarce ten years old."

"Yes, yes; it would be incredible."

She was evidently grateful for such a profession. "See him, Miss, first. *Then* believe it!" I felt forthwith a new impatience to see him; it was the beginning of a curiosity that, for all the next hours, was to deepen almost to pain. Mrs. Grose was aware, I could judge, of what she had produced in me, and she followed it up with assurance. "You might as well believe it of the little lady. Bless her," she added the next moment—"*look* at her!"

I turned and saw that Flora, whom, ten minutes before, I had established in the schoolroom with a sheet of white paper, a pencil, and a copy of nice "round O's," now presented herself to view at the open door. She expressed in her little way an extraordinary detachment from disagreeable duties, looking to me, however, with a great childish light that seemed to offer it as a mere result of the affection she had conceived for my person, which had rendered necessary that she should follow me. I needed nothing more than this to feel the full force of Mrs. Grose's comparison, and, catching my pupil in my arms, covered her with kisses in which there was a sob of atonement.

None the less, the rest of the day, I watched for further occasion to approach my colleague, especially as, toward evening, I began to fancy she rather sought to avoid me. I overtook her, I remember, on the staircase; we went down together, and at the bottom I detained her, holding her there with a hand on her arm. "I take what you said to me at noon as a declaration that *you've* never known him to be bad."

She threw back her head; she had clearly, by this time, and very honestly, adopted an attitude. "Oh, never known him—I don't pretend *that!*"

I was upset again. "Then you *have* known him—?"

"Yes indeed, Miss, thank God!"

On reflection I accepted this. "You mean that a boy who never is—?"

"Is no boy for *me!*"

I held her tighter. "You like them with the spirit to be

naughty?" Then, keeping pace with her answer, "So do I!"
I eagerly brought out. "But not to the degree to contaminate—"

"To contaminate?"—my big word left her at a loss. I
explained it. "To corrupt."

She stared, taking my meaning in: but it produced in her
an odd laugh. "Are you afraid he'll corrupt *you?*" She put
the question with such a fine bold humour that, with a
laugh, a little silly doubtless, to match her own, I gave way
for the time to the apprehension of ridicule.

But the next day, as the hour for my drive approached, I
cropped up in another place. "What was the lady who was
here before?"

"The last governess? She was also young and pretty—
almost as young and almost as pretty, Miss, even as you."

"Ah, then, I hope her youth and her beauty helped her!"
I recollect throwing off. "He seems to like us young and
pretty!"

"Oh, he *did*," Mrs. Grose assented: "it was the way he
liked everyone!" She had no sooner spoken indeed than
she caught herself up. "I mean that's *his* way—the master's."

I was struck. "But of whom did you speak first?"

She looked blank, but she coloured. "Why, of *him*."

"Of the master?"

"Of who else?"

There was so obviously no one else that the next moment
I had lost my impression of her having accidentally said
more than she meant; and I merely asked what I wanted to
know. "Did *she* see anything in the boy—?"

"That wasn't right? She never told me."

I had a scruple,° but I overcame it. "Was she careful—
particular?"

Mrs. Grose appeared to try to be conscientious. "About
some things—yes."

"But not about all?"

Again she considered. "Well, Miss—she's gone. I won't
tell tales."

"I quite understand your feeling," I hastened to reply;

but I thought it, after an instant, not opposed to this concession to pursue: "Did she die here?"

"No—she went off."

I don't know what there was in this brevity of Mrs. Grose's that struck me as ambiguous. "Went off to die?" Mrs. Grose looked straight out of the window, but I felt that, hypothetically, I had a right to know what young persons engaged for Bly were expected to do. "She was taken ill, you mean, and went home?"

"She was not taken ill, so far as appeared, in this house. She left it, at the end of the year, to go home, as she said, for a short holiday, to which the time she had put in had certainly given her a right. We had then a young woman—a nursemaid who had stayed on and who was a good girl and clever; and *she* took the children altogether for the interval. But our young lady never came back, and at the very moment I was expecting her I heard from the master that she was dead."

I turned this over. "But of what?"

"He never told me! But please, Miss," said Mrs. Grose, "I must get to my work."

III

Her thus turning her back on me was fortunately not, for my just preoccupations, a snub that could check the growth of our mutual esteem. We met, after I had brought home little Miles, more intimately than ever on the ground of my stupefaction, my general emotion: so monstrous was I then ready to pronounce it that such a child as had now been revealed to me should be under an interdict.° I was a little late on the scene, and I felt, as he stood wistfully looking out for me before the door of the inn at which the coach had put him down, that I had seen him, on the instant, without and within, in the great glow of freshness, the same positive fragrance of purity, in which I had, from the first moment, seen his little sister. He was incredibly beautiful, and Mrs. Grose had put her finger on it: everything but a sort of passion of tenderness for him was swept away by his presence. What I then and there took him to my heart for was something divine that I have never found to the same degree in any child — his indescribable little air of knowing nothing in the world but love. It would have been impossible to carry a bad name with a greater sweetness of innocence, and by the time I had got back to Bly with him I remained merely bewildered — so far, that is, as I was not outraged — by the sense of the horrible letter locked up in my room, in a drawer. As soon as I could compass° a private word with Mrs. Grose I declared to her that it was grotesque.

She promptly understood me. "You mean the cruel charge — ?"

"It doesn't live an instant. My dear woman, *look* at him!"

She smiled at my pretension to have discovered his charm. "I assure you, Miss, I do nothing else! What will you say, then?" she immediately added.

"In answer to the letter?" I had made up my mind. "Nothing."

"And to his uncle?"

I was incisive. "Nothing."

"And to the boy himself?"

I was wonderful. "Nothing."

She gave with her apron a great wipe to her mouth. "Then I'll stand by you. We'll see it out."

"We'll see it out!" I ardently echoed, giving her my hand to make it a vow.

She held me there a moment, then whisked up her apron again with her detached hand. "Would you mind, Miss, if I used the freedom — "

"To kiss me? No!" I took the good creature in my arms and, after we had embraced like sisters, felt still more fortified and indignant.

This, at all events, was for the time: a time so full that, as I recall the way it went, it reminds me of all the art I now need to make it a little distinct. What I look back at with amazement is the situation I accepted. I had undertaken, with my companion, to see it out, and I was under a charm, apparently, that could smooth away the extent and the far and difficult connections of such an effort. I was lifted aloft on a great wave of infatuation and pity. I found it simple, in my ignorance, my confusion, and perhaps my conceit, to assume that I could deal with a boy whose education for the world was all on the point of beginning. I am unable even to remember at this day what proposal I framed for the end of his holidays and the resumption of his studies. Lessons with me, indeed, that charming summer, we all had a theory that he was to have; but I now feel that, for weeks, the lessons must have been rather my own. I learnt something — at first certainly — that had not been one of the teachings of my small, smothered life; learnt to be amused, and even amusing, and not to think for the morrow. It was the first time, in a manner, that I had known space and air and freedom, all the music of summer and all the mystery of nature. And then there was consideration — and consideration was sweet. Oh, it was a trap — not designed, but deep — to my imagination, to my delicacy, perhaps to my vanity; to whatever, in me, was most excitable. The best way to picture it all is to say that I was off my guard. They gave me so little trouble — they were of a gentleness so extraordinary. I used to speculate — but even this with a dim disconnectedness — as to how the rough future (for all futures are rough!) would handle them and might bruise them. They had the bloom of health and happiness; and yet, as if I had been in charge of a pair of little grandees,° of princes of the blood, for whom everything, to be right, would have to be enclosed and protected, the only form that, in my fancy, the after-years could take for them was that of a romantic, a really royal extension of the garden and the park. It may be, of course, above all, that what suddenly broke into this gives the previous time a charm of stillness — that hush in which something gathers or crouches. The change was actually like the spring of a beast.

In the first weeks the days were long; they often, at their finest, gave me what I used to call my own hour, the hour when, for my pupils, tea-time and bed-time having come and gone, I had, before my final retirement, a small interval alone. Much as I liked my companions, this hour was the thing in the day I liked most; and I liked it best of all when, as the light faded—or rather, I should say, the day lingered and the last calls of the last birds sounded, in a flushed sky, from the old trees—I could take a turn into the grounds and enjoy, almost with a sense of property that amused and flattered me, the beauty and dignity of the place. It was a pleasure at these moments to feel myself tranquil and justified; doubtless, perhaps, also to reflect that by my discretion, my quiet good sense and general high propriety, I was giving pleasure—if he ever thought of it!—to the person to whose pressure I had responded. What I was doing was what he had earnestly hoped and directly asked of me, and that I *could*, after all, do it proved even a greater joy than I had expected. I dare say I fancied myself, in short, a remarkable young woman and took comfort in the faith that this would more publicly appear. Well, I needed to be remarkable to offer a front to the remarkable things that presently gave their first sign.

It was plump, one afternoon, in the middle of my very hour: the children were tucked away and I had come out for my stroll. One of the thoughts that, as I don't in the least shrink now from noting, used to be with me in these wanderings was that it would be as charming as a charming story suddenly to meet someone. Someone would appear there at the turn of a path and would stand before me and smile and approve. I didn't ask more than that—I only asked that he should *know;* and the only way to be sure he knew would be to see it, and the kind light of it, in his handsome face. That was exactly present to me—by which I mean the face was—when, on the first of these occasions, at the end of a long June day, I stopped short on emerging from one of the plantations and coming into view of the house. What arrested me on the spot—and with a shock much greater than any vision had allowed for—was the sense that my imagination had, in a flash, turned real. He did stand there!—but high up, beyond the lawn and at the very top of the tower to which, on that first morning, little Flora had conducted me. This tower was one of a pair—square, incongruous, crenelated° structures—that were distinguished, for some reason, though I could see little

difference, as the new and the old. They flanked opposite
ends of the house and were probably architectural absurdi-
ties, redeemed in a measure indeed by not being wholly
disengaged nor of a height too pretentious, dating, in their
gingerbread antiquity, from a romantic revival that was
already a respectable past. I admired them, had fancies
about them, for we could all profit in a degree, especially
when they loomed through the dusk, by the grandeur of
their actual battlements; yet it was not at such an elevation
that the figure I had so often invoked seemed most in place.

It produced in me, this figure, in the clear twilight, I
remember, two distinct gasps of emotion, which were,
sharply, the shock of my first and that of my second surprise.
My second was a violent perception of the mistake of my
first: the man who met my eyes was not the person I had
precipitately supposed. There came to me thus a bewilderment of vision of which, after these years, there is no living
view that I can hope to give. An unknown man in a lonely
place is a permitted object of fear to a young woman privately bred; and the figure that faced me was—a few more
seconds assured me—as little anyone else I knew as it was
the image that had been in my mind. I had not seen it in
Harley Street—I had not seen it anywhere. The place,
moreover, in the strangest way in the world, had, on the
instant, and by the very fact of its appearance, become a
solitude. To me at least, making my statement here with a
deliberation with which I have never made it, the whole
feeling of the moment returns. It was as if, while I took in—
what I did take in—all the rest of the scene had been
stricken with death. I can hear again, as I write, the intense
hush in which the sounds of evening dropped. The rooks
stopped cawing in the golden sky and the friendly hour lost,
for the minute, all its voice. But there was no other change
in nature, unless indeed it were a change that I saw with a
stranger sharpness. The gold was still in the sky, the
clearness in the air, and the man who looked at me over the
battlements was as definite as a picture in a frame. That's
how I thought, with extraordinary quickness, of each person
that he might have been and that he was not. We were

confronted across our distance quite long enough for me to ask myself with intensity who then he was and to feel, as an effect of my inability to say, a wonder that in a few instants more became intense.

The great question, or one of these, is, afterwards, I know, with regard to certain matters, the question of how long they have lasted. Well, this matter of mine, think what you will of it, lasted while I caught at a dozen possibilities, none of which made a difference for the better, that I could see, in there having been in the house — and for how long, above all? — a person of whom I was in ignorance. It lasted while I just bridled° a little with the sense that my office demanded that there should be no such ignorance and no such person. It lasted while this visitant, at all events — and there was a touch of the strange freedom, as I remember, in the sign of familiarity of his wearing no hat — seemed to fix me, from his position, with just the question, just the scrutiny through the fading light, that his own presence provoked. We were too far apart to call to each other, but there was a moment at which, at shorter range, some challenge between us, breaking the hush, would have been the right result of our straight mutual stare. He was in one of the angles, the one away from the house, very erect, as it struck me, and with both hands on the ledge. So I saw him as I see the letters I form on this page; then, exactly, after a minute, as if to add to the spectacle, he slowly changed his place — passed, looking at me hard all the while, to the opposite corner of the platform. Yes, I had the sharpest sense that during this transit he never took his eyes from me, and I can see at this moment the way his hand, as he went, passed from one of the crenelations to the next. He stopped at the other corner, but less long, and even as he turned away still markedly fixed me. He turned away; that was all I knew.

IV

It was not that I didn't wait, on this occasion, for more, for I was rooted as deeply as I was shaken. Was there a "secret" at Bly — a mystery of Udolpho or an insane, an unmentionable relative kept in unsuspected confinement? I can't say how long I turned it over, or how long, in a confusion of curiosity and dread, I remained where I had had my collision; I only recall that when I re-entered the house darkness had quite closed in. Agitation, in the interval, certainly had held me and driven me, for I must, in circling about the place, have walked three miles; but I was to be, later on, so much more overwhelmed that this mere dawn of alarm was a comparatively human chill. The most singular part of it in fact — singular as the rest had been — was the part I became, in the hall, aware of in meeting Mrs. Grose. This picture comes back to me in the general train — the impression, as I received it on my return, of the wide white panelled space, bright in the lamplight and with its portraits and red carpet, and of the good surprised look of my friend, which immediately told me she had missed me. It came to me straightway, under her contact, that, with plain heartiness, mere relieved anxiety at my appearance, she knew nothing whatever that could bear upon the incident I had there ready for her. I had not suspected in advance that her comfortable face would pull me up, and I somehow measured the importance of what I had seen by my thus finding myself hesitate to mention it. Scarce anything in the whole history seems to me so odd as this fact that my real beginning of fear was one, as I may say, with the instinct of sparing my companion. On the spot, accordingly, in the pleasant hall and with her eyes on me, I, for a reason that I couldn't then have phrased, achieved an inward revolution — offered a vague pretext for my lateness and, with the plea of the beauty of the night and of the heavy dew and wet feet, went as soon as possible to my room.

Here it was another affair; here, for many days after, it was a queer affair enough. There were hours, from day to day — or at least there were moments, snatched even from clear duties — when I had to shut myself up to think. It was not so much yet that I was more nervous than I could bear to be as that I was remarkably afraid of becoming so; for the truth I had now to turn over was, simply and clearly, the truth that I could arrive at no account whatever of the visitor with whom I had been so inexplicably and yet, as it seemed to me, so intimately concerned. It took little time to see that I could sound without forms of inquiry and without exciting remark any domestic complication. The shock I had suffered must have sharpened all my senses; I felt sure, at the end of three days and as the result of mere closer attention, that I had not been practised upon by the servants nor made the object of any "game." Of whatever it was that I knew nothing was known around me. There was but one sane inference: someone had taken a liberty rather gross. That was what, repeatedly, I dipped into my room and locked the door to say to myself. We had been, collectively, subject to an intrusion; some unscrupulous traveller, curious in old houses, had made his way in unobserved, enjoyed the prospect from the best point of view, and then stolen out as he came. If he had given me such a bold hard stare, that was but a part of his indiscretion. The good thing, after all, was that we should surely see no more of him.

This was not so good a thing, I admit, as not to leave me to judge that what, essentially, made nothing else much signify was simply my charming work. My charming work was just my life with Miles and Flora, and through nothing could I so like it as through feeling that I could throw myself into it in trouble. The attraction of my small charges was a constant joy, leading me to wonder afresh at the vanity of my original fears, the distaste I had begun by entertaining for the probable grey prose of my office. There was to be no grey prose, it appeared, and no long grind; so how could work not be charming that presented itself as daily beauty? It was all the romance of the nursery and the poetry of the schoolroom. I don't mean by this, of course, that we studied only fiction and verse; I mean I can express no otherwise the sort of interest my companions inspired. How can I describe that except by saying that instead of growing used to them—and it's a marvel for a governess: I call the sisterhood to witness!—I made constant fresh discoveries. There was one direction, assuredly, in which these discoveries stopped: deep obscurity continued to cover the region of the boy's conduct at school. It had been promptly given me, I have noted, to face that mystery without a pang.

Perhaps even it would be nearer the truth to say that—
without a word—he himself had cleared it up. He had
made the whole charge absurd. My conclusion bloomed
there with the real rose-flush of his innocence: he was only
too fine and fair for the little horrid, unclean school-world,
and he had paid a price for it. I reflected acutely that the
sense of such differences, such superiorities of quality,
always, on the part of the majority—which could include
even stupid, sordid head-masters—turns infallibly to the
vindictive.

Both the children had a gentleness (it was their only fault,
and it never made Miles a muff)² that kept them—how shall
I express it?—almost impersonal and certainly quite unpun-
ishable. They were like the cherubs of the anecdote, who
had—morally, at any rate—nothing to whack! I remember
feeling with Miles in especial as if he had had, as it were, no
history. We expect of a small child a scant one, but there
was in this beautiful little boy something extraordinarily
sensitive, yet extraordinarily happy, that, more than in any
creature of his age I have seen, struck me as beginning
anew each day. He had never for a second suffered. I took
this as a direct disproof of his having really been chastised.
If he had been wicked he would have "caught" it, and I
should have caught it by the rebound—I should have found
the trace. I found nothing at all, and he was therefore angel.
He never spoke of his school, never mentioned a comrade
or a master; and I, for my part, was quite too much disgusted
to allude to them. Of course I was under the spell, and the
wonderful part is that, even at the time, I perfectly knew I
was. But I gave myself up to it; it was an antidote to any
pain, and I had more pains than one. I was in receipt in
these days of disturbing letters from home, where things
were not going well. But with my children, what things in
the world mattered? That was the question I used to put to
my scrappy retirements. I was dazzled by their loveliness.

There was a Sunday—to get on—when it rained with
such force and for so many hours that there could be no

²One who is awkward in sports; a bungler.

procession to church; in consequence of which, as the day
declined, I had arranged with Mrs. Grose that, should the
evening show improvement, we would attend together the
late service. The rain happily stopped, and I prepared for
our walk, which, through the park and by the good road to
the village, would be a matter of twenty minutes. Coming
downstairs to meet my colleague in the hall, I remembered
a pair of gloves that had required three stitches and that had
received them—with a publicity perhaps not edifying—
while I sat with the children at their tea, served on Sundays,
by exception, in that cold, clean temple of mahogany and
brass, the "grown-up" dining-room. The gloves had been
dropped there, and I turned in to recover them. The day
was grey enough, but the afternoon light still lingered, and
it enabled me, on crossing the threshold, not only to
recognise, on a chair near the wide window, then closed,
the articles I wanted, but to become aware of a person on
the other side of the window and looking straight in. One
step into the room had sufficed; my vision was instantaneous; it was all there. The person looking straight in was the
person who had already appeared to me. He appeared thus
again with I won't say greater distinctness, for that was
impossible, but with a nearness that represented a forward
stride in our intercourse and made me, as I met him, catch
my breath and turn cold. He was the same—he was the
same, and seen, this time, as he had been seen before, from
the waist up, the window, though the dining-room was on
the ground-floor, not going down to the terrace on which he
stood. His face was close to the glass, yet the effect of this
better view was, strangely, only to show me how intense
the former had been. He remained but a few seconds—long
enough to convince me he also saw and recognised; but it
was as if I had been looking at him for years and had known
him always. Something, however, happened this time that
had not happened before; his stare into my face, through
the glass and across the room, was as deep and hard as then,
but it quitted me for a moment during which I could still
watch it, see it fix successively several other things. On the
spot there came to me the added shock of a certitude that it

was not for me he had come there. He had come for someone else.

The flash of this knowledge – for it was knowledge in the midst of dread – produced in me the most extraordinary effect, started, as I stood there, a sudden vibration of duty and courage. I say courage because I was beyond all doubt already far gone. I bounded straight out of the door again, reached that of the house, got, in an instant, upon the drive, and, passing along the terrace as fast as I could rush, turned a corner and came full in sight. But it was in sight of nothing now – my visitor had vanished. I stopped, I almost dropped, with the real relief of this; but I took in the whole scene – I gave him time to reappear. I call it time, but how long was it? I can't speak to the purpose today of the duration of these things. That kind of measure must have left me: they couldn't have lasted as they actually appeared to me to last. The terrace and the whole place, the lawn and the garden beyond it, all I could see of the park, were empty with a great emptiness. There were shrubberies and big trees, but I remember the clear assurance I felt that none of them concealed him. He was there or was not there: not there if I didn't see him. I got hold of this; then, instinctively, instead of returning as I had come, went to the window. It was confusedly present to me that I ought to place myself where he had stood. I did so; I applied my face to the pane and looked, as he had looked, into the room. As if, at this moment, to show me exactly what his range had been, Mrs. Grose, as I had done for himself just before, came in from the hall. With this I had the full image of a repetition of what had already occurred. She saw me as I had seen my own visitant; she pulled up short as I had done; I gave her something of the shock that I had received. She turned white, and this made me ask myself if I had blanched as much. She stared, in short, and retreated on just *my* lines, and I knew she had then passed out and come round to me and that I should presently meet her. I remained where I was, and while I waited I thought of more things than one. But there's only one I take space to mention. I wondered why *she* should be scared.

V

Oh, she let me know as soon as, round the corner of the house, she loomed again into view. "What in the name of goodness is the matter — ?" She was now flushed and out of breath.

I said nothing till she came quite near. "With me?" I must have made a wonderful face. "Do I show it?"

"You're as white as a sheet. You look awful."

I considered; I could meet on this, without scruple, any innocence. My need to respect the bloom of Mrs. Grose's had dropped, without a rustle, from my shoulders, and if I wavered for the instant it was not with what I kept back. I put out my hand to her and she took it; I held her hard a little, liking to feel her close to me. There was a kind of support in the shy heave of her surprise. "You came for me for church, of course, but I can't go."

"Has anything happened?"

"Yes. You must know now. Did I look very queer?"

"Through this window? Dreadful!"

"Well," I said, "I've been frightened." Mrs. Grose's eyes expressed plainly that *she* had no wish to be, yet also that she knew too well her place not to be ready to share with me any marked inconvenience. Oh, it was quite settled that she *must* share! "Just what you saw from the dining-room a minute ago was the effect of that. What *I* saw — just before — was much worse."

Her hand tightened. "What was it?"

"An extraordinary man. Looking in."

"What extraordinary man?"

"I haven't the least idea."

Mrs. Grose gazed round us in vain. "Then where is he gone?"

"I know still less."

"Have you seen him before?"

"Yes — once. On the old tower."

She could only look at me harder. "Do you mean he's a stranger?"

"Oh, very much!"

"Yet you didn't tell me?"

"No — for reasons. But now that you've guessed —"

Mrs. Grose's round eyes encountered this charge. "Ah, I haven't guessed!" She said very simply. "How can I if *you* don't imagine?"

"I don't in the very least."

"You've seen him nowhere but on the tower?"

"And on this spot just now."

Mrs. Grose looked round again. "What was he doing on the tower?"

"Only standing there and looking down at me."

She thought a minute. "Was he a gentleman?"

I found I had no need to think. "No." She gazed in deeper wonder. "No."

"Then nobody about the place? Nobody from the village?"

"Nobody—nobody. I didn't tell you, but I made sure."

She breathed a vague relief: this was, oddly, so much to the good. It only went indeed a little way. "But if he isn't a gentleman—"

"What *is* he? He's a horror."

"A horror?"

"He's—God help me if I know *what* he is!"

Mrs. Grose looked round once more; she fixed her eyes on the duskier distance, then, pulling herself together, turned to me with abrupt inconsequence. "It's time we should be at church."

"Oh, I'm not fit for church!"

"Won't it do you good?"

"It won't do *them*—!" I nodded at the house.

"The children?"

"I can't leave them now."

"You're afraid—?"

I spoke boldly. "I'm afraid of *him*."

Mrs. Grose's large face showed me, at this, for the first time, the far-away faint glimmer of a consciousness more acute: I somehow made out in it the delayed dawn of an idea I myself had not given her and that was as yet quite obscure to me. It comes back to me that I thought instantly of this as something I could get from her; and I felt it to be connected with the desire she presently showed to know more. "When was it—on the tower?"

"About the middle of the month. At this same hour."

"Almost at dark?" said Mrs. Grose.

"Oh, no, not nearly. I saw him as I see you."

"Then how did he get in?"

"And how did he get out?" I laughed. "I had no opportunity to ask him! This evening, you see," I pursued, "he has not been able to get in."

"He only peeps?"

"I hope it will be confined to that!" She had now let go my hand; she turned away a little. I waited an instant; then I brought out: "Go to church. Good-bye. I must watch."

Slowly she faced me again. "Do you fear for them?"

We met in another long look. "Don't *you?*" Instead of answering she came nearer to the window and, for a minute, applied her face to the glass. "You see how he could see," I meanwhile went on.

She didn't move. "How long was he here?"

"Till I came out. I came to meet him."

Mrs. Grose at last turned round, and there was still more in her face. "*I* couldn't have come out."

"Neither could I!" I laughed again. "But I did come. I have my duty."

"So have I mine," she replied; after which she added: "What is he like?"

"I've been dying to tell you. But he's like nobody."

"Nobody?" she echoed.

"He has no hat." Then seeing in her face that she already, in this, with a deeper dismay, found a touch of picture, I quickly added stroke to stroke. "He has red hair, very red, close-curling, and a pale face, long in shape, with straight, good features and little, rather queer whiskers that are as red as his hair. His eyebrows are, somehow, darker; they look particularly arched and as if they might move a good deal. His eyes are sharp, strange—awfully; but I only know clearly that they're rather small and very fixed. His mouth's wide, and his lips are thin, and except for his little whiskers he's quite clean-shaven. He gives me a sort of sense of looking like an actor."

"An actor!" It was impossible to resemble one less, at least, than Mrs. Grose at that moment.

"I've never seen one, but so I suppose them. He's tall, active, erect," I continued, "but never—no, never!—a gentleman."

My companion's face had blanched as I went on; her round eyes started and her mild mouth gaped. "A gentleman?" she gasped, confounded, stupefied: "a gentleman *he*?"

"You know him then?"

She visibly tried to hold herself. "But he *is* handsome?"

I saw the way to help her. "Remarkably!"

"And dressed—?"

"In somebody's clothes. They're smart, but they're not his own."

She broke into a breathless affirmative groan. "They're the master's!"

I caught it up. "You *do* know him?"

She faltered but a second. "Quint!" she cried.

"Quint?"

"Peter Quint—his own man, his valet, when he was here!"

"When the master was?"

Gaping still, but meeting me, she pieced it all together. "He never wore his hat, but he did wear—well, there were waistcoats missed! They were both here—last year. Then the master went, and Quint was alone."

I followed, but halting a little. "Alone?"

"Alone with *us*." Then, as from a deeper depth, "In charge," she added.

"And what became of him?"

She hung fire so long that I was still more mystified. "He went too," she brought out at last.

"Went where?"

Her expression, at this, became extraordinary. "God knows where! He died."

"Died?" I almost shrieked.

She seemed fairly to square herself, plant herself more firmly to utter the wonder of it. "Yes. Mr. Quint is dead."

VI

It took of course more than that particular passage to place us together in presence of what we had now to live with as we could — my dreadful liability to impressions of the order so vividly exemplified, and my companion's knowledge, henceforth — a knowledge half consternation and half compassion — of that liability. There had been, this evening, after the revelation that left me, for an hour, so prostrate — there had been, for either of us, no attendance on any service but a little service of tears and vows, of prayers and promises, a climax to the series of mutual challenges and pledges that had straightway ensued on our retreating together to the schoolroom and shutting ourselves up there to have everything out. The result of our having everything out was simply to reduce our situation to the last rigour of its elements. She herself had seen nothing, not the shadow of a shadow, and nobody in the house but the governess was in the governess's plight; yet she accepted without directly impugning° my sanity the truth as I gave it to her, and ended by showing me, on this ground, an awe-stricken tenderness, an expression of the sense of my more than questionable privilege, of which the very breath has remained with me as that of the sweetest of human charities.

What was settled between us, accordingly, that night, was that we thought we might bear things together; and I was not even sure that, in spite of her exemption, it was she who had the best of the burden. I knew at this hour, I think, as well as I knew later what I was capable of meeting to shelter my pupils; but it took me some time to be wholly sure of what my honest ally was prepared for to keep terms with so compromising a contract. I was queer company enough — quite as queer as the company I received; but as I trace over what we went through I see how much common ground we must have found in the one idea that, by good fortune, *could* steady us. It was the idea, the second movement, that led me straight out, as I may say, of the inner chamber of my dread. I could take the air in the court, at least, and there Mrs. Grose could join me. Perfectly can I recall now the particular way strength came to me before we separated for the night. We had gone over and over every feature of what I had seen.

"He was looking for someone else, you say — someone who was not you?"

"He was looking for little Miles." A portentous clearness now possessed me. *"That's* whom he was looking for."

"But how do you know?"

"I know, I know, I know!" My exaltation grew. "And *you* know, my dear!"

She didn't deny this, but I required, I felt, not even so much telling as that. She resumed in a moment, at any rate: "What if *he* should see him?"

"Little Miles? That's what he wants!"

She looked immensely scared again. "The child?"

"Heaven forbid! The man. He wants to appear to *them.*" That he might was an awful conception, and yet, somehow, I could keep it at bay; which, moreover, as we lingered there, was what I succeeded in practically proving. I had an absolute certainty that I could see again what I had already seen, but something within me said that by offering myself bravely as the sole subject of such experience, by accepting, by inviting, by surmounting it all, I should serve as an expiatory° victim and guard the tranquillity of my companions. The children, in especial, I should thus fence about and absolutely save. I recall one of the last things I said that night to Mrs. Grose.

"It does strike me that my pupils have never mentioned—"

She looked at me hard as I musingly pulled up. "His having been here and the time they were with him?"

"The time they were with him, and his name, his presence, his history, in any way."

"Oh, the little lady doesn't remember. She never heard or knew."

"The circumstances of his death?" I thought with some intensity. "Perhaps not. But Miles would remember — Miles would know."

"Ah, don't try him!" broke from Mrs. Grose.

I returned her the look she had given me. "Don't be afraid." I continued to think. "It *is* rather odd."

"That he has never spoken of him?"

"Never by the least allusion. And you tell me they were 'great friends'?"

"Oh, it wasn't *him!*" Mrs. Grose with emphasis declared. "It was Quint's own fancy. To play with him, I mean—to spoil him." She paused a moment; then she added: "Quint was much too free."

This gave me, straight from my vision of his face—*such* a face!—a sudden sickness of disgust. "Too free with *my* boy?"

"Too free with everyone!"

I forebore, for the moment, to analyse this description further than by the reflection that a part of it applied to several of the members of the household, of the half-dozen maids and men who were still of our small colony. But there was everything, for our apprehension, in the lucky fact that no discomfortable legend, no perturbation of scul- lions,° had ever, within anyone's memory, attached to the kind old place. It had neither bad name nor ill fame, and Mrs. Grose, most apparently, only desired to cling to me and to quake in silence. I even put her, the very last thing of all, to the test. It was when, at midnight, she had her hand on the schoolroom door to take leave. "I have it from you then—for it's of great importance—that he was defin- itely and admittedly bad?"

"Oh, not admittedly. *I* knew it—but the master didn't."

"And you never told him?"

"Well, he didn't like tale-bearing—he hated complaints. He was terribly short with anything of that kind, and if people were all right to *him*—"

"He wouldn't be bothered with more?" This squared well enough with my impresssion of him: he was not a trouble-loving gentleman, nor so very particular perhaps about some of the company *he* kept. All the same, I pressed my interlocutress. "I promise you *I* would have told!"

She felt my discrimination. "I dare say I was wrong. But, really, I was afraid."

"Afraid of what?"

"Of things that man could do. Quint was so clever—he was so deep."

I took this in still more than, probably, I showed. "You weren't afraid of anything else? Not of his effect—?"

"His effect?" she repeated with a face of anguish and waiting while I faltered.

"On innocent little precious lives. They were in your charge."

"No, they were not in mine!" she roundly and distressfully returned. "The master believed in him and placed him here because he was supposed not to be well and the country air so good for him. So he had everything to say. Yes"—she let me have it—"even about *them*."

"Them—that creature?" I had to smother a kind of howl. "And you could bear it!"

"No. I couldn't—and I can't now!" And the poor woman burst into tears.

A rigid control, from the next day, was, as I have said, to follow them; yet how often and how passionately, for a week, we came back together to the subject! Much as we had discussed it that Sunday night, I was, in the immediate later hours in especial—for it may be imagined whether I slept—still haunted with the shadow of something she had not told me. I myself had kept back nothing, but there was a word Mrs. Grose had kept back. I was sure, moreover, by morning, that this was not from a failure of frankness, but because on every side there were fears. It seems to me indeed, in retrospect, that by the time the morrow's sun was high I had restlessly read into the facts before us almost all the meaning they were to receive from subsequent and more cruel occurrences. What they gave me above all was just the sinister figure of the living man—the dead one would keep awhile!—and of the months he had continuously passed at Bly, which, added up, made a formidable stretch. The limit of this evil time had arrived only when, on the dawn of a winter's morning, Peter Quint was found, by a labourer going to early work, stone dead on the road from the village: a catastrophe explained—superficially at

least — by a visible wound to his head; such a wound as
might have been produced — and as, on the final evidence,
had been — by a fatal slip, in the dark and after leaving the
public house, on the steepish icy slope, a wrong path,
altogether, at the bottom of which he lay. The icy slope, the
turn mistaken at night and in liquor, accounted for much —
practically, in the end and after the inquest and boundless
chatter, for everything; but there had been matters in his
life — strange passages and perils, secret disorders, vices
more than suspected — that would have accounted for a
good deal more.

I scarce know how to put my story into words that shall be
a credible picture of my state of mind; but I was in these
days literally able to find a joy in the extraordinary flight of
heroism the occasion demanded of me. I now saw that I
had been asked for a service admirable and difficult; and
there would be a greatness in letting it be seen — oh, in the
right quarter! — that I could succeed where many another
girl might have failed. It was an immense help to me — I
confess I rather applaud myself as I look back! — that I saw
my service so strongly and so simply. I was there to protect
and defend the little creatures in the world the most be-
reaved and the most loveable, the appeal of whose helplessness had suddenly become only too explicit, a deep, constant ache of one's own committed heart. We were cut off,
really, together; we were united in our danger. They had
nothing but me and I — well, I had *them*. It was in short a
magnificent chance. This chance presented itself to me in
an image richly material. I was a screen — I was to stand
before them. The more I saw, the less they would. I began
to watch them in a stifled suspense, a disguised excitement
that might well, had it continued too long, have turned to
something like madness. What saved me, as I now see, was
that it turned to something else altogether. It didn't last as
suspense — it was superseded by horrible proofs. Proofs, I
say, yes — from the moment I really took hold.

This moment dated from an afternoon hour that I happened to spend in the grounds with the younger of my
pupils alone. We had left Miles indoors, on the red cushion

of a deep window-seat; he had wished to finish a book, and I had been glad to encourage a purpose so laudable in a young man whose only defect was an occasional excess of the restless. His sister, on the contrary, had been alert to come out, and I strolled with her half an hour, seeking the shade, for the sun was still high and the day exceptionally warm. I was aware afresh, with her, as we went, of how, like her brother, she contrived—it was the charming thing in both children—to let me alone without appearing to drop me and to accompany me without appearing to surround. They were never importunate° and yet never listless. My attention to them all really went to seeing them amuse themselves immensely without me: this was a spectacle they seemed actively to prepare and that engaged me as an active admirer. I walked in a world of their invention—they had no occasion whatever to draw upon mine; so that my time was taken only with being, for them, some remarkable person or thing that the game of the moment required and that was merely, thanks to my superior, my exalted stamp, a happy and highly distinguished sinecure.° I forget what I was on the present occasion; I only remember that I was something very important and very quiet and that Flora was playing very hard. We were on the edge of the lake, and, as we had lately begun geography, the lake was the Sea of Azof.

Suddenly, in these circumstances, I became aware that, on the other side of the Sea of Azof, we had an interested spectator. The way this knowledge gathered in me was the strangest thing in the world—the strangest, that is, except the very much stranger in which it quickly merged itself. I had sat down with a piece of work—for I was something or other that could sit—on the old stone bench which over-looked the pond; and in this position I began to take in with certitude, and yet without direct vision, the presence, at a distance, of a third person. The old trees, the thick shrub-bery, made a great and pleasant shade, but it was all suffused with the brightness of the hot, still hour. There was no ambiguity° in anything; none whatever, at least, in the conviction I from one moment to another found myself forming as to what I should see straight before me and across the lake as a consequence of raising my eyes. They were attached at this juncture to the stitching in which I was engaged, and I can feel once more the spasm of my effort not to move them till I should so have steadied myself as to be able to make up my mind what to do. There was an alien object in view—a figure whose right of presence I instantly, passionately questioned. I recollect counting over perfectly the possibilities, reminding myself that nothing was more natural, for instance, than the appearance of one of the men about the place, or even of a messenger, a postman or a tradesman's boy, from the village. That reminder had as little effect on my practical certitude as I was conscious—still even without looking—of its having upon the character and attitude of our visitor. Nothing was more natural than that these things should be the other things that they absolutely were not.

Of the positive identity of the apparition I would assure myself as soon as the small clock of my courage should have ticked out the right second; meanwhile, with an effort that was already sharp enough, I transferred my eyes straight to little Flora, who, at the moment, was about ten yards away. My heart had stood still for an instant with the wonder and terror of the question whether she too would see; and I held my breath while I waited for what a cry from her, what some sudden innocent sign either of interest or of alarm, would tell me. I waited, but nothing came; then, in the first place —and there is something more dire in this, I feel, than in anything I have to relate—I was determined by a sense that, within a minute, all sounds from her had previously dropped; and, in the second, by the circumstance that, also within the minute, she had, in her play, turned her back to the water. This was her attitude when I at last looked at her —looked with the confirmed conviction that we were still, together, under direct personal notice. She had picked up a small flat piece of wood, which happened to have in it a little hole that had evidently suggested to her the idea of sticking in another fragment that might figure as a mast and make the thing a boat. This second morsel, as I watched her, she was very markedly and intently attempting to tighten in its place. My apprehension of what she was doing sustained me so that after some seconds I felt I was ready for more. Then I again shifted my eyes — I faced what I had to face.

VII

I got hold of Mrs. Grose as soon after this as I could; and I can give no intelligible account of how I fought out the interval. Yet I still hear myself cry as I fairly threw myself into her arms: "They *know* — it's too monstrous: they know, they know!"

"And what on earth — ?" I felt her incredulity as she held me.

"Why, all that *we* know — and heaven knows what else besides!" Then, as she released me, I made it out to her, made it out perhaps only now with full coherency even to myself. "Two hours ago, in the garden" — I could scarce articulate — "Flora *saw!*"

Mrs. Grose took it as she might have taken a blow in the stomach. "She has told you?" she panted.

"Not a word — that's the horror. She kept it to herself! The child of eight, *that* child!" Unutterable still, for me, was the stupefaction of it.

Mrs. Grose, of course, could only gape the wider. "Then how do you know?"

"I was there — I saw with my eyes: saw that she was perfectly aware."

"Do you mean aware of *him?*"

"No — of *her.*" I was conscious as I spoke that I looked prodigious things, for I got the slow reflection of them in my companion's face. "Another person — this time; but a figure of quite as unmistakeable horror and evil: a woman in black, pale and dreadful — with such an air also, and such a face! — on the other side of the lake. I was there with the child — quiet for the hour; and in the midst of it she came."

"Came how — from where?"

"From where they come from! She just appeared and stood there — but not so near."

"And without coming nearer?"

"Oh, for the effect and the feeling, she might have been as close as you!"

My friend, with an odd impulse, fell back a step. "Was she someone you've never seen?"

"Yes. But someone the child has. Someone *you* have." Then, to show how I had thought it all out: "My predecessor—the one who died."

"Miss Jessel?"

"Miss Jessel. You don't believe me?" I pressed.

She turned right and left in her distress. "How can you be sure?"

This drew from me, in the state of my nerves, a flash of impatience. "Then ask Flora—*she's* sure!" But I had no sooner spoken than I caught myself up. "No, for God's sake, *don't!* She'll say she isn't—she'll lie!"

Mrs. Grose was not too bewildered instinctively to protest. "Ah, how *can* you?"

"Because I'm clear. Flora doesn't want me to know."

"It's only then to spare you."

"No, no—there are depths, depths! The more I go over it, the more I see in it, and the more I see in it the more I fear. I don't know what I *don't* see—what I *don't* fear!"

Mrs. Grose tried to keep up with me. "You mean you're afraid of seeing her again?"

"Oh, no; that's nothing—now!" Then I explained. "It's of *not* seeing her."

But my companion only looked wan. "I don't understand you."

"Why, it's that the child may keep it up—and that the child assuredly *will*—without my knowing it."

At the image of this possibility Mrs. Grose for a moment collapsed, yet presently to pull herself together again, as if from the positive force of the sense of what, should we yield an inch, there would really be to give way to. "Dear, dear—we must keep our heads! And after all, if she doesn't mind it—!" She even tried a grim joke. "Perhaps she likes it!"

"Likes *such* things—a scrap of an infant!"

"Isn't it just a proof of her blessed innocence?" my friend bravely inquired.

She brought me, for the instant, almost round. "Oh, we must clutch at *that*—we must cling to it! If it isn't a proof of what you say, it's a proof of—God knows what! For the woman's a horror of horrors."

Mrs. Grose, at this, fixed her eyes a minute on the ground; then at last raising them, "Tell me how you know," she said.

"Then you admit it's what she was?" I cried.

"Tell me how you know," my friend simply repeated.

"Know! By seeing her! By the way she looked."

"At you, do you mean—so wickedly?"

"Dear me, no—I could have borne that. She gave me never a glance. She only fixed the child."

Mrs. Grose tried to see it. "Fixed her?"

"Ah, with such awful eyes!"

She stared at mine as if they might really have resembled them. "Do you mean of dislike?"

"God help us, no. Of something much worse."

"Worse than dislike?"—this left her indeed at a loss.

"With a determination—indescribable. With a kind of fury of intention."

I made her turn pale. "Intention?"

"To get hold of her." Mrs. Grose—her eyes just lingering on mine—gave a shudder and walked to the window; and while she stood there looking out I completed my statement. *"That's* what Flora knows."

After a little she turned round. "The person was in black, you say?"

"In mourning—rather poor, almost shabby. But—yes—with extraordinary beauty." I now recognised to what I had at last, stroke by stroke, brought the victim of my confidence, for she quite visibly weighed this. "Oh, handsome—very, very," I insisted; "wonderfully handsome. But infamous."

She slowly came back to me. "Miss Jessel—*was* infamous." She once more took my hand in both her own, holding it as tight as if to fortify me against the increase of alarm I might draw from this disclosure. "They were both infamous," she finally said.

So, for a little, we faced it once more together; and I found absolutely a degree of help in seeing it now so straight. "I appreciate," I said, "the great decency of your not having hitherto spoken; but the time has certainly come to give me the whole thing." She appeared to assent to this, but still only in silence; seeing which I went on: "I must have it now. Of what did she die? Come, there was something between them."

"There was everything."

"In spite of the difference — ?"

"Oh, of their rank, their condition" — she brought it woefully out. "*She* was a lady."

I turned it over; I again saw. "Yes — she was a lady."

"And he so dreadfully below," said Mrs. Grose.

I felt that I doubtless needn't press too hard, in such company, on the place of a servant in the scale; but there was nothing to prevent an acceptance of my companion's own measure of my predecessor's abasement. There was a way to deal with that, and I dealt; the more readily for my full vision — on the evidence — of our employer's late clever, good-looking "own" man; impudent, assured, spoiled, depraved. "The fellow was a hound."

Mrs. Grose considered as if it were perhaps a little a case for a sense of shades. "I've never seen one like him. He did what he wished."

"With *her*?"

"With them all."

It was as if now in my friend's own eyes Miss Jessel had again appeared. I seemed at any rate, for an instant, to see their evocation of her as distinctly as I had seen her by the pond; and I brought out with decision: "It must have been also what *she* wished!"

Mrs. Grose's face signified that it had been indeed, but she said at the same time: "Poor woman — she paid for it!"

"Then you do know what she died of?" I asked.

"No — I know nothing. I wanted not to know; I was glad enough I didn't; and I thanked heaven she was well out of this!"

"Yet you had, then, your idea—"

"Of her real reason for leaving? Oh, yes—as to that. She couldn't have stayed. Fancy it here—for a governess! And afterwards I imagined—and I still imagine. And what I imagine is dreadful."

"Not so dreadful as what *I* do," I replied; on which I must have shown her—as I was indeed but too conscious—a front of miserable defeat. It brought out again all her compassion for me, and at the renewed touch of her kindness my power to resist broke down. I burst, as I had, the other time, made her burst, into tears; she took me to her motherly breast, and my lamentation overflowed. "I don't do it!" I sobbed in despair; "I don't save or shield them. It's far worse than I dreamed—they're lost!"

VIII

What I had said to Mrs. Grose was true enough: there were in the matter I had put before her depths and possibilities that I lacked resolution to sound; so that when we met once more in the wonder of it we were of a common mind about the duty of resistance to extravagant fancies. We were to keep our heads if we should keep nothing else—difficult indeed as that might be in the face of what, in our prodigious experience, was least to be questioned. Late that night, while the house slept, we had another talk in my room, when she went all the way with me as to its being beyond doubt that I had seen exactly what I had seen. To hold her perfectly in the pinch of that, I found I had only to ask her how, if I had "made it up," I came to be able to give, of each of the persons appearing to me, a picture disclosing, to the last detail, their special marks—a portrait on the exhibition of which she had instantly recognised and named them. She wished, of course—small blame to her!—to sink the whole subject; and I was quick to assure her that my own interest in it had now violently taken the form of a search for the way to escape from it. I encountered her on the ground of a probability that with recurrence—for recurrence we took for granted—I should get used to my danger, distinctly professing that my personal exposure had suddenly become the least of my discomforts. It was my new

suspicion that was intolerable; and yet even to this complication the later hours of the day had brought a little ease.

On leaving her, after my first outbreak, I had of course
returned to my pupils, associating the right remedy for my
dismay with that sense of their charm which I had already
found to be a thing I could positively cultivate and which
had never failed me yet. I had simply, in other words,
plunged afresh into Flora's special society and there become aware — it was almost a luxury! — that she could put her
little conscious hand straight upon the spot that ached. She
had looked at me in sweet speculation and then had ac-
cused me to my face of having "cried." I had supposed I
had brushed away the ugly signs: but I could literally — for
the time, at all events — rejoice, under this fathomless
charity, that they had not entirely disappeared. To gaze
into the depths of blue of the child's eyes and pronounce
their loveliness a trick of premature cunning was to be
guilty of a cynicism in preference to which I naturally
preferred to abjure° my judgment and, so far as might be,
my agitation. I couldn't abjure for merely wanting to, but I
could repeat to Mrs. Grose — as I did there, over and over, in
the small hours — that with their voices in the air, their
pressure on one's heart and their fragrant faces against one's
cheek, everything fell to the ground but their incapacity
and their beauty. It was a pity that, somehow, to settle this
once for all, I had equally to re-enumerate the signs of
subtlety that, in the afternoon, by the lake, had made a
miracle of my show of self-possession. It was a pity to be
obliged to re-investigate the certitude of the moment itself
and repeat how it had come to me as a revelation that the
inconceivable communion I then surprised was a matter,
for either party, of habit. It was a pity that I should have had
to quaver out again the reasons for my not having, in my
delusion, so much as questioned that the little girl saw our
visitant even as I actually saw Mrs. Grose herself, and that
she wanted, by just so much as she did thus see, to make me
suppose she didn't, and at the same time, without showing
anything, arrive at a guess as to whether I myself did! It
was a pity that I needed once more to describe the porten-

tous little activity by which she sought to divert my attention—the perceptible increase of movement, the greater intensity of play, the singing, the gabbling of nonsense, and the invitation to romp.

Yet if I had not indulged, to prove there was nothing in it, in this review, I should have missed the two or three dim elements of comfort that still remained to me. I should not, for instance, have been able to asseverate° to my friend that I was certain—which was so much to the good—that *I* at least had not betrayed myself. I should not have been prompted, by stress of need, by desperation of mind—I scarce know what to call it—to invoke such further aid to intelligence as might spring from pushing my colleague fairly to the wall. She had told me, bit by bit, under pressure, a great deal; but a small shifty spot on the wrong side of it all still sometimes brushed my brow like the wing of a bat; and I remember how on this occasion—for the sleeping house and the concentration alike of our danger and our watch seemed to help—I felt the importance of giving the last jerk to the curtain. "I don't believe anything so horrible," I recollect saying; "no, let us put it definitely, my dear, that I don't. But if I did, you know, there's a thing I should require now, just without sparing you the least bit more—oh, not a scrap, come!—to get out of you. What was it you had in mind when, in our distress, before Miles came back, over the letter from his school, you said, under my insistence, that you didn't pretend for him that he had not literally *ever* been 'bad'? He has *not* literally 'ever,' in these weeks that I myself have lived with him and so closely watched him; he has been an imperturbable little prodigy of delightful, loveable goodness. Therefore you might perfectly have made the claim for him if you had not, as it happened, seen an exception to take. What was your exception, and to what passage in your personal observation of him did you refer?"

It was a dreadfully austere inquiry, but levity was not our note, and, at any rate, before the grey dawn admonished us to separate I had got my answer. What my friend had had in mind proved to be immensely to the purpose. It was neither more nor less than the circumstance that for a period of several months Quint and the boy had been perpetually together. It was in fact the very appropriate truth that she had ventured to criticise the propriety, to hint at the incongruity, of so close an alliance, and even to go so far on the subject as a frank overture to Miss Jessel. Miss Jessel had, with a most strange manner, requested her to mind her business, and the good woman had, on this, directly approached little Miles. What she had said to him, since I pressed, was that *she* liked to see young gentlemen not forget their station.

I pressed again, of course, at this. "You reminded him that Quint was only a base menial?"

"As you might say! And it was his answer, for one thing, that was bad."

"And for another thing?" I waited. "He repeated your words to Quint?"

"No, not that. It's just what he *wouldn't!*" she could still impress upon me. "I was sure, at any rate," she added, "that he didn't, But he denied certain occasions."

"What occasions?"

"When they had been about together quite as if Quint were his tutor—and a very grand one—and Miss Jessel only for the little lady. When he had gone off with the fellow, I mean, and spent hours with him."

"He then prevaricated about it—he said he hadn't?" Her assent was clear enough to cause me to add in a moment: "I see. He lied."

"Oh!" Mrs. Grose mumbled. This was a suggestion that it didn't matter; which indeed she backed up by a further remark. "You see, after all, Miss Jessel didn't mind. She didn't forbid him."

I considered. "Did he put that to you as a justification?"

At this she dropped again. "No, he never spoke of it."

"Never mentioned her in connection with Quint?"

She saw, visibly flushing, where I was coming out. "Well, he didn't show anything. He denied," she repeated; "he denied."

Lord, how I pressed her now! "So that you could see he knew what was between the two wretches?"

"I don't know—I don't know!" the poor woman groaned.

"You do know, you dear thing," I replied; "only you haven't my dreadful boldness of mind, and you keep back, out of timidity and modesty and delicacy, even the impression that, in the past, when you had, without my aid, to flounder about in silence, most of all made you miserable. But I shall get it out of you yet! There was something in the boy that suggested to you," I continued, "that he covered and concealed their relation."

"Oh, he couldn't prevent—"

"Your learning the truth? I dare say! But, heavens," I fell, with vehemence, a-thinking, "what it shows that they must, to that extent, have succeeded in making of him!"

"Ah nothing that's not nice *now!*" Mrs. Grose lugubriously pleaded.

"I don't wonder you looked queer," I persisted, "when I mentioned to you the letter from his school!"

"I doubt if I looked as queer as you!" she retorted with homely force. "And if he was so bad then as that comes to, how is he such an angel now?"

"Yes, indeed—and if he was a fiend at school! How, how, how? Well," I said in my torment, "you must put it to me again, but I shall not be able to tell you for some days. Only, put it to me again!" I cried in a way that made my friend stare. "There are directions in which I must not for the present let myself go." Meanwhile I returned to her first example—the one to which she had just previously referred—of the boy's happy capacity for an occasional slip. "If Quint—on your remonstrance at the time you speak of— was a base menial, one of the things Miles said to you, I find myself guessing, was that you were another." Again her admission was so adequate that I continued: "And you forgave him that?"

"Wouldn't *you?*"

"Oh, yes!" And we exchanged there, in the stillness, a sound of the oddest amusement. Then I went on: "At all events, while he was with the man—"

"Miss Flora was with the woman. It suited them all!"

It suited me too, I felt, only too well; by which I mean that it suited exactly the particularly deadly view I was in the very act of forbidding myself to entertain. But I so far succeeded in checking the expression of this view that I wilł throw, just here, no further light on it than may be offered by the mention of my final observation to Mrs. Grose. "His having lied and been impudent are, I confess, less engaging specimens than I had hoped to have from you of the outbreak in him of the little natural man. Still," I mused, "they must do, for they make me feel more than ever that I must watch."

It made me blush, the next minute, to see in my friend's face how much more unreservedly she had forgiven him than her anecdote struck me as presenting to my own tenderness an occasion for doing. This came out when, at the schoolroom door, she quitted me. "Surely you don't accuse *him*—"

"Of carrying on an intercourse that he conceals from me? Ah, remember that, until further evidence, I now accuse nobody." Then, before shutting her out to go, by another passage, to her own place, "I must just wait," I wound up.

IX

I waited and waited, and the days, as they elapsed, took something from my consternation. A very few of them, in fact, passing, in constant sight of my pupils, without a fresh incident, sufficed to give to grievous fancies and even to odious memories a kind of brush of the sponge. I have spoken of the surrender to their extraordinary childish grace as a thing I could actively cultivate, and it may be imagined if I neglected now to address myself to this source for whatever it would yield. Stranger than I can express, certainly, was the effort to struggle against my new lights; it would doubtless have been, however, a greater tension still had it not been so frequently successful. I used to wonder how my little charges could help guessing that I thought strange things about them; and the circumstance that these things only made them more interesting was not by itself a direct aid to keeping them in the dark. I trembled lest they should see that they *were* so immensely more interesting. Putting things at the worst, at all events, as in meditation I so often did, any clouding of their innocence could only be — blameless and foredoomed as they were — a reason the more for taking risks. There were moments when, by an irresistible impulse, I found myself catching them up and pressing them to my heart. As soon as I had done so I used to say to myself: "What will they think of that? Doesn't it betray too much?" It would have been easy to get into a sad, wild tangle about how much I might betray; but the real account, I feel, of the hours of peace that I could still enjoy was that the immediate charm of my companions was a beguilement still effective even under the shadow of the possibility that it was studied. For if it occurred to me that I might occasionally excite suspicion by the little outbreaks of my sharper passion for them, so too I remember wondering if I mightn't see a queerness in the traceable increase of their own demonstrations.

They were at this period extravagantly and preternaturally fond of me; which, after all, I could reflect, was no more than a graceful response in children perpetually bowed over and hugged. The homage of which they were so lavish succeeded, in truth, for my nerves, quite as well as if I never appeared to myself, as I may say, literally to catch them at a purpose in it. They had never, I think, wanted to do so many things for their poor protectress; I mean — though they got their lessons better and better, which was naturally what would please her most — in the way of diverting, entertaining, surprising her; reading her passages, telling her stories, acting her charades, pouncing out at her, in disguises, as animals and historical characters, and above all astonishing her by the "pieces" they had secretly got by heart and could interminably recite. I should never get to the bottom — were I to let myself go even now — of the prodigious private commentary, all under still more private correction, with which, in these days, I overscored their full hours. They had shown me from the first a facility for everything, a general faculty which, taking a fresh start, achieved remarkable flights. They got their little tasks as if they loved them, and indulged, from the mere exuberance of the gift, in the most unimposed little miracles of memory.

They not only popped out at me as tigers and as Romans, but as Shakespeareans, astronomers, and navigators. This was so singularly the case that it had presumably much to do with the fact as to which, at the present day, I am at a loss for a different explanation: I allude to my unnatural composure on the subject of another school for Miles. What I remember is that I was content not, for the time, to open the question, and that contentment must have sprung from the sense of his perpetually striking show of cleverness. He was too clever for a bad governess, for a parson's daughter, to spoil; and the strangest if not the brightest thread in the pensive embroidery I just spoke of was the impression I might have got, if I had dared to work it out, that he was under some influence operating in his small intellectual life as a tremendous incitement.

If it was easy to reflect, however, that such a boy could postpone school, it was at least as marked that for such a boy to have been "kicked out" by a school-master was a mystification without end. Let me add that in their company now —and I was careful almost never to be out of it—I could follow no scent very far. We lived in a cloud of music and love and success and private theatricals. The musical sense in each of the children was of the quickest, but the elder in especial had a marvellous knack of catching and repeating. The schoolroom piano broke into all gruesome fancies; and when that failed there were confabulations in corners, with a sequel of one of them going out in the highest spirits in order to "come in" as something new. I had had brothers myself, and it was no revelation to me that little girls could be slavish idolaters of little boys. What surpassed everything was that there was a little boy in the world who could have for the inferior age, sex, and intelligence so fine a consideration. They were extraordinarily at one, and to say that they never either quarrelled or complained is to make the note of praise coarse for their quality of sweetness. Sometimes, indeed, when I dropped into coarseness, I perhaps came across traces of little understandings between them by which one of them should keep me occupied while the other slipped away. There is a *naïf* side, I suppose, in all diplomacy; but if my pupils practised upon me, it was surely with the minimum of grossness. It was all in the other quarter that, after a lull, the grossness broke out.

I find that I really hang back; but I must take my plunge. In going on with the record of what was hideous at Bly, I not only challenge the most liberal faith—for which I little care; but—and this is another matter—I renew what I myself suffered, I again push my way through it to the end. There came suddenly an hour after which, as I look back, the affair seems to me to have been all pure suffering; but I have at least reached the heart of it, and the straightest road out is doubtless to advance. One evening—with nothing to lead up or to prepare it—I felt the cold touch of the impression that had breathed on me the night of my arrival and which, much lighter then, as I have mentioned, I should probably have made little of in memory had my subsequent sojourn been less agitated. I had not gone to bed; I sat reading by a couple of candles. There was a roomful of old books at Bly—last-century fiction, some of it, which, to the extent of a distinctly deprecated renown, but never to so much as that of a stray specimen, had reached the sequestered home and appealed to the unavowed curiosity of my youth. I remember that the book I had in my hand was Fielding's *Amelia;* also that I was wholly awake. I recall further both a general conviction that it was horribly late and a particular objection to looking at my watch. I figure, finally, that the white curtain draping, in the fashion of those days, the head of Flora's little bed, shrouded, as I had assured myself long before, the perfection of childish rest. I recollect in short that, though I was deeply interested in my author, I found myself, at the turn of a page and with his spell all scattered, looking straight up from him and hard at the door of my room. There was a moment during which I listened, reminded of the faint sense I had had, the first night, of there being something undefineably astir in the house, and noted the soft breath of the open casement just move the half-drawn blind. Then, with all the marks of a deliberation that must have seemed magnificent had there been anyone to admire it, I laid down my book, rose to my feet, and, taking a candle, went straight out of the room and, from the passage, on which my light made little impression, noiselessly closed and locked the door.

I can say now neither what determined nor what guided me, but I went straight along the lobby, holding my candle high, till I came within sight of the tall window that presided over the great turn of the staircase. At this point I precipitately found myself aware of three things. They were practically simultaneous, yet they had flashes of succession. My candle, under a bold flourish, went out, and I perceived, by the uncovered window, that the yielding dusk of earliest morning rendered it unnecessary. Without it, the next instant, I saw that there was someone on the stair. I speak of sequences, but I required no lapse of seconds to stiffen myself for a third encounter with Quint. The apparition had reached the landing halfway up and was therefore on the spot nearest the window, where at sight of me, it stopped short and fixed me exactly as it had fixed me from the tower and from the garden. He knew me as well as I knew him; and so, in the cold, faint twilight, with a glimmer in the high glass and another on the polish of the oak stair below, we faced each other in our common intensity. He was absolutely, on this occasion, a living, detestable, dangerous presence. But that was not the wonder of wonders; I reserve this distinction for quite another circumstance: the circumstance that dread had unmistakeably quitted me and that there was nothing in me there that didn't meet and measure him.

I had plenty of anguish after that extraordinary moment, but I had, thank God, no terror. And he knew I had not — I found myself at the end of an instant magnificently aware of this. I felt, in a fierce rigour of confidence, that if I stood my ground a minute I should cease — for the time, at least — to have him to reckon with; and during the minute, accordingly, the thing was as human and hideous as a real interview: hideous just because it *was* human, as human as to have met alone, in the small hours, in a sleeping house, some enemy, some adventurer, some criminal. It was the dead silence of our long gaze at such close quarters that gave the whole horror, huge as it was, its only note of the unnatural. If I had met a murderer in such a place and at such an hour, we still at least would have spoken. Something would have passed, in life, between us; if nothing had passed one of us would have moved. The moment was so prolonged that it would have taken but little more to make me doubt if even *I* were in life. I can't express what followed it save by saying that the silence itself—which was indeed in a manner an attestation of my strength—became the element into which I saw the figure disappear; in which I definitely saw it turn as I might have seen the low wretch to which it had once belonged turn on receipt of an order, and pass, with my eyes on the villainous back that no hunch could have more disfigured, straight down the staircase and into the darkness in which the next bend was lost.

X

I remained awhile at the top of the stair, but with the effect presently of understanding that when my visitor had gone, he had gone: then I returned to my room. The foremost thing I saw there by the light of the candle I had left burning was that Flora's little bed was empty; and on this I caught my breath with all the terror that, five minutes before, I had been able to resist. I dashed at the place in which I had left her lying and over which (for the small silk counterpane and the sheets were disarranged) the white curtains had been deceivingly pulled forward; then my step, to my unutterable relief, produced an answering sound: I perceived an agitation of the window-blind, and the child, ducking down, emerged rosily from the other side of it. She stood there in so much of her candour and so little of her nightgown, with her pink bare feet and the golden glow of her curls. She looked intensely grave, and I had never had such a sense of losing an advantage acquired (the thrill of which had just been so prodigious) as on my consciousness that she addressed me with a reproach. "You naughty: where *have* you been?"—instead of challenging her own irregularity I found myself arraigned and explaining. She herself explained, for that matter, with the loveliest, eagerest simplicity. She had known suddenly, as she lay there, that I was out of the room, and had jumped up to see what had become of me. I had dropped, with the joy of her reappearance, back into my chair—feeling then, and then only, a little faint; and she had pattered straight over to me, thrown herself upon my knee, given herself to be held with the flame of the candle full in the wonderful little face that was still flushed with sleep. I remember closing my eyes an instant, yieldingly, consciously, as before the excess of something beautiful that shone out of the blue of her own. "You were looking for me out of the window?" I said. "You thought I might be walking in the grounds?"

"Well, you know, I thought someone was"—she never blanched as she smiled out that at me.

Oh, how I looked at her now! "And did you see anyone?"

"Ah, *no!*" she returned, almost with the full privilege of childish inconsequence, resentfully, though with a long sweetness in her little drawl of the negative.

At that moment, in the state of my nerves, I absolutely believed she lied; and if I once more closed my eyes it was before the dazzle of the three or four possible ways in which I might take this up. One of these, for a moment, tempted me with such singular intensity that, to withstand it, I must have gripped my little girl with a spasm that, wonderfully, she submitted to without a cry or a sign of fright. Why not break out at her on the spot and have it all over?— give it to her straight in her lovely little lighted face? "You see, you see, you *know* that you do and that you already quite suspect I believe it; therefore why not frankly confess it to me, so that we may at least live with it together and learn perhaps, in the strangeness of our fate, where we are and what it means?" This solicitation dropped, alas, as it came: if I could immediately have succumbed to it I might have spared myself—well you'll see what. Instead of succumbing I sprang again to my feet, looked at her bed, and took a helpless middle way. "Why did you pull the curtain over the place to make me think you were still there?"

Flora luminously considered; after which, with her little divine smile: "Because I don't like to frighten you!"

"But if I had, by your idea, gone out—?"

She absolutely declined to be puzzled; she turned her eyes to the flame of the candle as if the question were as irrelevant, or at any rate as impersonal, as Mrs. Marcet[3] or nine-times-nine. "Oh, but you know," she quite adequately answered, "that you might come back, you dear, and that you *have!*" And after a little, when she had got into bed, I had, for a long time, by almost sitting on her to hold her hand, to prove that I recognised the pertinence of my return.

You may imagine the general complexion, from that moment, of my nights. I repeatedly sat up till I didn't know when; I selected moments when my room-mate unmistakeably slept, and, stealing out, took noiseless turns in the passage and even pushed as far as to where I had last met Quint. But I never met him there again; and I may as well say at once that I on no other occasion saw him in the house. I just missed, on the staircase, on the other hand, a different adventure. Looking down it from the top I once recognised the presence of a woman seated on one of the lower steps with her back presented to me, her body half bowed and her head, in an attitude of woe, in her hands. I had been there but an instant, however, when she vanished without looking round at me. I knew, none the less, exactly what dreadful face she had to show; and I wondered whether, if instead of being above I had been below, I should have had, for going up, the same nerve I had lately shown Quint. Well, there continued to be plenty of chance for nerve. On the eleventh night after my latest encounter with that gentleman—they were all numbered now—I had an alarm that perilously skirted it and that indeed, from the particular quality of its unexpectedness, proved quite my sharpest shock. It was precisely the first night during this series that, weary with watching, I had felt that I might again without laxity lay myself down at my old hour. I slept immediately and, as I afterwards know, till about one o'clock; but when I woke it was to sit straight up, as completely roused as if a

[3]Mrs. Jane Marcet (1769-1858), the author of numerous books for children. She wrote popular works on scientific, economic, and many other subjects.

hand had shook me. I had left a light burning, but it was now out, and I felt an instant certainty that Flora had extinguished it. This brought me to my feet and straight, in the darkness, to her bed, which I found she had left. A glance at the window enlightened me further, and the striking of a match completed the picture.

The child had again got up—this time blowing out the taper, and had again, for some purpose of observation or response, squeezed in behind the blind and was peering out into the night. That she now saw—as she had not, I had satisfied myself, the previous time—was proved to me by the fact that she was disturbed neither by my re-illumination nor by the haste I made to get into slippers and into a wrap. Hidden, protected, absorbed, she evidently rested on the sill—the casement opened forward—and gave herself up. There was a great still moon to help her, and this fact had counted in my quick decision. She was face to face with the apparition we had met at the lake, and could now communicate with it as she had not then been able to do. What I, on my side, had to care for was, without disturbing her, to reach, from the corridor, some other window in the same quarter. I got to the door without her hearing me; I got out of it, closed it and listened, from the other side, for some sound from her. While I stood in the passage I had my eyes on her brother's door, which was but ten steps off and which, indescribably, produced in me a renewal of the strange impulse that I lately spoke of as my temptation. What if I should go straight in and march to *his* window?— what if, by risking to his boyish bewilderment a revelation of my motive, I should throw across the rest of the mystery the long halter of my boldness?

This thought held me sufficiently to make me cross to his threshold and pause again. I preternaturally listened; I figured to myself what might portentously be; I wondered if his bed were also empty and he too were secretly at watch. It was a deep, soundless minute, at the end of which my impulse failed. He was quiet; he might be innocent; the risk was hideous; I turned away. There was a figure in the grounds—a figure prowling for a sight, the visitor with whom Flora was engaged; but it was not the visitor most concerned with my boy. I hesitated afresh, but on other grounds and only a few seconds; then I had made my choice. There were empty rooms at Bly, and it was only a question of choosing the right one. The right one suddenly presented itself to me as the lower one—though high above the gardens—in the solid corner of the house that I have spoken of as the old tower. This was a large, square chamber, arranged with some state as a bedroom, the extravagant size of which made it so inconvenient that it had not for years, though kept by Mrs. Grose in exemplary order, been occupied. I had often admired it and I knew my way about in it; I had only after just faltering at the first chill gloom of its disuse, to pass across it and unbolt as quietly as I could one of the shutters. Achieving this transit, I uncovered the glass without a sound and, applying my face to the pane, was able, the darkness without being much less than within, to see that I commanded the right direction. Then I saw something more. The moon made the night extraordinarily penetrable and showed me on the lawn a person, diminished by distance, who stood there motionless and as if fascinated, looking up to where I had appeared—looking, that is, not so much straight at me as at something that was apparently above me. There was clearly another person above me—there was a person on the tower; but the presence on the lawn was not in the least what I had conceived and had confidently hurried to meet. The presence on the lawn—I felt sick as I made it out—was poor little Miles himself.

XI

It was not till late next day that I spoke to Mrs. Grose; the rigour with which I kept my pupils in sight making it often difficult to meet her privately, and the more as we each felt the importance of not provoking—on the part of the servants quite as much as on that of the children—any suspicion of a secret flurry or of a discussion of mysteries. I drew a great security in this particular from her mere smooth aspect. There was nothing in her fresh face to pass on to others my horrible confidences. She believed me, I was sure, absolutely: if she hadn't I don't know what would have become of me, for I couldn't have borne the business alone. But she was a magnificent monument to the blessing of a want of imagination, and if she could see in our little charges nothing but their beauty and amiability, their happiness and cleverness, she had no direct communication with the sources of my trouble. If they had been at all visibly blighted or battered, she would doubtless have grown, on tracing it back, haggard enough to match them; as matters stood, however, I could feel her, when she surveyed them, with her large white arms folded and the habit of serenity in all her look, thank the Lord's mercy that if they were ruined the pieces would still serve. Flights of fancy gave place, in her mind, to a steady fireside glow, and I had already begun to perceive how, with the development of the conviction that—as time went on without a public accident—our young things could, after all, look out for themselves, she addressed her greatest solicitude to the sad case presented by their instructress. That, for myself, was a sound simplification: I could engage that, to the world, my face should tell no tales, but it would have been, in the conditions, an immense added strain to find myself anxious about hers.

At the hour I now speak of she has joined me, under pressure, on the terrace, where, with the lapse of the season, the afternoon sun was now agreeable; and we sat there together while, before us, at a distance, but within call if we wished, the children strolled to and fro in one of their most manageable moods. They moved slowly, in unison, below us, over the lawn, the boy, as they went, reading aloud from a storybook and passing his arm round his sister to keep her quite in touch. Mrs. Grose watched them with positive placidity; then I caught the suppressed intellectual creak with which she conscientiously turned to take from me a view of the back of the tapestry. I had made her a receptacle of lurid things, but there was an odd recognition of my superiority—my accomplishments and my function—in her patience under my pain. She offered her mind to my disclosures as, had I wished to mix a witch's broth and proposed it with assurance, she would have held out a large clean saucepan. This had become thoroughly her attitude by the time that, in my recital of the events of the night, I reached the point of what Miles had said to me when, after seeing him, at such a monstrous hour, almost on the very spot where he happened now to be, I had gone down to bring him in; choosing then, at the window, with a concentrated need of not alarming the house, rather that method than a signal more resonant. I had left her meanwhile in little doubt of my small hope of representing with success even to her actual sympathy my sense of the real splendour of the little inspiration with which, after I had got him into the house, the boy met my final articulate challenge. As soon as I appeared in the moonlight on the terrace, he had come to me as straight as possible; on which I had taken his hand without a word and led him, through the dark spaces, up the staircase where Quint had so hungrily hovered for him, along the lobby where I had listened and trembled, and so to his forsaken room.

Not a sound, on the way, had passed between us, and I had wondered—oh, *how* I had wondered!—if he were groping about in his little mind for something plausible and not too grotesque. It would tax his invention, certainly, and I felt, this time, over his real embarrassment, a curious thrill of triumph. It was a sharp trap for the inscrutable! He couldn't play any longer at innocence; so how the deuce would he get out of it? There beat in me indeed, with the passionate throb of this question, an equal dumb appeal as to how the deuce *I* should. I was confronted at last, as never yet, with all the risk attached even now to sounding my own horrid note. I remember in fact that as we pushed into his little chamber, where the bed had not been slept in at all and the window, uncovered to the moonlight, made the place so clear that there was no need of striking a match—I remember how I suddenly dropped, sank upon the edge of the bed from the force of the idea that he must know how he really, as they say, "had" me. He could do what he liked, with all his cleverness to help him, so long as I should continue to defer to the old tradition of the criminality of those caretakers of the young who minister to superstitions and fears. He "had" me indeed, and in a cleft stick; for who would ever absolve me, who would consent that I should go unhung, if, by the faintest tremor of an overture, I were the first to introduce into our perfect intercourse an element so dire? No, no: it was useless to attempt to convey to Mrs. Grose, just as it is scarcely less so to attempt to suggest here, how, in our short, stiff brush in the dark, he fairly shook me with admiration. I was of course thoroughly kind and merciful; never, never yet had I placed on his little shoulders hands of such tenderness as those with which, while I rested against the bed, I held him there well under fire. I had no alternative but, in form at least, to put it to him.

"You must tell me now — and all the truth. What did you go out for? What were you doing there?"

I can still see his wonderful smile, the whites of his beautiful eyes, and the uncovering of his little teeth shine to me in the dusk. "If I tell you why, will you understand?" My heart, at this, leaped into my mouth. *Would* he tell me why? I found no sound on my lips to press it, and I was aware of replying only with a vague, repeated, grimacing nod. He was gentleness itself, and while I wagged my head at him he stood there more than ever a little fairy prince. It was his brightness indeed that gave me a respite. Would it be so great if he were really going to tell me? "Well," he said at last, "just exactly in order that you should do this."

"Do what?"

"Think me — for a change — *bad!*" I shall never forget the sweetness and gaiety with which he brought out the word, nor how, on top of it, he bent forward and kissed me. It was practically the end of everything. I met his kiss and I had to make, while I folded him for a minute in my arms, the most stupendous effort not to cry. He had given exactly the account of himself that permitted least of my going behind it, and it was only with the effect of confirming my acceptance of it that, as I presently glanced about the room, I could say —

"Then you didn't undress at all?"

He fairly glittered in the gloom. "Not at all. I sat up and read."

"And when did you go down?"

"At midnight. When I'm bad I *am* bad!"

"I see, I see—it's charming. But how could you be sure I would know it?"

"Oh, I arranged that with Flora." His answers rang out with a readiness! "She was to get up and look out."

"Which is what she did do." It was I who fell into the trap!

"So she disturbed you, and, to see what she was looking at, you also looked—you saw."

"While you," I concurred, "caught your death in the night air!"

He literally bloomed so from this exploit that he could afford radiantly to assent. "How otherwise should I have been bad enough?" he asked. Then, after another embrace, the incident and our interview closed on my recognition of all the reserves of goodness that, for his joke, he had been able to draw upon.

XII

The particular impression I had received proved in the morning light, I repeat, not quite successfully presentable to Mrs. Grose, though I reinforced it with the mention of still another remark that he had made before we separated. "It all lies in half-a-dozen words," I said to her, "words that really settle the matter. 'Think, you know, what I *might* do!' He threw that off to show me how good he is. He knows down to the ground what he 'might' do. That's what he gave them a taste of at school."

"Lord, you do change!" cried my friend.

"I don't change—I simply make it out. The four, depend upon it, perpetually meet. If on either of these last nights you had been with either child, you would clearly have understood. The more I've watched and waited the more I've felt that if there were nothing else to make it sure it would be made so by the systematic silence of each. *Never,* by a slip of the tongue, have they so much as alluded to either of their old friends, any more than Miles has alluded to his expulsion. Oh yes, we may sit here and look at them, and they may show off to us there to their fill; but even while they pretend to be lost in their fairy-tale they're steeped in their vision of the dead restored. He's not reading to her," I declared; "they're talking of *them—* they're talking horrors! I go on, I know, as if I were crazy; and it's a wonder I'm not. What I've seen would have made *you* so; but it has only made me more lucid, made me get hold of still other things."

My lucidity must have seemed awful, but the charming creatures who were victims of it, passing and repassing in their interlocked sweetness, gave my colleague something to hold on by; and I felt how tight she held as, without stirring in the breath of my passion, she covered them still with her eyes. "Of what other things have you got hold?"

"Why, of the very things that have delighted, fascinated, and yet, at bottom, as I now so strangely see, mystified and troubled me. Their more than earthly beauty, their absolutely unnatural goodness. It's a game," I went on; "it's a policy and a fraud!"

"On the part of little darlings—?"

"As yet mere lovely babies? Yes, mad as that seems!" The very act of bringing it out really helped me to trace it— follow it all up and piece it all together. "They haven't been good—they've only been absent. It has been easy to live with them, because they're simply leading a life of their own. They're not mine—they're not ours. They're his and they're hers!"

"Quint's and that woman's?"

"Quint's and that woman's. They want to get to them."

Oh, how, at this, poor Mrs. Grose appeared to study them! "But for what?"

"For the love of all the evil that, in those dreadful days, the pair put into them. And to ply them with that evil still, to keep up the work of demons, is what brings the others back."

"Laws!" said my friend under her breath. The exclamation was homely, but it revealed a real acceptance of my further proof of what, in the bad time—for there had been a worse even than this!—must have occurred. There could have been no such justification for me as the plain assent of her experience to whatever depth of depravity I found credible in our brace of scoundrels. It was in obvious submission of memory that she brought out after a moment: "They *were* rascals! But what can they now do?" she pursued.

"Do?" I echoed so loud that Miles and Flora, as they passed at their distance, paused an instant in their walk and looked at us. "Don't they do enough?" I demanded in a lower tone, while the children, having smiled and nodded and kissed hands to us, resumed their exhibition. We were held by it a minute; then I answered: "They can destroy them!" At this my companion did turn, but the inquiry she launched was a silent one, the effect of which was to make me more explicit. "They don't know, as yet, quite how — but they're trying hard. They're seen only across, as it were, and beyond — in strange places and on high places, the top of towers, the roof of houses, the outside of windows, the further edge of pools; but there's a deep design, on either side, to shorten the distance and overcome the obstacle; and the success of the tempters is only a question of time. They've only to keep to their suggestions of danger."

"For the children to come?"

"And perish in the attempt!" Mrs. Grose slowly got up, and I scrupulously added: "Unless, of course, we can prevent!"

Standing there before me while I kept my seat, she visibly turned things over. "Their uncle must do the preventing. He must take them away."

"And who's to make him?"

She had been scanning the distance, but she now dropped on me a foolish face. "You, Miss."

"By writing to him that his house is poisoned and his little nephew and niece mad?"

"But if they *are*, Miss?"

"And if I am myself, you mean? That's charming news to be sent him by a governess whose prime undertaking was to give him no worry."

Mrs. Grose considered, following the children again. "Yes, he do hate worry. That was the great reason — "

"Why those fiends took him in so long? No doubt, though

his indifference must have been awful. As I'm not a fiend, at any rate, I shouldn't take him in."

My companion, after an instant and for all answer, sat down again and grasped my arm. "Make him at any rate come to you."

I stared. "To *me?*" I had a sudden fear of what she might do. " 'Him'?"

"He ought to *be* here—he ought to help."

I quickly rose, and I think I must have shown her a queerer face than ever yet. "You see me asking him for a visit?" No, with her eyes on my face she evidently couldn't. Instead of it even—as a woman reads another—she could see what I myself saw: his derision, his amusement, his contempt for the break-down of my resignation at being left alone and for the fine machinery I had set in motion to attract his attention to my slighted charms. She didn't know —no one knew—how proud I had been to serve him and to stick to our terms; yet she none the less took the measure, I think, of the warning I now gave her. "If you should so lose your head as to appeal to him for me—"

She was really frightened. "Yes, Miss?"

"I would leave, on the spot, both him and you."

XIII

It was all very well to join them, but speaking to them proved quite as much as ever an effort beyond my strength —offered, in close quarters, difficulties as insurmountable as before. This situation continued a month, and with new aggravations and particular notes, the note above all, sharper and sharper, of the small ironic consciousness on the part of my pupils. It was not, I am as sure today as I was sure then, my mere infernal imagination: it was absolutely traceable that they were aware of my predicament and that this strange relation made, in a manner, for a long time, the air in which we moved. I don't mean that they had their tongues in their cheeks or did anything vulgar, for that was not one of their dangers: I do mean, on the other hand, that the element of the unnamed and untouched became, be-

tween us, greater than any other, and that so much avoidance could not have been so successfully effected without a
great deal of tacit° arrangement. It was as if, at moments, we
were perpetually coming into sight of subjects before which
we must stop short, turning suddenly out of alleys that we
perceived to be blind, closing with a little bang that made
us look at each other—for, like all bangs, it was something
louder than we had intended—the doors we had indis-
creetly opened. All roads lead to Rome, and there were
times when it might have struck us that almost every branch
of study or subject of conversation skirted forbidden
ground. Forbidden ground was the question of the return
of the dead in general and of whatever, in especial, might
survive, in memory, of the friends little children had lost.
There were days when I could have sworn that one of them
had, with a small invisible nudge, said to the other: "She
thinks she'll do it this time—but she *won't!*" To "do it"
would have been to indulge, for instance—and for once in a
way—in some direct reference to the lady who had prepared them for my discipline. They had a delightful endless appetite for passages in my own history, to which I
had again and again treated them; they were in possession
of everything that had ever happened to me, had had, with
every circumstance, the story of my smallest adventures
and of those of my brothers and sisters and of the cat and the
dog at home, as well as many particulars of the eccentric
nature of my father, of the furniture and arrangement of our
house, and of the conversation of the old women of our
village. There were things enough, taking one with
another, to chatter about, if one went very fast and knew by
instinct when to go round. They pulled with an art of their
own the strings of my invention and my memory; and
nothing else perhaps, when I thought of such occasions
afterwards, gave me so the suspicion of being watched from
under cover. It was in any case over *my* life, *my* past, and
my friends alone that we could take anything like our ease
—a state of affairs that led them sometimes without the least
pertinence to break out into sociable reminders. I was
invited—with no visible connection—to repeat afresh

Goody Gosling's celebrated *mot°* or to confirm the details already supplied as to the cleverness of the vicarage pony.

It was partly at such junctures as these and partly at quite different ones that, with the turn my matters had now taken, my predicament, as I have called it, grew most sensible. The fact that the days passed for me without another encounter ought, it would have appeared, to have done something toward soothing my nerves. Since the light brush, that second night on the upper landing, of the presence of a woman at the foot of the stair, I had seen nothing, whether in or out of the house, that one had better not have seen. There was many a corner round which I expected to come upon Quint, and many a situation that, in a merely sinister way, would have favoured the appearance of Miss Jessel. The summer had turned, the summer had gone; the autumn had dropped upon Bly and had blown out half our lights. The place, with its grey sky and withered garlands, its bared spaces and scattered dead leaves, was like a theatre after the performance—all strewn with crumpled playbills. There were exactly states of the air, conditions of sound and of stillness, unspeakable impressions of the *kind* of ministering moment, that brought back to me, long enough to catch it, the feeling of the medium in which, that June evening out-of-doors, I had had my first sight of Quint, and in which, too, at those other instants, I had, after seeing him through the window, looked for him in vain in the circle of shrubbery. I recognised the signs, the portents—I recognised the moment, the spot. But they remained unaccompanied and empty, and I continued unmolested; if unmolested one could call a young woman whose sensibility had, in the most extraordinary fashion, not declined but deepened. I had said in my talk with Mrs. Grose on that horrid scene of Flora's by the lake—and had perplexed her by so saying—that it would from that moment distress me much more to lose my power than to keep it. I had then expressed what was vividly in my mind: the truth that, whether the children really saw or not—since, that is, it was not yet definitely proved—I greatly preferred, as a safeguard, the fullness of my own exposure. I was ready to know the very worst that was to be known. What I had then had an ugly glimpse of was that my eyes might be sealed just while theirs were most opened. Well, my eyes *were* sealed, it appeared, at present—a consummation for which it seemed blasphemous not to thank God. There was, alas, a difficulty about that: I would have thanked him with all my soul had I not had in a proportionate measure this conviction of the secret of my pupils.

How can I retrace today the strange steps of my obsession? There were times of our being together when I would have been ready to swear that, literally, in my presence, but with my direct sense of it closed, they had visitors who were known and were welcome. Then it was that, had I not been deterred by the very chance that such an injury might prove greater than the injury to be averted, my exultation would have broken out. "They're here, they're here, you little wretches," I would have cried, "and you can't deny it now!" The little wretches denied it with all the added volume of their sociability and their tenderness, in just the crystal depths of which—like the flash of a fish in a stream— the mockery of their advantage peeped up. The shock, in truth, had sunk into me still deeper than I knew on the night when, looking out to see either Quint or Miss Jessel under the stars, I had beheld the boy over whose rest I watched and who had immediately brought in with him— had straightway, there, turned it on me—the lovely upward look with which, from the battlements above me, the hideous apparition of Quint had played. If it was a question of a scare, my discovery on this occasion had scared me more than any other, and it was in the condition of nerves produced by it that I made my actual inductions. They harassed me so that sometimes, at odd moments, I shut myself up audibly to rehearse—it was at once a fantastic relief and a renewed despair—the manner in which I might come to the point. I approached it from one side and the other while, in my room, I flung myself about, but I always broke down in the monstrous utterance of names. As they died away on my lips, I said to myself that I should indeed help them to represent something infamous, if by pronouncing them, I should violate as rare a little case of instinctive delicacy as any schoolroom, probably, had ever known. When I said to myself: "*They* have the manners to be silent, and you, trusted as you are, the baseness to speak!" I felt myself crimson and I covered my face with my hands. After these secret scenes I chattered more than ever, going on volubly enough 'til one of our prodigious, palpable° hushes occurred —I can call them nothing else—the strange, dizzy lift or swim (I try for terms!) into a stillness, a pause of all life, that had nothing to do with the more or less noise that at the moment we might be engaged in making and that I could hear through any deepened exhilaration or quickened recitation or louder strum of the piano. Then it was that the others, the outsiders, were there. Though they were not angels, they "passed," as the French say, causing me, while they stayed, to tremble with the fear of their addressing to their younger victims some yet more infernal message or more vivid image than they had thought good enough for myself.

What it was most impossible to get rid of was the cruel idea that, whatever I had seen, Miles and Flora saw *more*— things terrible and unguessable and that sprang from dreadful passages of intercourse in the past. Such things naturally left on the surface, for the time, a chill which we vociferously denied that we felt; and we had, all three, with repetition, got into such splendid training that we went, each time, almost automatically, to mark the close of the incident, through the very same movements. It was striking of the children, at all events, to kiss me inveterately with a kind of wild irrelevance and never to fail—one or the other —of the precious question that had helped us through many a peril. "When do you think he *will* come? Don't you think we *ought* to write?"—there was nothing like that inquiry, we found by experience, for carrying off an awkwardness. "He" of course was their uncle in Harley Street; and we lived in much profusion of theory that he might at any moment arrive to mingle in our circle. It was impossible to have given less encouragement than he had done to such a doctrine, but if we had not had the doctrine to fall back upon we should have deprived each other of some of our finest exhibitions. He never wrote to them — that may have been selfish, but it was a part of the flattery of his trust of me; for the way in which a man pays his highest tribute to a woman is apt to be but by the more festal celebration of one of the sacred laws of his comfort; and I held that I carried out the spirit of the pledge given not to appeal to him when I let my charges understand that their own letters were but charming literary exercises. They were too beautiful to be posted; I kept them myself; I have them all to this hour. This was a rule indeed which only added to the satiric effect of my being plied with the supposition that he might at any moment be among us. It was exactly as if my charges knew how almost more awkward than anything else that might be for me. There appears to me, moreover, as I look back, no note in all this more extraordinary than the mere fact that, in spite of my tension and of their triumph, I never lost patience with them. Adorable they must in truth have been, I now reflect, that I didn't in these days hate them! Would exasperation, however, if relief had longer been postponed, finally have betrayed me? It little matters, for relief arrived. I call it relief, though it was only the relief that a snap brings to a strain or the burst of a thunderstorm to a day of suffocation. It was at least change, and it came with a rush.

XIV

Walking to church a certain Sunday morning, I had little Miles at my side and his sister, in advance of us and at Mrs. Grose's, well in sight. It was a crisp, clear day, the first of its order for some time; the night had brought a touch of frost, and the autumn air, bright and sharp, made the church-bells almost gay. It was an odd accident of thought that I should have happened at such a moment to be particularly and very gratefully struck with the obedience of my little charges. Why did they never resent my inexorable, my perpetual society? Something or other had brought nearer home to me that I had all but pinned the boy to my shawl and that, in the way our companions were marshalled before me, I might have appeared to provide against some danger of rebellion. I was like a gaoler° with an eye to possible surprises and escapes. But all this belonged—I mean their magnificent little surrender—just to the special array of the facts that were most abysmal.° Turned out for Sunday by his uncle's tailor, who had had a free hand and a notion of pretty waistcoats and of his grand little air, Miles's whole title to independence, the rights of his sex and situation, were so stamped upon him that if he had suddenly struck for freedom I should have had nothing to say. I was by the strangest of chances wondering how I should meet him when the revolution unmistakeably occurred. I call it a revolution because I now see how, with the word he spoke, the curtain rose on the last act of my dreadful drama and the catastrophe was precipitated.° "Look here, my dear, you know," he charmingly said, "when in the world, please, am I going back to school?"

Transcribed here the speech sounds harmless enough, particularly as uttered in the sweet, high, casual pipe with which, at all interlocutors, but above all at his eternal governess, he threw off intonations as if he were tossing roses. There was something in them that always made one "catch," and I caught, at any rate, now so effectually that I stopped as short as if one of the trees of the park had fallen across the road. There was something new, on the spot, between us, and he was perfectly aware that I recognised it, though, to enable me to do so, he had no need to look a whit less candid and charming than usual. I could feel in him how he already, from my at first finding nothing to reply, perceived the advantage he had gained. I was so slow to find anything that he had plenty of time, after a minute, to continue with his suggestive but inconclusive smile: "You know, my dear, that for a fellow to be with a lady al-ways—!" His "my dear" was constantly on his lips for me, and nothing could have expressed more the exact shade of the sentiment with which I desired to inspire my pupils than its fond familiarity. It was so respectfully easy.

But, oh, how I felt that at present I must pick my own phrases! I remember that, to gain time, I tried to laugh, and I seemed to see in the beautiful face with which he watched me how ugly and queer I looked. "And always with the same lady?" I returned.

He neither blenched nor winked. The whole thing was virtually out between us. "Ah, of course, she's a jolly, 'perfect' lady; but, after all, I'm a fellow, don't you see? that's—well, getting on."

I lingered there with him an instant ever so kindly. "Yes, you're getting on." Oh, but I felt helpless!

I have kept to this day the heartbreaking little idea of how he seemed to know that and to play with it. "And you can't say I've not been awfully good, can you?"

I laid my hand on his shoulder, for, though I felt how much better it would have been to walk on, I was not yet quite able. "No, I can't say that, Miles."

"Except just that one night, you know—!"

"That one night?" I couldn't look as straight as he.

"Why, when I went down—went out of the house."

"Oh, yes. But I forget what you did it for."

"You forget?"—he spoke with the sweet extravagance of childish reproach. "Why, it was to show you I could!"

"Oh, yes, you could."

"And I can again."

I felt that I might, perhaps, after all succeed in keeping my wits about me. "Certainly. But you won't."

"No, not *that* again. It was nothing."

"It was nothing," I said. "But we must go on."

He resumed our walk with me, passing his hand into my arm. "Then when *am* I going back?"

I wore, in turning it over, my most responsible air. "Were you very happy at school?"

He just considered. "Oh, I'm happy enough anywhere!"

"Well, then," I quavered, "if you're just as happy here—!"

"Ah, but that isn't everything! Of course *you* know a lot—"

"But you hint that you know almost as much?" I risked as he paused.

"Not half I want to!" Miles honestly professed. "But it isn't so much that."

"What is it, then?"

"Well—I want to see more life."

"I see; I see." We had arrived within sight of the church and of various persons, including several of the household of Bly, on their way to it and clustered about the door to see us go in. I quickened our step; I wanted to get there before the question between us opened up much further; I reflected hungrily that, for more than an hour, he would have to be silent; and I thought with envy of the comparative dusk of the pew and of the almost spiritual help of the hassock on which I might bend my knees. I seemed literally to be running a race with some confusion to which he was about to reduce me, but I felt that he had got in first when, before we had even entered the churchyard, he threw out—

"I want my own sort!"

It literally made me bound forward. "There are not many of your own sort, Miles!" I laughed. "Unless perhaps dear little Flora!"

"You really compare me to a baby girl?"

This found me singularly weak. "Don't you, then, *love* our sweet Flora?"

"If I didn't—and you too; if I didn't—!" he repeated as if retreating for a jump, yet leaving his thought so unfinished that, after we had come into the gate, another stop, which he imposed on me by the pressure of his arm, had become inevitable. Mrs. Grose and Flora had passed into the church, the other worshippers had followed, and we were, for the minute, alone among the old, thick graves. We had paused, on the path from the gate, by a low, oblong, table-like tomb.

"Yes. If you didn't—?"

He looked, while I waited, about at the graves. "Well, you know what!" But he didn't move, and he presently produced something that made me drop straight down on the stone slab, as if suddenly to rest. "Does my uncle think what *you* think?"

I markedly rested. "How do you know what I think?"

"Ah, well, of course I don't; for it strikes me you never tell me. But I mean does *he* know?"

"Know what, Miles?"

"Why, the way I'm going on."

I perceived quickly enough that I could make, to this inquiry, no answer that would not involve something of a sacrifice of my employer. Yet it appeared to me that we were all, at Bly, sufficiently sacrificed to make that venial.° "I don't think your uncle much cares."

Miles, on this, stood looking at me. "Then don't you think he can be made to?"

"In what way?"

"Why, by his coming down."

"But who'll get him to come down?"

"*I* will!" the boy said with extraordinary brightness and emphasis. He gave me another look charged with that expression and then marched off alone into church.

XV

The business was practically settled from the moment I never followed him. It was a pitiful surrender to agitation, but my being aware of this had somehow no power to restore me. I only sat there on my tomb and read into what my little friend had said to me the fullness of its meaning; by the time I had grasped the whole of which I had also embraced, for absence, the pretext that I was ashamed to offer my pupils and the rest of the congregation such an example of delay. What I said to myself above all was that Miles had got something out of me and that the proof of it, for him, would be just this awkward collapse. He had got out of me that there was something I was much afraid of and that he should probably be able to make use of my fear to gain, for his own purpose, more freedom. My fear was of having to deal with the intolerable question of the grounds of his dismissal from school, for that was really but the question of the horrors gathered behind. That his uncle should arrive to treat with me of these things was a solution that, strictly speaking, I ought now to have desired to bring on; but I could so little face the ugliness and the pain of it that I simply procrastinated° and lived from hand to mouth. The boy, to my deep discomposure, was immensely in the right, was in a position to say to me: "Either you clear up with my guardian the mystery of this interruption of my studies, or you cease to expect me to lead with you a life that's so unnatural for a boy." What was so unnatural for the particular boy I was concerned with was this sudden revelation of a consciousness and a plan.

That was what really overcame me, what prevented my going in. I walked round the church, hesitating, hovering; I reflected that I had already, with him, hurt myself beyond repair. Therefore I could patch up nothing, and it was too extreme an effort to squeeze beside him into the pew: he would be so much more sure than ever to pass his arm into mine and make me sit there for an hour in close, silent contact with his commentary on our talk. For the first minute since his arrival I wanted to get away from him. As I paused beneath the high east window and listened to the sounds of worship, I was taken with an impulse that might master me, I felt, completely should I give it the least encouragement. I might easily put an end to my predicament by getting away altogether. Here was my chance; there was no one to stop me; I could give the whole thing up—turn my back and retreat. It was only a question of hurrying again, for a few preparations, to the house which the attendance at church of so many of the servants would practically have left unoccupied. No one, in short, could blame me if I should just drive desperately off. What was it to get away if I got away only till dinner? That would be in a couple of hours, at the end of which—I had the acute prevision—my little pupils would play at innocent wonder about my non-appearance in their train.

"What *did* you do, you naughty, bad thing? Why in the world, to worry us so—and take our thoughts off too, don't you know?—did you desert us at the very door?" I couldn't meet such questions nor, as they asked them, their false little lovely eyes; yet it was all so exactly what I should have to meet that, as the prospect grew sharp to me, I at last let myself go.

I got, so far as the immediate moment was concerned, away; I came straight out of the churchyard and, thinking hard, retraced my steps through the park. It seemed to me that by the time I reached the house I had made up my mind I would fly. The Sunday stillness both of the approaches and of the interior, in which I met no one, fairly excited me with a sense of opportunity. Were I to get off quickly, this way, I should get off without a scene, without a word. My quickness would have to be remarkable, however, and the question of a conveyance was the great one to settle. Tormented, in the hall, with difficulties and obstacles, I remember sinking down at the foot of the staircase—suddenly collapsing there on the lowest step and then, with a revulsion, recalling that it was exactly where more than a month before, in the darkness of night and just so bowed with evil things, I had seen the spectre of the most horrible of women. At this I was able to straighten myself; I went the rest of the way up; I made, in my bewilderment, for the schoolroom, where there were objects belonging to me that I should have to take. But I opened the door to find again, in a flash, my eyes unsealed. In the presence of what I saw I reeled straight back upon my resistance.

Seated at my own table in clear noonday light I saw a person whom, without my previous experience, I should have taken at the first blush for some housemaid who might have stayed at home to look after the place and who, availing herself of rare relief from observation and of the schoolroom table and my pens, ink, and paper, had applied herself to the considerable effort of a letter to her sweetheart. There was an effort in the way that, while her arms rested on the table, her hand with evident weariness supported her head; but at the moment I took this in I had already become aware that, in spite of my entrance, her attitude strangely persisted. Then it was—with the very act of its announcing itself—that her identity flared up in a change of posture. She rose, not as if she had heard me, but with an indescribable grand melancholy of indifference and detachment, and, within a dozen feet of me, stood there as my vile predecessor. Dishonoured and tragic, she was all before me; but even as I fixed and, for memory, secured it, the awful image passed away. Dark as midnight in her black dress, her haggard beauty and her unutterable woe, she had looked at me long enough to appear to say that her right to sit at my table was as good as mine to sit at hers. While these instants lasted indeed I had the extraordinary chill of a feeling that it was I who was the intruder. It was as a wild protest against it that, actually addressing her—"You terrible, miserable woman!"—I heard myself break into a sound that, by the open door, rang through the long passage and the empty house. She looked at me as if she heard me, but I had recovered myself and cleared the air. There was nothing in the room the next minute but the sunshine and a sense that I must stay.

XVI

I had so perfectly expected that the return of my pupils would be marked by a demonstration that I was freshly upset at having to take into account that they were dumb about my absence. Instead of gaily denouncing and caressing me, they made no allusion to my having failed them, and I was left, for the time, on perceiving that she too said nothing, to study Mrs. Grose's odd face. I did this to such purpose that I made sure they had in some way bribed her to silence; a silence that, however, I would engage to break down on the first private opportunity. This opportunity came before tea: I secured five minutes with her in the houskeeper's room, where, in the twilight, amid a smell of lately-baked bread, but with the place all swept and garnished, I found her sitting in pained placidity before the fire. So I see her still, so I see her best: facing the flame from her straight chair in the dusky, shining room, a large clean image of the "put away"—of drawers closed and locked and rest without a remedy.

"Oh, yes, they asked me to say nothing; and to please them—so long as they were there—of course I promised. But what had happened to you?"

"I only went with you for the walk," I said. "I had then to come back to meet a friend."

She showed her surprise. "A friend—*you*?"

"Oh, yes, I have a couple!" I laughed. "But did the children give you a reason?"

"For not alluding to your leaving us? Yes; they said you would like it better. Do you like it better?"

My face had made her rueful. "No, I like it worse!" But after an instant I added: "Did they say why I should like it better?"

"No; Master Miles only said, 'We must do nothing but what she likes'!"

"I wish indeed he would! And what did Flora say?"

"Miss Flora was too sweet. She said, 'Oh, of course, of course!'—and I said the same."

I thought a moment. "You were too sweet too—I can hear you all. But none the less, between Miles and me, it's now all out."

"All out?" My companion stared. "But what, Miss?"

"Everything. It doesn't matter. I've made up my mind. I came home, my dear," I went on, "for a talk with Miss Jessel."

I had by this time formed the habit of having Mrs. Grose literally well in hand in advance of my sounding that note; so that even now, as she bravely blinked under the signal of my word, I could keep her comparatively firm. "A talk! Do you mean she spoke?"

"It came to that. I found her, on my return, in the schoolroom."

"And what did she say?" I can hear the good woman still, and the candour of her stupefaction.

"That she suffers the torments—!"

It was this, of a truth, that made her, as she filled out my picture, gape. "Do you mean," she faltered, "—of the lost?"

"Of the lost. Of the damned. And that's why, to share them—" I faltered myself with the horror of it.

But my companion, with less imagination, kept me up. "To share them—?"

"She wants Flora." Mrs. Grose might, as I gave it to her, fairly have fallen away from me had I not been prepared. I still held her there, to show I was. "As I've told you, however, it doesn't matter."

"Because you've made up your mind? But to what?"

"To everything."

"And what do you call 'everything'?"

"Why, sending for their uncle."

"Oh, Miss, in pity do," my friend broke out.

"Ah, but I will, I *will!* I see it's the only way. What's 'out,' as I told you, with Miles is that if he thinks I'm afraid to—and has ideas of what he gains by that—he shall see he's mistaken. Yes, yes; his uncle shall have it here from me on the spot (and before the boy himself if necessary) that if I'm to be reproached with having done nothing again about more school!—"

"Yes, Miss—" my companion pressed me.

"Well, there's that awful reason."

There were now clearly so many of these for my poor colleague that she was excusable for being vague. "But—a—which?"

"Why, the letter from his old place."

"You'll show it to the master?"

"I ought to have done so on the instant."

"Oh, no!" said Mrs. Grose with decision.

"I'll put it before him," I went on inexorably, "that I can't undertake to work the question on behalf of a child who has been expelled—"

"For we've never in the least known what!" Mrs. Grose declared.

"For wickedness. For what else—when he's so clever and beautiful and perfect? Is he stupid? Is he untidy? Is he infirm? Is he ill-natured? He's exquisite—so it can be only *that;* and that would open up the whole thing. After all," I said, "it's their uncle's fault. If he left here such people—!"

"He didn't really in the least know them. The fault's mine." She had turned quite pale.

"Well, you shan't suffer," I answered.

"The children shan't!" she emphatically returned.

I was silent awhile; we looked at each other. "Then what am I to tell him?"

"You needn't tell him anything. *I'll* tell him."

I measured this. "Do you mean you'll write—?" Remembering she couldn't, I caught myself up. "How do you communicate?"

"I tell the bailiff. *He* writes."

"And should you like him to write our story?"

My question had a sarcastic force that I had not fully intended, and it made her, after a moment, inconsequently break down. The tears were again in her eyes. "Ah, Miss, *you* write!"

"Well—tonight," I at last answered; and on this we separated.

XVII

I went so far, in the evening, as to make a beginning. The weather had changed back, a great wind was abroad, and beneath the lamp, in my room, with Flora at peace beside me, I sat for a long time before a blank sheet of paper and listened to the lash of the rain and the batter of the gusts. Finally I went out, taking a candle; I crossed the passage and listened a minute at Miles's door. What, under my endless obsession, I had been impelled to listen for was some betrayal of his not being at rest, and I presently caught one, but not in the form I had expected. His voice tinkled out. "I say, you there—come in." It was a gaiety in the gloom!

I went in with my light and found him, in bed, very wide awake, but very much at his ease. "Well, what are *you* up to?" he asked with a grace of sociability in which it occurred to me that Mrs. Grose, had she been present, might have looked in vain for proof that anything was "out."

I stood over him with my candle. "How did you know I was there?"

"Why, of course I heard you. Did you fancy you made no noise? You're like a troop of cavalry!" he beautifully laughed.

"Then you weren't asleep?"

"Not much! I lie awake and think."

I had put my candle, designedly, a short way off, and then, as he held out his friendly old hand to me, had sat down on the edge of his bed. "What is it," I asked, "that you think of?"

"What in the world, my dear, but *you*?"

"Ah, the pride I take in your appreciation doesn't insist on that! I had so far rather you slept."

"Well, I think also, you know, of this queer business of ours."

I marked the coolness of his firm little hand. "Of what queer business, Miles?"

"Why, the way you bring me up. And all the rest!"

I fairly held my breath a minute, and even from my glimmering taper there was light enough to show how he smiled up at me from his pillow. "What do you mean by all the rest?"

"Oh, you know, you know!"

I could say nothing for a minute, though I felt, as I held his hand and our eyes continued to meet, that my silence had all the air of admitting his charge and that nothing in the whole world of reality was perhaps at that moment so fabulous as our actual relation. "Certainly you shall go back to school," I said, "if it be that that troubles you. But not to the old place—we must find another, a better. How could I know it did trouble you, this question, when you never told me so, never spoke of it at all?" His clear, listening face, framed in its smooth whiteness, made him for the minute as appealing as some wistful patient in a children's hospital; and I would have given, as the resemblance came to me, all I possessed on earth really to be the nurse or the sister of charity who might have helped to cure him. Well, even as it was, I perhaps might help! "Do you know you've never said a word to me about your school—I mean the old one; never mentioned it in any way?"

He seemed to wonder; he smiled with the same loveliness. But he clearly gained time; he waited, he called for guidance. "Haven't I?" It wasn't for me to help him—it was for the thing I had met!

Something in his tone and the expression of his face, as I got this from him, set my heart aching with such a pang as it had never yet known; so unutterably touching was it to see his little brain puzzled and his little resources taxed to play, under the spell laid on him, a part of innocence and consistency. "No, never—from the hour you came back. You've never mentioned to me one of your masters, one of your comrades, nor the least little thing that ever happened to you at school. Never, little Miles—no, never—have you given me an inkling of anything that *may* have happened there. Therefore you can fancy how much I'm in the dark. Until you came out, that way, this morning, you had, since the first hour I saw you, scarce even made a reference to anything in your previous life. You seemed so perfectly to accept the present." It was extraordinary how my absolute conviction of his secret precocity° (or whatever I might call the poison of an influence that I dared but half to phrase) made him, in spite of the faint breath of his inward trouble, appear as accessible as an older person—imposed him almost as an intellectual equal. "I thought you wanted to go on as you are."

It struck me that at this he just faintly coloured. He gave, at any rate, like a convalescent slightly fatigued, a languid shake of his head. "I don't—I don't. I want to get away."

"You're tired of Bly?"

"Oh, no, I like Bly."

"Well, then—?"

"Oh, *you* know what a boy wants!"

I felt that I didn't know so well as Miles, and I took temporary refuge. "You want to go to your uncle?"

Again, at this, with his sweet ironic face, he made a movement on the pillow. "Ah, you can't get off with that!"

I was silent a little, and it was I, now, I think, who changed colour. "My dear, I don't want to get off!"

"You can't, even if you do. You can't, you can't!"—he lay beautifully staring. "My uncle must come down, and you must completely settle things."

"If we do," I returned with some spirit, "you may be sure it will be to take you quite away."

"Well, don't you understand that that's exactly what I'm working for? You'll have to tell him—about the way you've let it all drop: you'll have to tell him a tremendous lot!"

The exultation with which he uttered this helped me somehow, for the instant, to meet him rather more. "And how much will *you*, Miles, have to tell him? There are things he'll ask you!"

He turned it over. "Very likely. But what things?"

"The things you've never told me. To make up his mind what to do with you. He can't send you back—"

"Oh, I don't want to go back!" he broke in. "I want a new field."

He said it with admirable serenity, with positive unimpeachable gaiety; and doubtless it was that very note that most evoked for me the poignancy, the unnatural childish tragedy, of his probable reappearance at the end of three months with all this bravado and still more dishonour. It overwhelmed me now that I should never be able to bear that, and it made me let myself go. I threw myself upon him and in the tenderness of my pity I embraced him. "Dear little Miles, dear little Miles—!"

My face was close to his, and he let me kiss him, simply taking it with indulgent good-humour. "Well, old lady?"

"Is there nothing—nothing at all that you want to tell me?"

He turned off a little, facing round toward the wall and holding up his hand to look at as one had seen sick children look. "I've told you—I told you this morning."

Oh, I was sorry for him! "That you just want me not to worry you?"

He looked round at me now, as if in recognition of my understanding him; then ever so gently, "To let me alone," he replied.

There was even a singular little dignity in it, something that made me release him, yet, when I had slowly risen, linger beside him. God knows I never wished to harass him, but I felt that merely, at this, to turn my back on him was to abandon or, to put it more truly, to lose him. "I've just begun a letter to your uncle," I said.

"Well, then, finish it!"

I waited a minute. "What happened before?"

He gazed up at me again. "Before what?"

"Before you came back. And before you went away."

For some time he was silent, but he continued to meet my eyes. "What happened?"

It made me, the sound of the words, in which it seemed to me that I caught for the very first time a small faint quaver of consenting consciousness — it made me drop on my knees beside the bed and seize once more the chance of possessing him. "Dear little Miles, dear little Miles, if you *knew* how I want to help you! It's only that, it's nothing but that, and I'd rather die than give you a pain or do you a wrong — I'd rather die than hurt a hair of you. Dear little Miles" — oh, I brought it out now even if I *should* go too far — "I just want you to help me to save you!" But I knew in a moment after this that I had gone too far. The answer to my appeal was instantaneous, but it came in the form of an extraordinary blast and chill, a gust of frozen air and a shake of the room as great as if, in the wild wind, the casement had crashed in. The boy gave a loud, high shriek, which, lost in the rest of the shock of sound, might have seemed, indistinctly, though I was so close to him, a note either of jubilation or of terror. I jumped to my feet again and was conscious of darkness. So for a moment we remained, while I stared about me and saw that the drawn curtains were unstirred and the window tight. "Why, the candle's out!" I then cried.

"It was I who blew it, dear!" said Miles.

XVIII

The next day, after lessons, Mrs. Grose found a moment to say to me quietly: "Have you written, Miss?"

"Yes — I've written." But I didn't add — for the hour — that my letter, sealed and directed, was still in my pocket. There would be time enough to send it before the messenger should go to the village. Meanwhile there had been, on the part of my pupils, no more brilliant, more exemplary morning. It was exactly as if they had both had at heart to gloss over any recent little friction. They performed the dizziest feats of arithmetic, soaring quite out of *my* feeble range, and perpetrated, in higher spirits than ever, geographical and historical jokes. It was conspicuous of course in Miles in particular that he appeared to wish to show how easily he could let me down. This child, to my memory, really lives in a setting of beauty and misery that no words can translate; there was a distinction all his own in every impulse he revealed; never was a small natural creature, to the uninitiated eye all frankness and freedom, a more ingenious, a more extraordinary little gentleman. I had perpetually to guard against the wonder of contemplation into which my initiated view betrayed me; to check the irrelevant gaze and discouraged sigh in which I constantly both attacked and renounced the enigma of what such a little gentleman could have done that deserved a penalty. Say that, by the dark prodigy I knew, the imagination of all evil *had* been opened up to him: all the justice within me ached for the proof that it could ever have flowered into an act.

He had never, at any rate, been such a little gentleman as when, after our early dinner on this dreadful day, he came round to me and asked if I shouldn't like him, for half an hour, to play to me. David playing to Saul could never have shown a finer sense of the occasion. It was literally a charming exhibition of tact, of magnanimity, and quite tantamount° to his saying outright: "The true knights we love to read about never push an advantage too far. I know what you mean now: you mean that—to be let alone yourself and not followed up—you'll cease to worry and spy upon me, won't keep me so close to you, will let me go and come. Well, I 'come,' you see—but I don't go! There'll be plenty of time for that. I do really delight in your society, and I only want to show you that I contended for a principle." It may be imagined whether I resisted this appeal or failed to accompany him again, hand in hand, to the schoolroom. He sat down at the old piano and played as he had never played, and if there are those who think he had better have been kicking a football I can only say that I wholly agree with them. For at the end of a time that under his influence I had quite ceased to measure I started up with a strange sense of having literally slept at my post. It was after luncheon, and by the schoolroom fire, and yet I hadn't really, in the least, slept: I had only done something much worse—I had forgotten. Where, all this time, was Flora? When I put the question to Miles he played on a minute before answering, and then could only say: "Why, my dear,

how do I know?"—breaking moreover into a happy laugh
which, immediately after, as if it were a vocal accompaniment, he prolonged into incoherent, extravagant song.

I went straight to my room, but his sister was not there;
then, before going downstairs, I looked into several others.
As she was nowhere about she would surely be with Mrs.
Grose, whom, in the comfort of that theory, I accordingly
proceeded in quest of. I found her where I had found her
the evening before, but she met my quick challenge with
blank, scared ignorance. She had only supposed that, after
the repast, I had carried off both the children; as to which
she was quite in her right, for it was the very first time I had
allowed the little girl out of my sight without some special
provision. Of course now indeed she might be with the
maids, so that the immediate thing was to look for her
without an air of alarm. This we promptly arranged between us; but when, ten minutes later and in pursuance of
our arrangement, we met in the hall, it was only to report on
either side that after guarded inquiries we had altogether
failed to trace her. For a minute there, apart from observation, we exchanged mute alarms, and I could feel with what
high interest my friend returned me all those I had from the
first given her.

"She'll be above," she presently said—"in one of the
rooms you haven't searched."

"No; she's at a distance." I had made up my mind. "She
has gone out."

Mrs. Grose stared. "Without a hat?"

I naturally also looked volumes. "Isn't that woman always without one?"

"She's with *her?*"

"She's with *her!*" I declared. "We must find them."

My hand was on my friend's arm, but she failed for the
moment, confronted with such an account of the matter, to
respond to my pressure. She communed, on the contrary,
on the spot, with her uneasiness. "And where's Master
Miles?"

"Oh, *he's* with Quint. They're in the schoolroom."

"Lord, Miss!" My view, I was myself aware—and therefore I suppose my tone—had never yet reached so calm an assurance.

"The trick's played," I went on; "they've successfully worked their plan. He found the most divine little way to keep me quiet while she went off."

"'Divine'?" Mrs. Grose bewilderedly echoed.

"Infernal, then!" I almost cheerfully rejoined. "He has provided for himself as well. But come!"

She had helplessly gloomed at the upper regions. "You leave him—?"

"So long with Quint? Yes—I don't mind that now."

She always ended, at these moments, by getting possession of my hand, and in this manner she could at present still stay me. But after gasping an instant at my sudden resignation, "Because of your letter?" she eagerly brought out.

I quickly, by way of answer, felt for my letter, drew it forth, held it up, and then, freeing myself, went and laid it on the great hall-table. "Luke will take it," I said as I came back. I reached the house-door and opened it; I was already on the steps.

My companion still demurred: the storm of the night and the early morning had dropped, but the afternoon was damp and grey. I came down to the drive while she stood in the doorway. "You go with nothing on?"

"What do I care when the child has nothing? I can't wait to dress," I cried, "and if you must do so, I leave you. Try meanwhile, yourself, upstairs."

"With *them*?" Oh, on this, the poor woman promptly joined me!

XIX

We went straight to the lake, as it was called at Bly, and I dare say rightly called, though I reflect that it may in fact have been a sheet of water less remarkable than it appeared to my untravelled eyes. My acquaintance with sheets of water was small, and the pool of Bly, at all events on the few occasions of my consenting, under the protection of my pupils, to affront its surface in the old flat-bottomed boat moored there for our use, had impressed me both with its extent and its agitation. The usual place of embarkation was half a mile from the house, but I had an intimate conviction that, wherever Flora might be, she was not near home. She had not given me the slip for any small adventure, and, since the day of the very great one that I had shared with her by the pond, I had been aware, in our walks, of the quarter to which she most inclined. This was why I had now given to Mrs. Grose's steps so marked a direction — a direction that made her, when she perceived it, oppose a resistance that showed me she was freshly mystified. "You're going to the water, Miss? — you think she's *in* — ?"

"She may be, though the depth is, I believe, nowhere very great. But what I judge most likely is that she's on the spot from which, the other day, we saw together what I told you."

"When she pretended not to see — ?"

"With that astounding self-possession! I've always been sure she wanted to go back alone. And now her brother has managed it for her."

Mrs. Grose still stood where she had stopped. "You suppose they really *talk* of them?"

I could meet this with a confidence! "They say things that, if we heard them, would simply appall us."

"And if she *is* there — ?"

"Yes?"

"Then Miss Jessel is?"

"Beyond a doubt. You shall see."

"Oh, thank you!" my friend cried, planted so firm that, taking it in, I went straight on without her. By the time I reached the pool, however, she was close behind me, and I knew that, whatever, to her apprehension, might befall me, the exposure of my society struck her as her least danger. She exhaled a moan of relief as we at last came in sight of the greater part of the water without a sight of the child. There was no trace of Flora on that nearer side of the bank where my observation of her had been most startling, and none on the opposite edge, where, save for a margin of some twenty yards, a thick copse came down to the water.

The pond, oblong in shape, had a width so scant compared to its length that, with its ends out of view, it might have been taken for a scant river. We looked at the empty expanse, and then I felt the suggestion of my friend's eyes. I knew what she meant and I replied with a negative headshake.

"No, no; wait! She has taken the boat."

My companion stared at the vacant mooring-place and then again across the lake. "Then where is it?"

"Our not seeing it is the strongest of proofs. She has used it to go over, and then has managed to hide it."

"All alone—that child?"

"She's not alone, and at such times she's not a child: she's an old, old woman." I scanned all the visible shore while Mrs. Grose took again, into the queer element I offered her, one of her plunges of submission; then I pointed out that the boat might perfectly be in a small refuge formed by one of the recesses of the pool, an indentation masked, for the hither side, by a projection of the bank and by a clump of trees growing close to the water.

"But if the boat's there, where on earth's *she?*" my colleague anxiously asked.

"That's exactly what we must learn." And I started to walk further.

"By going all the way around?"

"Certainly, far as it is. It will take us but ten minutes, but it's far enough to have made the child prefer not to walk. She went straight over."

"Laws!" cried my friend again; the chain of my logic was ever too much for her. It dragged her at my heels even now, and when we had got half-way round—a devious, tiresome process, on ground much broken and by a path choked with overgrowth—I paused to give her breath. I sustained her with a grateful arm, assuring her that she might hugely help me; and this started us afresh, so that in the course of but a few minutes more we reached a point from which we found the boat to be where I had supposed it. It had been intentionally left as much as possible out of sight and was tied to one of the stakes of a fence that came, just there, down to the brink and that had been an assistance to disembarking. I recognised, as I looked at the pair of short, thick oars, quite safely drawn up, the prodigious character of the feat for a little girl; but I had lived, by this time, too long among wonders and had panted to too many livelier measures. There was a gate in the fence, through which we passed, and that brought us, after a trifling interval, more into the open. Then, "There she is!" we both exclaimed at once.

Flora, a short way off, stood before us on the grass and smiled as if her performance was now complete. The next thing she did, however, was to stoop straight down and pluck—quite as if it were all she was there for—a big, ugly spray of withered fern. I instantly became sure she had just come out of the copse. She waited for us, not herself taking a step, and I was conscious of the rare solemnity with which we presently approached her. She smiled and smiled, and we met; but it was all done in a silence by this time flagrantly ominous. Mrs. Grose was the first to break the spell: she threw herself on her knees and, drawing the child to her breast, clasped in a long embrace the little tender, yielding body. While this dumb convulsion lasted I could only watch it—which I did the more intently when I saw Flora's face peep at me over our companion's shoulder. It was serious now—the flicker had left it; but it strengthened the pang with which I at that moment envied Mrs. Grose the simplicity of *her* relation. Still, all this while, nothing more passed between us save that Flora had let her foolish fern again drop to the ground. What she and I had virtually said to each other was that pretexts were useless now. When Mrs. Grose finally got up she kept the child's hand, so that the two were still before me; and the singular reticence of our communion was even more marked in the frank look she launched me. "I'll be hanged," it said, "if *I'll* speak!"

It was Flora who, gazing all over me in candid wonder, was the first. She was struck with our bareheaded aspect. "Why, where are your things?"

"Where yours are, my dear!" I promptly returned.

She had already got back her gaiety, and appeared to take this as an answer quite sufficient. "And where's Miles?" she went on.

There was something in the small valour of it that quite finished me: these three words from her were, in a flash like the glitter of a drawn blade, the jostle of the cup that my hand, for weeks and weeks, had held high and full to the brim and that now, even before speaking, I felt overflow in a deluge. "I'll tell you if you'll tell *me*—" I heard myself say, then heard the tremor in which it broke.

"Well, what?"

Mrs. Grose's suspense blazed at me, but it was too late now, and I brought the thing out handsomely. "Where, my pet, is Miss Jessel?"

XX

Just as in the churchyard with Miles, the whole thing was upon us. Much as I had made of the fact that this name had never once, between us, been sounded, the quick, smitten glare with which the child's face now received it fairly likened my breach of the silence to the smash of a pane of glass. It added to the interposing cry, as if to stay the blow, that Mrs. Grose, at the same instant, uttered over my violence—the shriek of a creature scared, or rather wounded, which, in turn, within a few seconds, was completed by a gasp of my own. I seized my colleague's arm. "She's there, she's there!"

Miss Jessel stood before us on the opposite bank exactly as she had stood the other time, and I remember, strangely, as the first feeling now produced in me, my thrill of joy at having brought on a proof. She was there, and I was justified; she was there, and I was neither cruel nor mad. She was there for poor scared Mrs. Grose, but she was there most for Flora; and no moment of my monstrous time was perhaps so extraordinary as that in which I consciously threw out to her—with the sense that, pale and ravenous demon as she was, she would catch and understand it—an inarticulate message of gratitude. She rose erect on the spot my friend and I had lately quitted, and there was not, in all the long reach of her desire, an inch of her evil that fell

short. This first vividness of vision and emotion were
things of a few seconds, during which Mrs. Grose's dazed
blink across to where I pointed struck me as a sovereign
sign that she too at last saw, just as it carried my own eyes
precipitately to the child. The revelation then of the manner in which Flora was affected startled me, in truth, far
more than it would have done to find her also merely
agitated, for direct dismay was of course not what I had
expected. Prepared and on her guard as our pursuit had
actually made her, she would repress every betrayal; and I
was therefore shaken, on the spot, by my first glimpse of the
particular one for which I had not allowed. To see her,
without a convulsion of her small pink face, not even feign
to glance in the direction of the prodigy I announced, but
only, instead of that, turn at *me* an expression of hard, still
gravity, an expression absolutely new and unprecedented
and that appeared to read and accuse and judge me—this
was a stroke that somehow converted the little girl herself
into the very presence that could make me quail. I quailed
even though my certitude that she thoroughly saw was
never greater than at that instant, and in the immediate
need to defend myself I called it passionately to witness.
"She's there, you little unhappy thing—there, there, *there,*
and you see her as well as you see me!" I had said shortly
before to Mrs. Grose that she was not at these times a child,
but an old, old woman, and that description of her could
not have been more strikingly confirmed than in the way in
which, for all answer to this, she simply showed me, without a concession, an admission, of her eyes, a countenance
of deeper and deeper, of indeed suddenly quite fixed,
reprobation.° I was by this time—if I can put the whole
thing at all together—more appalled at what I may properly
call her manner than at anything else, though it was simultaneously with this that I became aware of having Mrs.
Grose also, and very formidably, to reckon with. My elder
companion, the next moment, at any rate, blotted out
everything but her own flushed face and her loud, shocked
protest, a burst of high disapproval. "What a dreadful turn,
to be sure, Miss! Where on earth do you see anything?"

I could only grasp her more quickly yet, for even while

she spoke the hideous plain presence stood undimmed and undaunted. It had already lasted a minute, and it lasted while I continued, seizing my colleague, quite thrusting her at it and presenting her to it, to insist with my pointing hand. "You don't see her exactly as *we* see?—you mean to say you don't now—*now*? She's as big as a blazing fire! Only look, dearest woman, *look*—!" She looked, even as I did, and gave me, with her deep groan of negation, repulsion, compassion—the mixture with her pity of her relief at her exemption—a sense, touching to me even then, that she would have backed me up if she could. I might well have needed that, for with this hard blow of the proof that her eyes were hopelessly sealed I felt my own situation horribly crumble, I felt—I saw—my livid° predecessor press, from her position, on my defeat, and I was conscious, more than all, of what I should have from this instant to deal with in the astounding little attitude of Flora. Into this attitude Mrs. Grose immediately and violently entered, breaking, even while there pierced through my sense of ruin a prodigious private triumph, into breathless reassurance.

."She isn't there, little lady, and nobody's there—and you never see nothing, my sweet! How can poor Miss Jessel? when poor Miss Jessel's dead and buried? *We* know, don't we, love?"—and she appealed, blundering in, to the child. "It's all a mere mistake and a worry and a joke—and we'll go home as fast as we can!"

Our companion, on this, had responded with a strange, quick primness of propriety, and they were again, with Mrs. Grose on her feet, united, as it were, in pained opposition to me. Flora continued to fix me with her small mask of reprobation, and even at that minute I prayed God to forgive me for seeming to see that, as she stood there holding tight to our friend's dress, her incomparable childish beauty had suddenly failed, had quite vanished. I've said it already—she was literally, she was hideously, hard; she had turned common and almost ugly. "I don't know what you mean. I see nobody. I see nothing. I never *have*. I think you're cruel. I don't like you!" Then, after this deliverance, which might have been that of a vulgarly pert little girl in the street, she hugged Mrs. Grose more closely and buried in her skirts the dreadful little face. In this position she produced an almost furious wail. "Take me away, take me away—oh, take me away from *her!*"

"From *me?*" I panted.

"From you—from you!" she cried.

Even Mrs. Grose looked across at me dismayed, while I had nothing to do but communicate again with the figure that, on the opposite bank, without a movement, as rigidly still as if catching, beyond the interval, our voices, was as vividly there for my disaster as it was not there for my service. The wretched child had spoken exactly as if she had got from some outside source each of her stabbing little words, and I could therefore, in the full despair of all I had to accept, but sadly shake my head at her. "If I had ever doubted, all my doubt would at present have gone. I've been living with the miserable truth, and now it has only too much closed round me. Of course I've lost you: I've interfered, and you've seen—under *her* dictation"—with which I faced, over the pool again, our infernal witness—"the easy and perfect way to meet it. I've done my best, but I've lost you. Good-bye." For Mrs. Grose I had an imperative, an almost frantic "Go, go!" before which, in infinite distress, but mutely possessed of the little girl and clearly convinced, in spite of her blindness, that something awful had occurred and some collapse engulfed us, she retreated, by the way we had come, as fast as she could move.

Of what first happened when I was left alone I had no subsequent memory. I only knew that at the end of, I suppose, a quarter of an hour, an odorous dampness and roughness, chilling and piercing my trouble, had made me understand that I must have thrown myself, on my face, on the ground and given way to a wildness of grief. I must have lain there long and cried and sobbed, for when I raised my head the day was almost done. I got up and looked a moment, through the twilight, at the grey pool and its blank, haunted edge, and then I took, back to the house, my dreary and difficult course. When I reached the gate in the fence,

the boat, to my surprise, was gone, so that I had a fresh
reflection to make on Flora's extraordinary command of the
situation. She passed that night, by the most tacit, and I
should add, were not the word so grotesque a false note,
the happiest of arrangements, with Mrs. Grose. I saw
neither of them on my return, but, on the other hand as by
an ambiguous compensation, I saw a great deal of Miles. I
saw—I can use no other phrase—so much of him that it was
as if it were more than it had ever been. No evening I had
passed at Bly had the portentous quality of this one; in spite
of which—and in spite also of the deeper depths of consternation that had opened beneath my feet—there was literally, in the ebbing actual, an extraordinarily sweet sadness.
On reaching the house I had never so much as looked for
the boy; I had simply gone straight to my room to change
what I was wearing and to take in, at a glance, much
material testimony to Flora's rupture. Her little belongings
had all been removed. When later, by the schoolroom fire, I
was served with tea by the usual maid, I indulged, on the
article of my other pupil, in no inquiry whatever. He had
his freedom now—he might have it to the end! Well, he did
have it; and it consisted—in part at least—of his coming in
at about eight o'clock and sitting down with me in silence.
On the removal of the tea-things I had blown out the
candles and drawn my chair closer: I was conscious of a
mortal coldness and felt as if I should never again be warm.
So, when he appeared, I was sitting in the glow with my
thoughts. He paused a moment by the door as if to look at
me; then—as if to share them—came to the other side of the
hearth and sank into a chair. We sat there in absolute
stillness; yet he wanted, I felt, to be with me.

XXI

Before a new day, in my room, had fully broken, my eyes
opened to Mrs. Grose, who had come to my bedside with
worse news. Flora was so markedly feverish that an illness
was perhaps at hand; she had passed a night of extreme
unrest, a night agitated above all by fears that had for their
subject not in the least her former, but wholly her present,

governess. It was not against the possible re-entrance of Miss Jessel on the scene that she protested—it was conspicuously and passionately against mine. I was promptly on my feet of course, and with an immense deal to ask; the more that my friend had discernibly now girded her loins to meet me once more. This I felt as soon as I had put to her the question of her sense of the child's sincerity as against my own. "She persists in denying to you that she saw, or has ever seen, anything?"

My visitor's trouble, truly, was great. "Ah, Miss, it isn't a matter on which I can push her! Yet it isn't either, I must say, as if I much needed to. It has made her, every inch of her, quite old."

"Oh, I see her perfectly from here. She resents, for all the world like some high little personage, the imputation° on her truthfulness and, as it were, her respectability. 'Miss Jessel indeed—*she!*' Ah, she's 'respectable,' the chit! The impression she gave me there yesterday was, I assure you, the very strangest of all; it was quite beyond any of the others. I *did* put my foot in it! She'll never speak to me again."

Hideous and obscure as it all was, it held Mrs. Grose briefly silent; then she granted my point with a frankness which, I made sure, had more behind it. "I think indeed, Miss, she never will. She do have a grand manner about it!"

"And that manner"—I summed it up—"is practically what's the matter with her now!"

Oh, that manner, I could see in my visitor's face, and not a little else besides! "She asks me every three minutes if I think you're coming in."

"I see—I see." I too, on my side, had so much more than worked it out. "Has she said to you since yesterday—except to repudiate her familiarity with anything so dreadful—a single other word about Miss Jessel?"

"Not one, Miss. And of course you know," my friend added, "I took it from her, by the lake, that, just then and there at least, there *was* nobody."

"Rather! And, naturally, you take it from her still."

"I don't contradict her. What else can I do?"

"Nothing in the world! You've the cleverest little person to deal with. They've made them—their two friends, I mean—still cleverer even than nature did; for it was wondrous material to play on! Flora has now her grievance, and she'll work it to the end."

"Yes, Miss; but to *what* end?"

"Why, that of dealing with me to her uncle. She'll make me out to him the lowest creature—!"

I winced at the fair show of the scene in Mrs. Grose's face; she looked for a minute as if she sharply saw them together. "And him who thinks so well of you!"

"He has an odd way—it comes over me now," I laughed, "—of proving it! But that doesn't matter. What Flora wants, of course, is to get rid of me."

My companion bravely concurred. "Never again to so much as look at you."

"So that what you've come to me now for," I asked, "is to speed me on my way?" Before she had time to reply, however, I had her in check. "I've a better idea—the result of my reflections. My going *would* seem the right thing, and on Sunday I was terribly near it. Yet that won't do. It's *you* who must go. You must take Flora."

My visitor, at this, did speculate. "But where in the world—?"

"Away from here. Away from *them*. Away, even most of all, now, from me. Straight to her uncle."

"Only to tell on you—?"

"No, not 'only'! To leave me, in addition, with my remedy."

She was still vague. "And what *is* your remedy?"

"Your loyalty, to begin with. And then Miles's."

She looked at me hard. "Do you think he—?"

"Won't if he has the chance, turn on me? Yes, I venture still to think it. At all events, I want to try. Get off with his sister as soon as possible and leave me with him alone." I was amazed, myself, at the spirit I had still in reserve, and therefore perhaps a trifle the more disconcerted at the way in which, in spite of this fine example of it, she hesitated. "There's one thing, of course," I went on: "they mustn't, before she goes, see each other for three seconds."

Then it came over me that, in spite of Flora's presumable sequestration° from the instant of her return from the pool, it might already be too late. "Do you mean," I anxiously asked, "that they *have* met?"

At this she quite flushed. "Ah, Miss, I'm not such a fool as that! If I've been obliged to leave her three or four times, it has been each time with one of the maids, and at present, though she's alone, she's locked in safe. And yet—and yet!" There were too many things.

"And yet what?"

"Well, are you so sure of the little gentleman?"

"I'm not sure of anything but *you*. But I have, since last evening, a new hope. I think he wants to give me an opening. I do believe that—poor little exquisite wretch!—he wants to speak. Last evening, in the firelight and the silence, he sat with me for two hours as if it were just coming."

Mrs. Grose looked hard, through the window, at the grey, gathering day. "And did it come?"

"No, though I waited and waited, I confess it didn't, and it was without a breach of the silence or so much as a faint allusion to his sister's condition and absence that we at last kissed for goodnight. All the same," I continued, "I can't, if her uncle sees her, consent to his seeing her brother without my having given the boy—and most of all because things have got so bad—a little more time."

My friend appeared on this ground more reluctant than I could quite understand. "What do you mean by more time?"

"Well, a day or two—really to bring it out. He'll then be on *my* side—of which you see the importance. If nothing comes, I shall only fail, and you will, at the worst, have helped me by doing, on your arrival in town, whatever you may have found possible." So I put it before her, but she continued for a little so inscrutably embarrassed that I came again to her aid. "Unless, indeed," I wound up, "you really want *not* to go."

I could see it, in her face, at last clear itself; she put out her hand to me as a pledge. "I'll go—I'll go. I'll go this morning."

I wanted to be very just. "If you *should* wish still to wait, I would engage she shouldn't see me."

"No, no: it's the place itself. She must leave it." She held me a moment with heavy eyes, then brought out the rest. "Your idea's the right one. I myself, Miss—"

"Well?"

"I can't stay."

The look she gave me with it made me jump at possibilities.

"You mean that, since yesterday, you *have* seen—?"

She shook her head with dignity. "I've *heard*—!"

"Heard?"

"From that child—horrors! There!" she sighed with tragic relief. "On my honour, Miss, she says things—!" But at this evocation she broke down; she dropped, with a sudden sob, upon my sofa and, as I had seen her do before, gave way to all the grief of it.

It was quite in another manner that I, for my part, let myself go. "Oh, thank God!"

She sprang up again at this, drying her eyes with a groan. "'Thank God'?"

"It so justifies me!"

"It does that, Miss!"

I couldn't have desired more emphasis, but I just hesitated. "She's so horrible?"

I saw my colleague scarce knew how to put it. "Really shocking."

"And about me?"

"About you, Miss—since you must have it. It's beyond everything, for a young lady; and I can't think wherever she must have picked up—"

"The appalling language she applied to me? I can, then!" I broke in with a laugh that was doubtless significant enough.

It only, in truth, left my friend still more grave. "Well, perhaps I ought to also—since I've heard some of it before! Yet I can't bear it," the poor woman went on while, with the same movement, she glanced, on my dressing-table, at the face of my watch. "But I must go back."

I kept her, however. "Ah, if you can't bear it—!"

"How can I stop with her, you mean? Why, just *for* that: to get her away. Far from this," she pursued, "Far from *them*—"

"She may be different? she may be free?" I seized her almost with joy. "Then, in spite of yesterday, you *believe*—"

"In such doings?" Her simple description of them required, in the light of her expression, to be carried no further, and she gave me the whole thing as she had never done. "I believe."

Yes, it was a joy, and we were still shoulder to shoulder: if I might continue sure of that I should care but little what else happened. My support in the presence of disaster would be the same as it had been in my early need of confidence, and if my friend would answer for my honesty, I would answer for all the rest. On the point of taking leave of her, none the less, I was to some extent embarrassed. "There's one thing of course—it occurs to me—to remember. My letter, giving the alarm, will have reached town before you."

I now perceived still more how she had been beating about the bush and how weary at last it had made her. "Your letter won't have got there. Your letter never went."

"What then became of it?"

"Goodness knows! Master Miles—"

"Do you mean *he* took it?" I gasped.

She hung fire, but she overcame her reluctance, "I mean that I saw yesterday, when I came back with Miss Flora, that it wasn't where you had put it. Later in the evening I had the chance to question Luke, and he declared that he had neither noticed nor touched it." We could only exchange, on this, one of our deeper mutual soundings, and it was Mrs. Grose who first brought up the plumb° with an almost elate "You see!"

"Yes, I see that if Miles took it instead he probably will have read it and destroyed it."

"And don't you see anything else?"

I faced her a moment with a sad smile. "It strikes me that by this time your eyes are open even wider than mine."

They proved to be so indeed, but she could still blush,

almost, to show it. "I make out now what he must have done at school." And she gave, in her simple sharpness, an almost droll disillusioned nod. "He stole!"

I turned it over—I tried to be more judicial. "Well— perhaps."

She looked as if she found me unexpectedly calm. "He stole *letters!*"

She couldn't know my reasons for a calmness after all pretty shallow; so I showed them off as I might. "I hope then it was to more purpose than in this case! The note, at any rate, that I put on the table yesterday," I pursued, "will have given him so scant an advantage—for it contained only the bare demand for an interview—that he is already much ashamed of having gone so far for so little, and that what he had on his mind last evening was precisely the need of confession." I seemed to myself, for the instant, to have mastered it, to see it all. "Leave us, leave us"—I was already, at the door, hurrying her off. "I'll get it out of him. He'll meet me—he'll confess. If he confesses, he's saved. And if he's saved—"

"Then *you* are?" The dear woman kissed me on this, and I took her farewell. "I'll save you without him!" she cried as she went.

XXII

Yet it was when she had got off—and I missed her on the spot—that the great pinch really came. If I had counted on what it would give me to find myself alone with Miles, I speedily perceived, at least, that it would give me a measure. No hour of my stay in fact was so assailed with apprehensions as that of my coming down to learn that the carriage containing Mrs. Grose and my younger pupil had already rolled out of the gates. Now I *was,* I said to myself, face to face with the elements, and for much of the rest of the day, while I fought my weakness, I could consider that I had been supremely rash. It was a tighter place still than I had yet turned round in; all the more that, for the first time, I could see in the aspect of others a confused reflection of the crisis. What had happened naturally caused them all to

stare; there was too little of the explained, throw out whatever we might, in the suddenness of my colleague's act.
The maids and the men looked blank; the effect of which
on my nerves was an aggravation until I saw the necessity of
making it a positive aid. It was precisely, in short, by just
clutching the helm that I avoided total wreck; and I dare say
that, to bear up at all, I became, that morning, very grand
and very dry. I welcomed the consciousness that I was
charged with much to do, and I caused it to be known as
well that, left thus to myself, I was quite remarkably firm. I
wandered with that manner, for the next hour or two, all
over the place and looked, I have no doubt, as if I were
ready for any onset. So, for the benefit of whom it might
concern, I paraded with a sick heart.

The person it appeared least to concern proved to be, till
dinner, little Miles himself. My perambulations° had given
me meanwhile, no glimpse of him, but they had tended to
make more public the change taking place in our relation as
a consequence of his having at the piano, the day before,
kept me, in Flora's interest, so beguiled and befooled. The
stamp of publicity had of course been fully given by her
confinement and departure, and the change itself was now
ushered in by our non-observance of the regular custom of
the schoolroom. He had already disappeared when, on my
way down, I pushed open his door, and I learned below that
he had breakfasted—in the presence of a couple of the
maids—with Mrs. Grose and his sister. He had then gone
out, as he said, for a stroll; than which nothing, I reflected,
could better have expressed his frank view of the abrupt
transformation of my office. What he would now permit this
office to consist of was yet to be settled: there was a queer
relief, at all events—I mean for myself in especial—in the
renouncement of one pretension. If so much had sprung to
the surface, I scarce put it too strongly in saying that what
had perhaps sprung highest was the absurdity of our pro-
longing the fiction that I had anything more to teach him. It
sufficiently stuck out that, by tacit little tricks in which even
more than myself he carried out the care for my dignity, I
had had to appeal to him to let me off straining to meet him

on the ground of his true capacity. He had at any rate his freedom now; I was never to touch it again; as I had amply shown, moreover, when, on his joining me in the school-room the previous night, I had uttered, on the subject of the interval just concluded, neither challenge nor hint. I had too much, from this moment, my other ideas. Yet when he at last arrived the difficulty of applying them, the accumulations of my problem, were brought straight home to me by the beautiful little presence on which what had occurred had as yet, for the eye, dropped neither stain nor shadow.

To mark, for the house, the high state I cultivated I decreed that my meals with the boy should be served, as we called it, downstairs; so that I had been awaiting him in the ponderous pomp of the room outside of the window of which I had had from Mrs. Grose, that first scared Sunday, my flash of something it would scarce have done to call light. Here at present I felt afresh—for I had felt it again and again—how my equilibrium depended on the success of my rigid will, the will to shut my eyes as tight as possible to the truth that what I had to deal with was, revoltingly, against nature. I could only get on at all by taking "nature" into my confidence and my account, by treating my monstrous ordeal as a push in a direction unusual, of course, and unpleasant, but demanding, after all, for a fair front, only another turn of the screw of ordinary human virtue. No attempt, none the less, could well require more tact than just this attempt to supply, one's self, *all* the nature. How could I put even a little of that article into a suppression of reference to what had occurred? How, on the other hand, could I make a reference without a new plunge into the hideous obscure? Well, a sort of answer, after a time, had come to me, and it was so far confirmed as that I was met, incontestably, by the quickened vision of what was rare in my little companion. It was indeed as if he had found even now—as he had so often found at lessons—still some other delicate way to ease me off. Wasn't there light in the fact which, as we shared our solitude, broke out with a specious glitter it had never yet quite worn?—the fact that (opportunity aiding, precious opportunity which had now come) it

would be preposterous, with a child so endowed, to forgo
the help one might wrest from absolute intelligence? What
had his intelligence been given him for but to save him?
Mightn't one, to reach his mind, risk the stretch of an
angular arm over his character? It was as if, when we were
face to face in the dining-room, he had literally shown me
the way. The roast mutton was on the table, and I had
dispensed with attendance. Miles, before he sat down,
stood a moment with his hands in his pockets and looked at
the joint, on which he seemed on the point of passing some
humorous judgment. But what he presently produced was:
"I say, my dear, is she really very awfully ill?"

"Little Flora? Not so bad but that she'll presently be
better. London will set her up. Bly had ceased to agree
with her. Come here and take your mutton."

He alertly obeyed me, carried the plate carefully to his
seat, and, when he was established, went on. "Did Bly
disagree with her so terribly suddenly?"

"Not so suddenly as you might think. One had seen it
coming on."

"Then why didn't you get her off before?"

"Before what?"

"Before she became too ill to travel."

I found myself prompt. "She's *not* too ill to travel: she
only might have become so if she had stayed. This was just
the moment to seize. The journey will dissipate the influence"—oh, I was grand!—"and carry it off."

"I see, I see"—Miles, for that matter, was grand too. He
settled to his repast with the charming little "table manner"
that, from the day of his arrival, had relieved me of all
grossness of admonition. Whatever he had been driven
from school for, it was not for ugly feeding. He was irre-
proachable, as always, today; but he was unmistakeably
more conscious. He was discernibly trying to take for
granted more things than he found, without assistance,
quite easy; and he dropped into peaceful silence while he
felt his situation. Our meal was of the briefest—mine a vain
pretence, and I had the things immediately removed.
While this was done Miles stood again with his hands in his

little pockets and his back to me — stood and looked out of the wide window through which, that other day, I had seen what pulled me up. We continued silent while the maid was with us — as silent, it whimsically occurred to me, as some young couple who, on their wedding-journey, at the inn, feel shy in the presence of the waiter. He turned round only when the waiter had left us. "Well — so we're alone!"

<h2 style="text-align:center">XXIII</h2>

"Oh, more or less." I fancy my smile was pale. "Not absolutely. We shouldn't like that!" I went on.

"No — I suppose we shouldn't. Of course we have the others."

"We have the others — we have indeed the others," I concurred.

"Yet even though we have them," he returned, still with his hands in his pockets and planted there in front of me, "they don't much count, do they?"

I made the best of it, but I felt wan. "It depends on what you call 'much'!"

"Yes" — with all accommodation — "everything depends!" On this, however, he faced to the window again and presently reached it with his vague, restless, cogitating step. He remained there awhile, with his forehead against the glass, in contemplation of the stupid shrubs I knew and the dull things of November. I had always my hypocrisy of "work," behind which, now, I gained the sofa. Steadying myself with it there as I had repeatedly done at those moments of torment that I have described as the moments of my knowing the children to be given to something from which I was barred, I sufficiently obeyed my habit of being prepared for the worst. But an extraordinary impression dropped on me as I extracted a meaning from the boy's embarrassed back — none other than the impression that I was not barred now. This inference grew in a few minutes to sharp intensity and seemed bound up with the direct perception that it was positively *he* who was. The frames and squares of the great window were a kind of image, for him, of a kind of failure. I felt that I saw him, at any rate, shut in or shut out. He was admirable, but not comfortable: I took it in with a throb of hope. Wasn't he looking, through the haunted pane, for something he couldn't see?—and wasn't it the first time in the whole business that he had known such a lapse? The first, the very first: I found it a splendid portent.° It made him anxious, though he watched himself; he had been anxious all day and, even while in his usual sweet little manner he sat at table, had needed all his small strange genius to give it a gloss. When he at last turned round to meet me, it was almost as if this genius had succumbed. "Well, I think I'm glad Bly agrees with *me!*"

"You would certainly seem to have seen, these twenty-four hours, a good deal more of it than for some time before. I hope," I went on bravely, "that you've been enjoying yourself."

"Oh, yes, I've been ever so far; all round about—miles and miles away. I've never been so free."

He had really a manner of his own, and I could only try to keep up with him. "Well, do you like it?"

He stood there smiling; then at last he put into two words—"Do *you?*"— more discrimination than I had ever heard two words contain. Before I had time to deal with that, however, he continued as if with the sense that this was an impertinence to be softened. "Nothing could be more charming than the way you take it, for of course if we're alone together now it's you that are alone most. But I hope," he threw in, "you don't particularly mind!"

"Having to do with you?" I asked. "My dear child, how can I help minding? Though I've renounced all claim to your company—you're so beyond me—I at least greatly enjoy it. What else should I stay on for?"

He looked at me more directly, and the expression of his face, graver now, struck me as the most beautiful I had ever found in it. "You stay on just for *that?*"

"Certainly. I stay on as your friend and from the tremendous interest I take in you till something can be done for you that may be more worth your while. That needn't surprise you." My voice trembled so that I felt it impossible to suppress the shake. "Don't you remember how I told you, when I came and sat on your bed the night of the storm, that there was nothing in the world I wouldn't do for you?"

"Yes, yes!" He, on his side, more and more visibly nervous, had a tone to master; but he was so much more successful than I that, laughing out through his gravity, he could pretend we were pleasantly jesting. "Only that, I think, was to get me to do something for you!"

"It was partly to get you to do something," I conceded. "But, you know, you didn't do it."

"Oh, yes," he said with the brightest superficial eagerness, "you wanted me to tell you something."

"That's it. Out, straight out. What you have on your mind, you know."

"Ah, then, is *that* what you've stayed over for?"

He spoke with a gaiety through which I could still catch the finest little quiver of resentful passion; but I can't begin to express the effect upon me of an implication of surrender even so faint. It was as if what I had yearned for had come at last only to astonish me. "Well, yes — I may as well make a clean breast of it. It was precisely for that."

He waited so long that I supposed it for the purpose of repudiating the assumption on which my action had been founded; but what he finally said was: "Do you mean now — here?"

"There couldn't be a better place or time." He looked round him uneasily, and I had the rare — oh, the queer! — impression of the very first symptom I had seen in him of the approach of immediate fear. It was as if he were suddenly afraid of me — which struck me indeed as perhaps the best thing to make him. Yet in the very pang of the effort I felt it vain to try sternness, and I heard myself the next instant so gentle as to be almost grotesque. "You want so to go out again?"

"Awfully!" He smiled at me heroically, and the touching little bravery of it was enhanced by his actually flushing with pain. He had picked up his hat, which he had brought in, and stood twirling it in a way that gave me, even as I was just nearly reaching port, a perverse horror of what I was doing. To do it in *any* way was an act of violence, for what did it consist of but the obtrusion of the idea of grossness and guilt on a small helpless creature who had been for me a revelation of the possibilities of beautiful intercourse? Wasn't it base to create for a being so exquisite a mere alien awkwardness? I suppose I now read into our situation a clearness it couldn't have had at the time, for I seem to see our poor eyes already lighted with some spark of a prevision of the anguish that was to come. So we circled about, with terrors and scruples, like fighters not daring to close. But it was for each other we feared! That kept us a little longer suspended and unbruised. "I'll tell you everything," Miles said — "I mean I'll tell you anything you like. You'll stay on with me, and we shall both be all right and I *will* tell you — I *will*. But not now."

"Why not now?"

My insistence turned him from me and kept him once more at his window in a silence during which, between us, you might have heard a pin drop. Then he was before me again with the air of a person for whom, outside, someone who had frankly to be reckoned with was waiting. "I have to see Luke."

I had not yet reduced him to quite so vulgar a lie, and I felt proportionately ashamed. But, horrible as it was, his lies made up my truth. I achieved thoughtfully a few loops of my knitting. "Well, then, go to Luke, and I'll wait for what you promise. Only, in return for that, satisfy, before you leave me, one very much smaller request."

He looked as if he felt he had succeeded enough to be able still a little to bargain. "Very much smaller — ?"

"Yes, a mere fraction of the whole. Tell me" — oh, my work preoccupied me, and I was off-hand! — "if, yesterday afternoon, from the table in the hall, you took, you know, my letter."

XXIV

My sense of how he received this suffered for a minute from something that I can describe only as a fierce split of my attention — a stroke that at first, as I sprang straight up, reduced me to the mere blind movement of getting hold of

him, drawing him close, and, while I just fell for support
against the nearest piece of furniture, instinctively keeping
him with his back to the window. The appearance was full
upon us that I had already had to deal with here: Peter
Quint had come into view like a sentinel before a prison.
The next thing I saw was that, from outside, he had reached
the window, and then I knew that, close to the glass and
glaring in through it, he offered once more to the room his
white face of damnation. It represents but grossly what
took place within me at the sight to say that on the second
my decision was made; yet I believe that no woman so
overwhelmed ever in so short a time recovered her grasp of
the *act*. It came to me in the very horror of the immediate
presence that the act would be, seeing and facing what I
saw and faced, to keep the boy himself unaware. The
inspiration—I can call it by no other name—was that I felt
how voluntarily, how transcendently, I *might*. It was like
fighting with a demon for a human soul, and when I had
fairly so appraised it I saw how the human soul—held out,
in the tremor of my hands, at arm's length—had a perfect
dew of sweat on a lovely childish forehead. The face that
was close to mine was as white as the face against the glass,
and out of it presently came a sound, not low nor weak, but
as if from much further away, that I drank like a waft of
fragrance.

"Yes—I took it."

At this, with a moan of joy, I enfolded, I drew him close;
and while I held him to my breast, where I could feel in the
sudden fever of his little body the tremendous pulse of his
little heart, I kept my eyes on the thing at the window and
saw it move and shift its posture. I have likened it to a
sentinel, but its slow wheel, for a moment, was rather the
prowl of a baffled beast. My present quickened courage,
however, was such that, not too much to let it through, I had
to shade, as it were, my flame. Meanwhile the glare of the
face was again at the window, the scoundrel fixed as if to
watch and wait. It was the very confidence that I might now
defy him, as well as the positive certitude, by this time, of
the child's unconsciousness, that made me go on. "What
did you take it for?"

"To see what you said about me."

"You opened the letter?"

"I opened it."

My eyes were now, as I held him off a little again, on Miles's own face, in which the collapse of mockery showed me how complete was the ravage of uneasiness. What was prodigious was that at last, by my success, his sense was sealed and his communication stopped: he knew that he was in presence, but knew not of what, and knew still less that I also was and that I did know. And what did this strain of trouble matter when my eyes went back to the window only to see that the air was clear again and—by my personal triumph—the influence quenched? There was nothing there. I felt that the cause was mine and that I should surely get *all*. "And you found nothing!"—I let my elation out.

He gave the most mournful, thoughtful little headshake. "Nothing."

"Nothing, nothing!" I almost shouted in my joy.

"Nothing, nothing," he sadly repeated.

I kissed his forehead; it was drenched. "So what have you done with it?"

"I've burnt it."

"Burnt it?" It was now or never. "Is that what you did at school?"

Oh, what this brought up! "At school?"

"Did you take letters?—or other things?"

"Other things?" He appeared now to be thinking of something far off and that reached him only through the pressure of his anxiety. Yet it did reach him. "Did I *steal?*"

I felt myself redden to the roots of my hair as well as wonder if it were more strange to put to a gentleman such a question or to see him take it with allowances that gave the very distance of his fall in the world. "Was it for that you mightn't go back?"

The only thing he felt was rather a dreary little surprise. "Did you know I mightn't go back?"

"I know everything."

He gave me at this the longest and strangest look. "Everything?"

"Everything. Therefore *did* you — ?" But I couldn't say it again.

Miles could, very simply. "No. I didn't steal."

My face must have shown him I believed him utterly; yet my hands — but it was for pure tenderness — shook him as if to ask him why, if it was all for nothing, he had condemned me to months of torment. "What then did you do?"

He looked in vague pain all round the top of the room and drew his breath, two or three times over, as if with difficulty. He might have been standing at the bottom of the sea and raising his eyes to some faint green twilight. "Well — I said things."

"Only that?"

"They thought it was enough!"

"To turn you out for?"

Never, truly, had a person "turned out" shown so little to explain it as this little person! He appeared to weigh my question, but in a manner quite detached and almost helpless. "Well, I suppose I oughtn't."

"But to whom did you say them?"

He evidently tried to remember, but it dropped — he had lost it. "I don't know!"

He almost smiled at me in the desolation of his surrender, which was indeed practically, by this time, so complete that I ought to have left it there. But I was infatuated — I was blind with victory, though even then the very effect that was to have brought him so much nearer was already that of added separation. "Was it to everyone?" I asked.

"No; it was only to — " But he gave a sick little headshake. "I don't remember their names."

"Were they then so many?"

"No — only a few. Those I liked."

Those he liked? I seemed to float not into clearness, but into a darker obscure, and within a minute there had come to me out of my very pity the appalling alarm of his being perhaps innocent. It was for the instant confounding and bottomless, for if he *were* innocent, what then on earth was *I?* Paralysed, while it lasted, by the mere brush of the question, I let him go a little, so that, with a deep-drawn sigh, he turned away from me again; which, as he faced toward the clear window, I suffered, feeling that I had nothing now there to keep him from. "And did they repeat what you said?" I went on after a moment.

He was soon at some distance from me, still breathing hard and again with the air, though now without anger for it, of being confined against his will. Once more, as he had done before, he looked up at the dim day as if, of what had hitherto sustained him, nothing was left but an unspeakable anxiety. "Oh, yes," he nevertheless replied—"they must have repeated them. To those *they* liked," he added.

There was, somehow, less of it than I had expected; but I turned it over. "And these things came round—?"

"To the masters? Oh, yes!" he answered very simply. "But I didn't know they'd tell."

"The masters? They didn't—they've never told. That's why I ask you."

He turned to me again his little beautiful fevered face. "Yes, it was too bad."

"Too bad?"

"What I suppose I sometimes said. To write home."

I can't name the exquisite pathos of the contradiction given to such a speech by such a speaker; I only know that the next instant I heard myself throw off with homely force: "Stuff and nonsense!" But the next after that I must have sounded stern enough. "What were these things?"

My sternness was all for his judge, his executioner; yet it made him avert himself again, and that movement made *me*, with a single bound and an irrepressible cry, spring straight upon him. For there again, against the glass, as if to blight his confession and stay his answer, was the hideous author of our woe—the white face of damnation. I felt a sick swim at the drop of my victory and all the return of my battle, so that the wildness of my veritable leap only served as a great betrayal. I saw him, from the midst of my act, meet it with a divination, and on the perception that even now he only guessed, and that the window was still to his own eyes free, I let the impulse flame up to convert the climax of his dismay into the very proof of his liberation.

"No more, no more, no more!" I shrieked, as I tried to press him against me, to my visitant.

"Is she *here*?" Miles panted as he caught with his sealed eyes the direction of my words. Then as his strange "she" staggered me and, with a gasp, I echoed it, "Miss Jessel, Miss Jessel!" he with a sudden fury gave me back.

I seized, stupefied, his supposition — some sequel to what we had done to Flora, but this made me only want to show him that it was better still than that. "It's not Miss Jessel! But it's at the window — straight before us. It's *there* — the coward horror, there for the last time!"

At this, after a second in which his head made the movement of a baffled dog's on a scent and then gave a frantic little shake for air and light, he was at me in a white rage, bewildered, glaring vainly over the place and missing wholly, though it now, to my sense, filled the room like the taste of poison, the wide, overwhelming presence. "It's *he*?"

I was so determined to have all my proof that I flashed into ice to challenge him. "Whom do you mean by 'he'?"

"Peter Quint — you devil!" His face gave again, round the room, its convulsed supplication. "*Where?*"

They are in my ears still, his supreme surrender of the name and his tribute to my devotion. "What does he matter now, my own? — what will he *ever* matter? *I* have you," I launched at the beast, "but he has lost you for ever!" Then, for the demonstration of my work, "There, *there!*" I said to Miles.

But he had already jerked straight round, stared, glared again, and seen but the quiet day. With the stroke of the loss I was so proud of he uttered the cry of a creature hurled over an abyss, and the grasp with which I recovered him might have been that of catching him in his fall. I caught him, yes, I held him — it may be imagined with what a passion; but at the end of a minute I began to feel what it truly was that I held. We were alone with the quiet day, and his little heart, dispossessed, had stopped.

Do especially Questions 1, 2, 10, 11, 15, 16, 41, 44, 45, 61, 73, 74, 75, 76, 77, 87, 88, 89, 90, 91, 92, 95, 99, 102, 103, 107, 109, 112, 114, 117, 133, 134, 137, 145, 147, 148, 154, and 157.

HENRY JAMES   1843-1916

A year before his death, Henry James became a British subject as a protest against America's neutrality during the first part of the World War, and became the first in a line of expatriate American authors who attempted to surmount the limits of a narrow regionalism and nationalism. The characters of his many great novels on international themes symbolize important phases in James's own international education and travel. He brought to his many volumes of novels, short stories, plays, travel books, and literary criticism a gift of psychological analysis that rivals the ability of his philosopher-brother William, and a rich convoluted style that has tried the patience of his admirers ever since. He was perhaps the most self-conscious and meticulous artist that America has ever produced. It is possible to study one of his major novels or short stories — such as *The American* (1877), *The Portrait of a Lady* (1881), or *The Turn of the Screw* (1898), for example — and turn to the two volumes of his letters, the intricate prefaces that he wrote for the New York Edition of his works (1907-1917), and the recently published volume of his *Notebooks,* and discover the attitude of the artist toward his work before, during, and after the creative process. For example, in his preface to *The Aspern Papers,* James has some revealing things to say about his intentions in creating *The Turn of the Screw:* "Only make the reader's general vision of evil intense enough, I said to myself — and that already is a charming job — and his own experience, his own imagination, his own sympathy (with the children) and horror (of their false friends) will supply him quite sufficiently with all the particulars. Make him *think* the evil, make him think it for himself, and you are released from weak specifications."

PROBLEM QUESTIONS

1. One interpretation of *The Turn of the Screw* is based on believing the governess' story. Another interpretation is based on an understanding of the governess as a psychotic spinster who has hallucinations and literally frightens Miles to death. Discuss the evidence *in the story* that supports one or both of these interpretations.

2. Considering the two interpretations of the character of the governess, evaluate the following characters: Miles, Flora, Mrs. Grose.

3. Decide which interpretation is, for you, more reliable. What, then, constitutes "evil" in the story?

4. Horror can often be achieved by the juxtaposition of things not normally associated with each other. For example, we normally associate childhood with innocence; therefore evil in a child is far more horrible to us than evil in an adult. This juxtaposition is one of many in *The Turn of the Screw*. Find as many others as you can and discuss how each heightens the effect of horror.

5. Develop some ideas as to what role Douglas might have in relation to the governess' story.

6. Of what value to the credibility of the story is the "story within a story" framework?

7. Select instances wherein James fails or succeeds in creating the effect Edgar Allan Poe recommended for short story writers. How does this story differ from the typical Poe tale of horror?

Preface to the
Dictionary of Questions

The "Dictionary of Questions for Understanding Literature" is an organized set of the important questions that
can be asked about any work of literature. It will serve
throughout the four years of high school as the basic source
for the questions that teachers and students will be asking
about the literature they read. In view of this long-con-
tinued reference to the "Dictionary," it seems reasonable
to suppose that you will develop the habit of asking yourself these important questions when you come to read
independently of teachers and textbooks.

The *organization* of the questions in the "Dictionary" is
simple. You move from your first general impression of a
work to classification and a tentative statement of the
theme; you then analyze the literary techniques used to
express and develop this theme; you conclude with a final
evaluation of the work in the light of the earlier steps in
the process.

The *purpose* of the "Dictionary of Questions" is simply
to teach habits of critical reading. It is devised to help you
form those habits which will serve you in whatever reading
you will have to do. Such habits will enable you to read
more intelligently and critically anything from the daily
newspaper or reports of a business meeting to the latest
significant novel or play. They will help you formulate and
express what would otherwise be vague feelings of satisfaction with a significant novel or general feelings of disappointment with a silly movie. In short, the purpose of
the "Dictionary of Questions" is to accustom you to ask
yourself the important questions you must answer if you
are to evaluate properly whatever you read.

The following comments about each of the seven steps
will give a quick overall view of the "Dictionary."

The *First View* elicits your first and perhaps superficial reaction after reading the work. In this View you try to familiarize yourself with the piece and begin to express your thoughts on it. The *Second View* asks you to classify the work among the various types of literature, a necessary step before any further analysis can take place. In the *Third View* you are asked a few general questions which will help you to state, at least in rough preliminary form, the theme of the work.

The *Fourth View* contains a series of questions which help you determine the overall structure of the work and the function each of its major divisions has in developing the theme. The *Fifth View*, which contains more than half of the questions in the "Dictionary," seeks a more detailed analysis of such points as style, imagery, figures of speech, characterization and plotting, and so forth. You will find in this View large blocks of questions relating specifically to lyric poetry, fiction, the drama, the film, television productions, and so forth.

The *Sixth View* contains questions about areas outside the work—history and biography, for example—which will help you to understand the work further and relate it to the culture that produced its author.

The *Seventh View*, the last one, offers questions for a final evaluation of the work in terms of comparison with other works and according to your own philosophy of life.

It would be an impossibly large task if all questions were to be asked of each work. There is a core of questions which will apply to any work of literature; but many questions are clearly labeled as applying only to one or other of the literary genres. Therefore, many of the 157 questions are eliminated early, when you decide (in the Second View) that the work belongs under one literary type rather than another.

The following consideration also reduces the number of questions that can be asked about any particular piece. Let us suppose that the work to be analyzed is a rather abstract essay. In that case you would skip over the questions relating to imagery and figures of speech, and concentrate more on those questions which analyze the thought processes and evaluate the moral and intellectual issues. On the other hand, if the poem is a simple lyric, the opposite will be true. There may be very little moral or philosophical content to the poem, whereas the imagery and figures will be the all-important carriers of the author's emotion. Summarily, not all 157 questions *can* be asked of every literary work.

SUMMARY OUTLINE OF THE DICTIONARY OF QUESTIONS

1. FIRST VIEW: **What is my first impression of the work as a total unit?** (Ques. 1)

2. SECOND VIEW: **Under which literary type would I classify the work from a first reading?** (Ques. 2-10)

3. THIRD VIEW: **What is my tentative expression of the *theme* of the work at this point?** (Ques. 11-20)

4. FOURTH VIEW: **How in general is the theme developed by the main parts of the work?** (Ques. 21-42)

5. FIFTH VIEW: **How in particular do the theme and its development give meaning to every part of the work?** (Ques. 43-132)
   A. *In all works* — **by feeling and thought, style, figures of speech and symbols?** (Ques. 44-61)
   B. *In poetry* — **by imagery, meter, rhyme?** (Ques. 62-72)
   C. *In narratives* — **by setting, plot, character?** (Ques. 73-117)
   D. *In drama* — **by dialogue, gesture, dramatic conventions?** (Ques. 118-127)
   E. *In movies and television plays* — **by pageantry, camera, editing?** (Ques. 128-132)

6. SIXTH VIEW: **How is the theme further clarified by knowledge of elements outside the work itself, such as the author's life and times?** (Ques. 133-146)

7. SEVENTH VIEW: **What is my final evaluation of the work? How does the work clarify, support, or contradict my own concept of what the "Good Life" is?** (Ques. 147-157)

Dictionary of Questions
for Understanding Literature

BY VERNON RULAND

FIRST VIEW

I. **What is my first impression of the work as a total unit?** I must try first to understand rather than to judge, to read the work with an open mind, to approach the author on his own terms no matter how much he might seem at first to differ with me.

SECOND VIEW

II. **Under which type in the following scheme would I classify the work from a first reading? Why?** I must remember, of course, that many works defy simple classification, even after much study. Placing a label on a work is not an end in itself, but merely a temporary decision about the direction my later questions for understanding will have to follow.

A. *An important preliminary:* **Does the work stand before me in its original state?** Although the editor's introduction will often answer this question, I must realize my distance from the original work in all my later analysis of this work. An author's vapid style might be merely the translator's; his apparent brevity might be the result of an editor's condensation.

   1. **Is the work before me in its original language, or is it a translation or "modernization" of the original? If a translation, is it an adequate one?**

   2. **Is my copy a "revised student edition" or an adaptation from which passages have been omitted? Is it an abridgement, a "Digest"?**

   3. **Is this work a chapter or excerpt from a complete work?**

   4. **Is this work meant primarily to be read, or to be heard as a poem read aloud and interpreted, or to be heard and seen as a drama in a stage performance?** Perhaps the work was written for an open Elizabethan stage, and loses much of its effect on our contemporary stage.

   5. **Is the present edition of the work accurate and trustworthy? What influence do its format, print, and illustrations exert on my analysis of the original work?**

B. **Is the *complete* work before me *nonimaginative* (nonfiction prose) or *imaginative* (prose fiction or poetry)?** In *nonimaginative works* (*nonfiction*) the author records and reports as scientist, scholar, historian, biographer: he develops already existing material and aims for factual accuracy in his work. In *imaginative works* (*prose fiction* or *poetry*) the author creates a world of his own; he forms his experience into an artistic whole that is more properly called a work of literature than is the nonfictional work.

C. **Under what more specific heading is the work best classified?**

TYPES OF LITERATURE

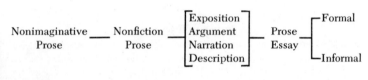

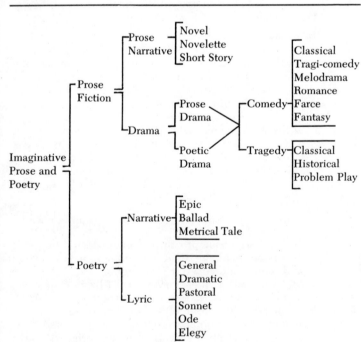

THIRD VIEW

III. **What is the theme of the work?** The theme of any work, best stated in a declarative sentence, is the essential meaning of the subject matter; it is the author's judgment about or attitude towards his subject matter. Any expression of a theme is correct that can justify itself from evidence in the work. Trying to state the theme of a work is *not* an effort to extract a moral or lesson from the work, nor should my statement be so final that it cannot be modified or enriched by further understanding.

    With the work already classified in my Second View, the following chart determines my choice of questions for the Third, Fourth, and Fifth Views. Answers to all questions are no stronger than the evidence quoted from the work to support them.

Type of Literature	*3rd View*	*4th View*	*5th View*
I. Nonimaginative Prose (or Nonfiction Prose)	Questions		
A. Exposition	12-14	22-31	44-61
B. Argument	12-14	22-31	44-61
C. Narration	15-20	22-31, 35-42	44-61, (73-117)
D. Description	12-14	22-31, 32-34	44-61
II. Imaginative Prose & Poetry			
A. Prose Fiction	15-20	35-42	44-61
1. Prose Narrative	15-20	35-42	73-117
2. Drama	15-20	35-42	44-61, 73-117, 118-127
3. (Movie & Television Drama)	15-20	35-42	44-61, 73-117, 118-127, 128-132
B. Poetry	15-20	35-42	44-61, 62-72, 73-117, 118-127
1. Narrative Poetry	15-20	(32-34) 35-42	44-61, 62-72, 73-117
2. Lyric Poetry	12-14	32-34	44-61, 62-72

11

A. *Questions for a Nonnarrative Work (12-14)*
     1. What in the subject matter causes the author to feel as
        he does—entranced, aloof, etc.? Or
     2. Why is the subject matter important to the author?
        What does it mean to him? Or
     3. What new insight into man and his world does the
        work seem most concerned about?

B. *Questions for a Narrative Work (15-20)*
     1. What does the author want me to generalize about the
        central character(s)?

        a. First, who is the central character?

        b. Next, what of major importance happened to him?
           (State the importance of the event in a declarative
           sentence with the central character(s) as subject.)
        c. Finally, is it probable that the author wants me to
           extend my preceding statement to "all men"; or to
           "every man in such a situation"?
     2. Or what important change or revelation occurred in
        the central character(s)?
     3. Or what new or significant vision of the world did I
        grasp through the eyes of the central character(s)?

FOURTH VIEW
  IV. How in general does the theme give order to the whole work?

     A. *Questions for All Nonimaginative Prose (22-31)*
          1. If the work is book-length, how does the theme of each
             chapter develop the theme of the whole book?
             a. What is the theme of the whole book? What chapter
                best expresses it?

             b. What is the theme of each chapter?

          2. If the work is a reasonably short essay, how is its theme
             developed?

             a. What is the topic paragraph?

             b. What overall pattern or method best explains how
                the remaining paragraphs develop the topic para-
                graph? E.g., enumeration, cause and effect, com-
                parison and contrast, circumstances, examples,
                repetition, etc.
             c. How does each paragraph fit into this unified
                scheme?

d. What method of *coherence* best explains the connection between successive paragraphs in this essay?

29

e. By what method(s) of *emphasis* does the essay give importance to the topic paragraph?

30

3. In the development of any given paragraph, how does the author achieve unity, coherence, emphasis, variety? How effective is the topic sentence?

31

B. *Questions for Descriptive Prose and Lyric Poetry (32-34)*

1. What in the work is the dominant physical *viewpoint* and the mental *viewpoint* (the author's attitude towards what he describes—sympathetic, ironic, casual, hostile, etc.)?

32

2. Record any noticeable shift from one physical or mental viewpoint to another, from one sense-appeal to another, from one emotional state to another. How do the theme and its method of development explain these changes?

33

3. If the work is a poem, do differing emotional states succeed one another and mark the poem into divisions? Does the poet use stanza divisions to mark changes in feelings and viewpoints, or does the theme develop independently of such divisions?

34

C. *Questions for All Narratives (35-42)*

1. What events or historical incidents are handled in each chapter of the book, or each scene and act of the drama?

35

2. If the work is biography, what important facts and judgments about the subject's life fall into the following time-divisions: (a) his cultural and family background, (b) his youth, (c) his education, (d) his maturity, (e) his decline, (f) his death, (g) a general analysis of his personality, (h) his achievements, and his effect on his own and later generations?

36

3. If the work is history, what important data belongs to one or more of the following convenient divisions?

37

a. Year-by-year, or century-by-century, or term-by-term of kingship or presidency or in terms of some characteristic hero of the period?

38

b. The data pertinent to the history of one nation, then another?

39

c. Subject-by-subject—the data of religious importance, then political, cultural, economic, etc.?

40

4. **If the work is prose fiction or narrative poetry, can I divide the material to indicate the growth and release of tension according to the following graph?**

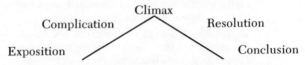

5. **Similarly, if the work is tragedy — drama or nondrama — can I construct a graph giving the exposition, rising action, climax, falling action, and catastrophe? What are the various inciting forces to account for the hero's rising action, the tragic forces accounting for the hero's falling action, the turning point in the climax, etc.?**

FIFTH VIEW
V. **How in particular do the theme and its development give meaning to every part of the work?**

A. *Questions for Understanding All Works (44-61)*
  1. **What feeling and thought does the work evoke?**
     a. **What emotions dominate the work — as signified in my expression of the theme? What emotions stand out in each division of the work — stanza or paragraph, for example — and how do they harmonize with the dominant feeling of the entire work?**
     b. **Are such emotions as strong as the subject matter and theme warrant, or are they excessive or deficient?**
     c. **Does the theme in any way so contradict my basic beliefs and convictions about man and the world, and man's place in the world, that I am hindered partially or entirely from sharing the feelings of the work? Or does it strengthen my beliefs and increase my sympathy for the work?**
  2. **How does the author's general style contribute to the development of the theme?**
     a. **What does the style tell me about the author's personality, and about the social caste, age group, and mentality of his audience?**
     b. **Are there qualities in the style that appear to be an aid or liability in developing the theme? Why?**
     c. **Is the style on a consistent level throughout the work, or does it shift to a higher or lower level of expression?**
     d. **Is the diction clear, simple, fresh, intense, subtle, purposeful; or labored, self-conscious, hackneyed, etc.?**

e. In expository and argumentative literature, is the logic lucid, mature? Does the author appeal to intellect and feelings both, or strictly to the intellect? Does he indulge in "loaded language" and in the other common fallacies of false argument?

3. Why does the author prefer the denotations and connotations of one word rather than those of another in developing his theme?

   a. What does the dictionary record as the exact logical definition, the pronunciation, syllabification, and etymology of the word?

   b. Assuming that the author chooses each word intelligently, preferring it to various synonyms, how does the meaning of any particular word affect a given context?

4. How does the author's use of figurative language and symbols affect the development of the theme?

   a. *Figures of speech*—What is their contribution to the theme?

      (1) Do I recognize the following figures of speech?

         (a) *Simile*—expressed comparison with "like" or "as"—"They went by like a jet."

         (b) *Metaphor*—implied comparison—"a snowball development" or "He has a thin jackal face."

         (c) *Personification*—giving human qualities to the nonhuman—"Death dropped in for a visit."

         (d) *Synecdoche*—part designates whole, whole a part—"All hands on deck!" *Metonymy*—word designates an associated relation—"I read Blake."

         (e) *Irony*—intended meaning is opposite of literal word-meaning—"I just love to lose a fight!"

         (f) *Hyperbole*—exaggeration for effect—"a night of pure hell."

         (g) *Litotes*—understatement for effect—"I finished the delicate little snack of five hamburgers."

         (h) *Paradox*—an apparent contradiction which is true upon examination—"We must die in order to live."

         (i) *Apostrophe*—words spoken in direct address to some abstract quality or nonexistent person—"Sing, Heavenly Muse! that on the secret top of Oreb..."

53

54

55

56

57

58

59

60

(2) **Once identified, is each particular figure of speech fresh and effective? If a literal prose statement were substituted in this passage for the figure, what values would be added or lost?**

b. *Symbols*—(A *symbol* is a word, person, action, or object which takes on a meaning in the work far beyond its ordinary meaning; allegory, fable, parable, and symbol are all extended metaphors.) **What is their contribution to the theme? Is there any central symbol or metaphor that gives organic unity and life to the work?**

61

B. *Questions for Understanding Poetry (62-72)*

1. Any short passage of a poem demands careful study of word denotations and connotations, figures of speech, symbols; turning complex grammatical constructions into normal word order; explaining difficult allusions. Once these preliminaries are finished, the most important questions remain: **Why did the author use this word or image or technique rather than another? What is the relationship between this brief passage analyzed on one hand—and on the other, the theme and the dominant feeling of the entire poem?**

62

2. **How does the imagery of the poem contribute to the shaping of the theme? Does the imagery unify the poem or merely enrich it as an ornament?**

63

a. **How varied and sharp is the appeal to each of the five senses?**

64

b. **What are the areas of experience that provide the sources for the metaphors, similes, and allusions in the poem?**

65

3. **How does the metrical pattern of the poem help shape the meaning of a particular passage or the total meaning of the poem?**

66

a. **How closely can I describe the general metrical pattern?** The four common *poetic feet* are:

Iambic (∪/)—"With whát | Ĭ móst | enjóy | con-ten- | těd leást."

Trochaic (/∪)—"Lăke ănd | rí-věr | bréak ă- | sún-děr."

Dactylic (/∪∪) —"Whére iš mў | lovelў ŏne | where iš mў | lovelíeš̆t"?

Anapestic (∪∪/)—"Ănd thě míght | ŏf thě Gén- | tĭle, ŭn-smóte | bў thě swórd."

67

A verse of one foot is monometer, two is dimeter, three is trimeter, four is tetrameter, five is pentameter, six is hexameter, seven is heptameter, eight is octameter.

b. The important question is: How do the tensions and pace of the metrical techniques in this poem contribute to its theme and effect? Would the effect be enhanced or weakened if I were to alter these techniques?

4. How do rhyme and other audial techniques contribute to the effect of a particular passage or the entire poem?

a. What is the rhyme scheme of the poem?

b. Is the rhyme scheme conventional to the stanza the poet has chosen? If no rhyme is used, are other audial effects used purposively? E.g.,

Alliteration — repetition of initial consonants — "brainy but bashful."

Assonance — similar vowel sound in two or more syllables (rhyme is exact in consonant — "wake-take"; assonance is approximate — "wake-fate").

Onomatopoeia — sound of words suggests their meaning — "sizzle" or "screech."

Refrain — a phrase or sentence of one or more lines repeated at intervals in a poem, often at the end of a stanza. See Jonson's "Hymn to Cynthia" in which the closing line of each stanza is "Goddess excellently bright."

c. Are rhyme, meter, imagery, and other techniques used with balanced regularity and variety?

C. Questions for Understanding All Narratives (73-117)

1. If the work is prose fiction or narrative poetry, what is the proportion of dialogue to description and comment? Is the plot cluttered by excessive descriptive detail? Does the story tell itself, or does the author himself intrude to editorialize or moralize?

2. In a brief paragraph, give a summary of the plot. What incidents are essential to the theme, which merely contributory?

3. Is the work primarily one of incident and surprise, character problems, or mood and local color; or are plot, character, and setting of equal importance?

4. How is the setting integrated with the theme?

a. What are the details of setting?

(1) The historical period, season, time of day?

(2) The nation, city, or section of the nation?

68
69
70
71
72
73
74
75
76
77
78
79

(3) The social class and occupation of the characters?

(4) The mood or atmosphere—tense, gloomy, care-free, etc.?

b. Are these details clearly presented? What is the contribution of the opening sentence to the setting? The closing sentence of the work?

c. What incidents in the story could have happened only in this particular setting; what could have happened at any time or place?

d. If the narrative begins in the middle of events, how does the author provide the reader with sufficient knowledge about characters' past lives and other incidents in order to follow the present story?

e. Are later plot changes in time and locality essential to the development of character and plot?

f. Does the environment described in the setting bring such social, economic, political, religious pressures to bear on the lives of the characters that these elements become essential to the shaping of the theme?

5. How is the plot integrated with the theme?

a. If the story has one single plot, are any episodes introduced that seem inessential—or even irrelevant—to the theme, characterization, or thread of the story?

b. What conflicts constitute the main action of the story? One emotion or state of mind against another, or one man against another, or man against his physical environment and society—or a combination of these conflicts? How are these conflicts resolved in the work? If unresolved, does some incident in the plot prevent a solution within the work, or does the author apparently want me to leave his work with a problem I must solve for myself?

c. What is the *climax* of the plot, and what bearing does it have on the theme of the work? Does the story end with the climax? If not, would the ending be more effective if the climax came earlier than it does?

d. If there is a *denouement* following the climax, does it attempt to squeeze an obtrusive moral from the story, or does it answer important questions raised in the work, summarize, hint at future events in the characters' lives?

e. *Foreshadowing and suspense* — What is their function in the work?   **92**

   (1) How and with what success does the author employ dramatic foreshadowing and suspense to grip the reader and urge him on to future movements in the story? Does he use *dramatic irony*?   **93**

   (2) If the work has a surprise ending, is the surprise essential to the theme of the story?   **94**

f. Is the plot convincing and plausible? If the work constructs a fantastic world of romance, does it sustain that world throughout the work? If the work strives for realism, on the contrary, is it marred by coincidences improbable in real life?   **95**

g. Are there significant contrasts in the work — between incidents in the plot (winning the first, losing the second game)? Between characters (the vindictive old woman and the congenial doctor)? Between moods (carnival gaiety followed by the terror of murder)? Do these contrasts contribute comic relief, irony, symbolism, or surprise to the total effect of the work?   **96**

h. How does the passage of time function in the plot?   **97**

   (1) Approximately what portion of the story is devoted to exposition, to the complication, to the climax, to the denouement?   **98**

   (2) Does the pace of the story entice the interest of the reader, but still allow sufficient time for plausible character growth and progress of events?   **99**

   (3) Does the plot progress chronologically, or are there skips ahead in time which are later filled in by "flashback" techniques?   **100**

6. How are the characters integrated with the theme?   **101**

a. Who is the central character in the work? How does the theme evolve out of this character in action? Is the work mainly the story of the central character's development or deterioration?   **102**

b. What are the dominant traits of the central character?   **103**

   (1) What is significant about his physical appearance, clothes, social status, personal habits?   **104**

   (2) What are the characteristics of his thoughts, speech, and actions?   **105**

106

(3) What is the relation between the character's judgment of himself and the judgment of him by others?

107

(4) What is the character's philosophy of life—his convictions and beliefs about man, the world, and human destiny? Does the author seem favorably inclined, critical, or noncommittal towards this philosophy?

108

(5) Do all these character traits harmonize into one plausible personality?

109

c. Who are the important subordinate characters? What are their chief traits? Are they distinct personalities, or are they mere surface types?

d. If the work is comedy, what is the exaggerated trait in the character of the hero or other characters which causes the complications of plot or provokes comic satire? If the work is tragedy, what personality trait is the "tragic flaw" from which the catastrophe emerges?

110

111

e. Is there real character change during the course of the work, or gradual self-realization and revelation of hitherto unknown qualities of character?

112

7. From what point of view is the story told?

113

a. Is the narrator the first or third person?

b. If first person, is the narrator an observer only or a participant in the action? If third person narrator, is the author omniscient—inspecting the most hidden motives of his characters, trying to keep his own personality out of the story—or does he tell the story only from inside the mind of one character?

114

115

c. Does the author maintain one consistent point of view throughout the story, or does he change it during the narrative—and, if so, does he do it plausibly?

116

d. What advantages and disadvantages result from the point of view chosen in this particular work?

8. Is it possible throughout the work to sympathize with the feelings of the central character(s) and the character through whose viewpoint the story is filtered? What in the work accounts for the ease or difficulty of my identification with the central character or others?

117

118

D. *Questions for Understanding Drama (118-132)*

1. What is the total effect of the play as a combined venture by author, director, actors, and stage technicians?

a. How closely does the stage performance achieve the ideals of the author's original script?

b. How effectively do author and director employ scenery, props, costumes, lighting, make-up, stage-groupings of characters, exits and entrances, etc.?

c. What are the names of the actors and the director? Are the actors well-cast—in physical appearance, voice, intelligent interpretation? Do they interact well as a unit?

2. How does the work *as a drama* develop its theme in setting, plot, and character?

a. How does the author respect the limitations and exploit the advantages of stage, television, radio, etc., in comparison with the novel or short-story form into which he might have chosen to cast his subject matter?

b. To what extent are the divisions (into scene and act) or lack of divisions in the play necessitated by the medium in which the author is creating?

c. How effectively do dialogue and gesture accomplish what the novelist more readily achieves by simple narrative and comment—viz., reveal internal states of mind, emphasize character differences, speed the pace and sustain the interest of the play?

3. How successfully does the author exploit the various dramatic stage-conventions to accomplish his theme and effects? E.g., asides and soliloquies, confidants, raisonneur, prologue and epilogue, Greek chorus, etc.?

4. If *poetic drama*, are the lines good poetry and good drama both? Do they become at times too reflective and complex to communicate themselves to an audience that is normally alert and experienced in appreciation of poetic drama?

E. *Questions for Understanding Movies and Television Plays (128-132)*

1. Is the film merely a photographed play that might just as well have been performed in a theater, or does the camera create a work with unique artistic value in itself?

2. Give examples of successful camera techniques—particular close-up studies of a face, fade-outs, etc. What is the effect of each technique on character portrayal, pace, setting, mood?

3. Does the pageantry of the setting have a value in itself, apart from plot and character?

119
120
121
122
123
124
125
126
127
128
129
130

131

4. Has the film been successfully edited to achieve continuity, pace, variety?

132

5. What contribution to the total effect of the work is made by the sound-track, color, the wide screen, or other techniques? Is the background music of good independent artistic value, or is it mere sound effects — muted violins for love scenes and kettle drums for suspense?

SIXTH VIEW

133

VI. How does my knowledge of elements outside the work contribute to further understanding of the work itself? Study beyond the limits of the work itself can suggest areas of scrutiny in the work I might otherwise have overlooked.

134

A. How do the author's notebooks, correspondence, and other comments on his own work shed light on his theme and other elements of the present work? Does this evidence limit, extend, or merely confirm my present conclusions?

135

B. What light do critical and biographical studies of the author shed on the meaning of the work?

136

1. Do these studies show me how the present work fits chronologically into the output of the author's entire career? Do his other works shed further understanding on this work, and this work shed further understanding on the others?

137

2. How does the present work agree with or contradict the author's philosophy of life — both as revealed in the general themes of his works, and as recorded in other documents?

138

3. Do the author's earlier editions or later revisions of the present work give insight into the meaning of the work?

139

4. How does a knowledge of the sources and analogues of the work contribute to a further understanding?

140

a. Are there people and experiences in the author's own life which bear close resemblance to — or have directly inspired — people and situations in the work?

141

b. Is the present work an adaptation of another's work, or has the author used his sources creatively?

142

5. How do the individual critic's reactions and interpretations of the work add to my understanding of the work?

143

C. How do other bodies of knowledge help me to understand the work?

1. How does the knowledge of the history of literature and the other arts contribute to my understanding of the work?   144

2. How does a knowledge of history and other sciences contribute to interpreting the work? Was the theme of the work—and the issues treated—something timely when the work first appeared? Are these issues vital today?   145

3. How does my understanding of the present work, on the other hand, contribute to an understanding of the politics, sociology, religion, etc., of the period? How does it contribute to further understanding of life in general? Does the author force me to reëvaluate institutions (marriage, the home, civil law, etc.) and philosophies that I respect? That is, are my ideals reaffirmed or are they attacked and ridiculed?   146

SEVENTH VIEW

VII. What is my final evaluation of the work? How does the work clarify, support, or contradict my own concept of what the "Good Life" is? I have a mental picture, vague or definite, of what would be for me an ideal life. In determining how this work of literature affects my idea of this life, I must first consider what kind of person I am, what kind of person I should like to be, what kinds of lives I admire, what ideas I respect. I am then concerned about whether the work helps me to understand my own personality, the character of others, or the nature of the world. I must consider whether the work disturbs me because it presents values and sympathies different from my own, whether it awakens in me a yearning for a different kind of life, or whether or not it makes me content with my present way of life.   147

A. How does a final reading of the work (considering it as a total unit after all of the analytical study has been completed) compare with my first unanalyzed impressions in the First View?   148

B. Is the development of the theme handled so intelligently that the work helps me to understand aspects of life previously confusing and inexplicable to me? Or, on the other hand, do the theme and important elements in the work represent, in my judgment, such an immature, distorted philosophy of life that I feel the work to be *artistically* inferior? When I compare the author's theme or view of a certain aspect of life with my own view, do I conclude that his notions are not only different from mine but also so extremely distorted that he has therefore produced a work of literature which is an artistic failure?   149

C. **How does the theme as it is developed in the work agree with my moral principles?** The following questions pertain chiefly to mature reading-experiences in later life, reading material beyond the scope of the present textbooks.

1. Am I judging the work solely on its own merits, unswayed by the author's known principles and conduct in his private life?

2. Characters in many realistic works use vulgar, obscene, blasphemous language. Is such language used with artistic purpose for realistic characterization? May it perhaps incite the normal reader to sensual thoughts or immoral behavior?

3. Are the scenes that describe immorality handled with restraint and artistic distance, and are they a true insight into the nature of immorality?

4. Is the immorality portrayed in the work presented as *some* type of human evil, or is it presented as the result of social pressures, or as a result of a personality flaw? Does the author recognize immorality as such, even if his characters do not? Moreover, in his work does he punish characters for their immoral behavior—if not, should he have done so? Is the immorality presented as evil only in a certain sense of the word? Is the main conflict in the work between actual moral good and evil, or between what is merely good and bad, pleasant and unpleasant, or socially or politically acceptable and unacceptable, etc.?

5. Does the work present a set of values so advanced or objectionable that it is to be recommended to mature readers only, or perhaps with a caution to others? Are the scenes or passages to which I object necessary to the artistic integrity of the work, or would the work be seriously mutilated by the omission of such passages?

6. How does my personal evaluation of the work compare with the judgment of other, more experienced, critics? In general, are my usual moral evaluations of literature more liberal or conservative—more tolerant or more severe—than their evaluation? In what ways might their conception of the normal reader's problems be more accurate than mine? In what ways less accurate?

D. **How does the present work, as I understand it, compare with other works I have read?** What difference, if any, is there between the rank I finally assign the work among my favorites, and the objective rank I have assigned it among the world's great pieces of literature?

Index